ANDREW MARTIN is an author, jo

previous books with Profile are Underground, Overground and
Belles and Whistles. He has written for the Guardian, Evening
Standard, Independent on Sunday, Daily Telegraph and New
Statesman, amongst many others. His 'Jim Stringer' series
of novels based around railways is published by Faber. His
latest novel, Soot, is set in late eighteenth-century York.

Praise for *Night Trains*

'You do not have to be a trainspotter to enjoy this book. It
is social history, a kind of epitaph to a way of travel that
seems to be lost, at least in Europe.' *Spectator*

'A delightful book ... charmingly combines Martin's own
travels, as he recreates journeys on famous trains such
as the Orient Express, with a serious, occasionally geeky,
history of those elegant *wagons lits* of the past ... Even if
you're not into the detail of rail gauges, this book is the
perfect companion as you wait for the 8.10 from Hove.'
Observer

'Excellent ... Mr Martin paints a vivid picture of this world
on rails ... he proves a witty companion who wears his
knowledge lightly' *Country Life*

'Andrew Martin has cornered the train market. He is
the Bard of the Buffer, the Balladeer of the Blue Train,
the Laureate of Lost Property ... I picked up *Night Trains*
knowing that I would be entertained, but also in the hope
that his many years of experience would teach me how to
sleep on a sleeper ... Andrew Martin is the best sort of travel
writer: inquisitive, knowledgeable, lively, congenial. He is
also very funny, while never letting the humour drive reality,
rather than vice versa. Every page has a good joke.' *Mail on
Sunday*

ALSO BY ANDREW MARTIN

NON-FICTION

Belles and Whistles (Profile)
Underground, Overground (Profile)
How to Get Things Really Flat
Ghoul Britannia
Flight by Elephant

FICTION

In the Jim Stringer series ...
The Necropolis Railway
The Blackpool Highflyer
The Lost Luggage Porter
Murder at Deviation Junction
Death on a Branch Line
The Last Train to Scarborough
The Somme Stations
The Baghdad Railway Club
Night Train to Jamalpur

Bilton
The Bobby Dazzlers
The Yellow Diamond
Soot (forthcoming)

NIGHT TRAINS

THE RISE AND FALL OF THE CITY SLEEPER

ANDREW MARTIN

P

PROFILE BOOKS

Copyright © Andrew Martin, 2017, 2018

1 3 5 7 9 10 8 6 4 2

Typeset in Quadraat by MacGuru Ltd
Printed and bound in Great Britain by CPI Group (UK) Ltd, Croydon CR0 4YY

The moral right of the author has been asserted.

A CIP catalogue record for this book is available from the British Library.

ISBN 978 1 78125 560 5
eISBN 978 1 78283 212 6

Mixed Sources
Product group from well-managed
forests and other controlled sources
www.fsc.org Cert no. TT-COC-002227
© 1996 Forest Stewardship Council

CONTENTS

The following passage is from *Railway Wonders of the World* magazine, October 1935. I intended to quote it ironically as soon as an official of one of the modern sleeper trains annoyed me:

It is no exaggeration to say that the popularity of the International Sleeping Car Company is partly due to the travelling officials in their smart brown uniforms (the dining car waiters wear immaculate white jackets). They deal daily with a large number of passengers belonging to all nations of the world, where each has his own peculiarities and requirements, expressed in many different languages. The passengers may consist of Royalties and crooks, artists and millionaires, diplomats and spies, scientists and generals, old ladies and film stars, infants in arms and death-defying octogenarians, thrown together within the narrow space of the railway carriage. To deal daily with such a kaleidoscopic multitude demands iron nerves, endless tact and an eternally good humour.

In the event, the passage was never required (which is not to say that all my journeys went smoothly), so I dedicate this book to the men and women who operate the surviving European sleepers.

INTRODUCTION

THE BLUE CARRIAGES AND ME

My father not only worked for British Rail (BR), he also believed in the railways, in spite of their unfashionability during most of his career. His enthusiasm probably owed something to the fact that he was entitled to free train travel at home and in Europe. He was one of those who took advantage of that European perk, and he was a member of the British Railwaymen's Touring Club (BRTC), which organised group holidays for BR workers and their dependants.

For three successive summers, between 1973 and 1975, my father, my sister and I (my mother had died in 1971) convened on what the BRTC men called 'the main "up" platform' of York station, and what normal people called 'platform three', to wait for a London train. We were on our way to 'the Continent', a term implying a certain remoteness that began to fall out of use when Britain joined the European Economic Community in 1973. Twice we went to Lido di Jesolo in Italy, once to Lloret de Mar in Spain. In the weeks before departure, my father, a Europhile, had been briefing me about the holiday ahead. He described the continental breakfast that awaited, which I was particularly excited about even though – considered objectively – it was bread and jam, albeit with real orange juice. ('The orange juice is a cocktail,' my dad counselled, 'you sip it.') He also held out the exciting prospect of an unusually thin soup called consommé (in which one put, strange as it may seem, grated cheese) while warning of very strong coffee served in very small cups, and a complete absence of tea.

I recall the cluster of suitcases on the York platform, the patterned summer frocks of the women, some of whom already had their sunglasses on. They took a maternal interest in my sister and me: 'Now you have brought your sunhats, haven't you?' I remember the freshly whitened plimsolls of the men, and the BRTC badges on the lapels of their summer jackets. The badge was circular, with the countries of Europe west of Russia shown in gold against a blue background. In the absence of my father, who died as I began writing this book, I might think I'd dreamt our railway jaunts were it not for that badge, which is the only thing that comes up when the words 'British Railwaymen's Touring Club' are put into the Internet. (The badges are offered for sale on various sites, with suggestions for starting bids around the three pound mark.)

The National Rail Museum in York reported no mention of the BRTC on their database, and suggested I contact an organisation called REPTA. This used to stand for Railway Employees' Privilege Ticket Association, a name that expressed the pride of the railwaymen of the 1920s, who had fought for travel concessions, and formed an association to protect them. Today, nobody calls themselves 'privileged', and the organisation has become the Railway Employees &

Public Transport Association. According to its spokesman, Colin Rolle, it is a 'benefits association for active and retired railwaymen', but the retired BR staff remain more privileged than those currently employed, who have concessionary travel within Britain only on the territory of their train operating company, and must clear high bureaucratic hurdles to access less generous European concessions than were enjoyed by my dad. According to Colin Rolle, 'The British Railwaymen's Touring Club wasn't part of British Rail. It was an independent tour company that organised package holidays for railwaymen, using their free travel. We don't have any mention of it in our records, but I think it folded in the early 80s.'

Now back to York station in 1973. When the train came in, I concentrated on looking nonchalant as we headed for first class. As a fairly senior man 'on the salaried side' (as he'd modestly say), my father's privilege tickets were all 'firsts'. We arrived at King's Cross – 'The Cross' to the BRTC men – at lunchtime. From there we transferred to Victoria by Underground. (The BRTC men had free travel on that as well, and I was always disappointed that there was no first class on the Tube, because if there had been, we'd have been in it.) At Victoria, we entrained for Dover. We then took a ferry operated by Sealink, the seagoing arm of BR. This we boarded at blustery Dover Marine station, which was located directly on the dock, and offered the classic conjunction of the boat–train era, which now seems dreamlike: a railway station with a ship alongside. It was customary for the railwaymen to point out to us children that the BR double arrow appeared the right way round on one side of the ferry's funnel, while being reversed on the other side so as to resemble an 'S' for Sealink.

We disembarked from the ferry at the French counterpart

3

to Dover Marine, Calais Maritime, which was demolished in the mid-1990s. Dover and Calais are now served by two stations located a ten-minute bus ride (if the bus is running that day) from the sea. The Calais Maritime I knew was a single-storey concrete building of 1956, almost Euston-like in its grey functionality. It appears in two films starring Alec Guinness: *The Lavender Hill Mob* and *The Detective*.

But still Calais Maritime was exciting, partly because Calais was exciting. For the British, it was where Europe began (whereas in recent years, migrants have thought it's where Britain begins). My dad always said Calais Maritime made him nervous, 'because if you got onto the wrong train you ended up in the wrong country'. I recall several trains waiting in that throbbing bunker, made up wholly or in part of dark-blue carriages with the words 'Compagnie Inter-nationale des Wagons-Lits' written above the windows in gold, so the colour scheme was the same as that of the BRTC badge. (It is also, come to think of it, the colour of the European Community flag.)

Having grown up in a railway family, I was vaguely aware of Wagons-Lits (W-L), so I took the first sighting of those carriages in my stride, as when seeing a famous person in the street, but they were impressive. They seemed huge, the French loading gauge (the permissible dimensions of a carriage) being bigger than our own. But what was striking was the blueness, an indulgently dark and romantic shade compared to the weak-blue-and-off-white livery being rolled out across British Rail just then.

These vehicles were marked either 'Wagon Restaurant' or 'Wagon-Lits', eating and sleeping being the decadent specialisms of the company. They seemed grown up, remote from the schoolboyish pedantry I had already come to associate with British railways. Much of that pedantry comes

4

from locomotives and their vital statistics, but Wagons-Lits ran no locomotives, so the student of the company is spared all that talk of steam pressures, horse power, wheel formations. (Strictly speaking, Wagon-Lits had *one* locomotive, an Austrian battery-electric four-wheeled shunter, built in 1903, and used for moving carriages about at its workshop at Inzersdorf near Vienna.)

When it came to the European expresses, the bluer the train the better. The most famous ones were entirely Wagons-Lits, entirely blue. Other trains might just have a W-L restaurant car, or a couple of sleepers. I can't remember the make-up of the train that took us to Paris on that first occasion. I do know that on arrival we took the Métro from Gare du Nord to Gare de Lyon, where, in the early evening, there were more of the blue carriages. I have been studying old editions of the *Thomas Cook Continental Timetable* in the British Library, trying to piece together what happened next ...

Incidentally, it is much more enjoyable to type 'Thomas Cook Continental Timetable', which is what the publication was called from 1873 to 1987 – except for the three years from 1977 to 1980 when it flung its net wider, becoming the *Thomas Cook International Timetable* – than it is to type 'Thomas Cook European Timetable', which is what it became after 1987. Cook's ceased to publish it in 2013, and today there is a weedily named 'European Rail Timetable' ('Produced by the former compilers of the Thomas Cook European Rail Timetable'), but we ought to be glad to have it, given what's happened to the timetable genre.

I think I have identified the train we took from Gare de Lyon, and it did have a name, albeit not a famous one. My note, made in the library with the excited urgency of a spy decoding a cryptogram, reads: 'The Lombardie Express. Depart Gare de Lyon 2137; arrive Lausanne 0340; arrive Brig 0520;

arrive Milan 0905.' No train of that name ever formed one of the Wagons-Lits expresses, and I slept in a couchette, which I thought, wrongly, was a term interchangeable with 'sleeper'.

Wagons-Lits sleepers were sleepers properly so called. Each compartment offered seating by day, and was convertible into either one to two comfortable beds. Some of the early sleepers of the company had compartments with four berths, but from the introduction of the S-class sleepers in 1922, a twin-berth compartment was the basic unit. There were also single-berth compartments, and singles or doubles could be turned into a two or a four by the unlocking of a connecting door. Wagons-Lits operated its own class system, which overlapped in a complicated way with the class systems of the national railways, but in essence the first-class price was paid by those seeking 'espace privatif', or sole occupancy, whether of a single-bed compartment specifically designed to facilitate that privilege, or a double, which you could have to yourself if you paid enough. From the 1940s, when the luxury rail market was in decline, an increasing number of three-berth compartments were offered by W-L. Particularly associated with three-berth occupancy was the Yt-class, and if things seem to be becoming rather algebraic, it must be admitted that, despite the absence of locomotive numbers to collect, Wagons-Lits did give an opening to the more pedantic sort of rail enthusiast, in the classification of their sleepers. I will keep discussion of S-class, Lx-class, Yt-class and so on to a minimum, not least because these terms are not as precise as they sound.

A sleeper, unlike a couchette, had – and has – a wash basin but almost never an en-suite bathroom, although in the case of the Wagons-Lits there was sometimes this discreet offer, in the form of a small notice: 'Sous le lavabo se trouve une vase'. It resembled a gravy boat, and was more useful to a gentleman than a lady, I would have thought. Each bed had blankets, a sheet and a pillow.

Couchettes were also convertible from seats. They were provided by the national rail companies rather than by the transnational W-L, which never dabbled in couchettes, just as there are no camp beds in the Ritz. In couchettes, there was no lavabo and no vase; the beds were harder than those on sleepers, and there would be four or six in a compartment depending on whether first or second class. So it was a matter of 'mucking in', and since you were likely to be sleeping with strangers, you kept your clothes on. Which is not to deny that plenty of sex must have occurred in couchettes, but it would have been less well upholstered than sex in a W-L compartment. In the *Thomas Cook Continental Timetable*, couchettes were indicated by a symbol resembling a plank, whereas sleepers were denoted by a drawing of a proper bed with headboard and plumped-up duvet. Being unaware of this discrepancy, I would drop the word 'couchette' at every opportunity when I got home to York. I remember sitting on the front lawn of our house with a group of my friends, who might have holidayed in Scarborough or Mablethorpe, lounging around me. My dad was mowing the lawn – always the first job on our return from holidays – as I held forth: 'While we were having our meal in the dining car, the guard came along and made up the couchettes!' and since they also didn't know the difference between a couchette and a sleeper, my friends were impressed, which in a way they were right to be.

At three in the morning on one of our jaunts, as our train approached the Simplon Tunnel, I raised the blind a few inches to see a perfect encapsulation of Switzerland: crescent moon, a handful of stars and a snow-capped mountain with a log chalet halfway up it. The journey was the highlight of my continental holidays, especially that first one to Lido di Jesolo, because, having got both a heat rash *and* a migraine on the beach on the second day (and I insist that I *was* wearing my sunhat), I spent the rest of the holiday in the hotel room with the curtains closed. I was mortified that my dad – looking dapper in the cravat he only ever wore abroad – felt obliged to spend the evenings with me, even though he had struck up a promising friendship with a pretty Japanese widow in our hotel, a romance my sister and I were keen to encourage so that we might become a normal family again. ('Mum wouldn't mind,' we agreed.)

The holiday ended badly: the Japanese widow's time in Lido di Jesolo was up before ours, and my sister disgustedly relayed to me that dad hadn't even taken her address. At least I had the journey back to look forward to; but I did not at that point become interested in European sleeper trains, so I missed the milestones of their decline.

In 1967, the Wagons-Lits et des Grands Express Européens had become the more suburban-sounding Compagnie Internationale des Wagons-Lits et du Tourisme. In 1976, when I was fourteen, it was none of my concern that the bar car was withdrawn from the blue train that was actually *called* the Blue Train. I was unaware, in the mid-1970s, that W-L had been selling off its carriages to the various national operators for some years, and that its only two British expresses would soon expire: the Golden Arrow in 1972, the Night Ferry in 1980. As for the Orient Express, that died various deaths, but I certainly didn't know that there was no longer any through service between Paris and Istanbul from 1977. If, in 1981, I read about the opening of the first French high-speed line, I can't remember doing so, and if the news did reach my ears, I failed to draw the obvious conclusion that here was a new generation of trains sufficiently fast that passengers would not need beds.

But as I began to write journalism about railways, I kept coming across this somnambulistic organisation, whose telegraphic addresses included 'Sleeping Monaco' and 'Sleeping Paris', and which was known in Britain as 'The International Sleeping Car Company'. It struck me as resembling a great narcotic conspiracy with its introduction into Europe, in 1880, of carriages mounted on smooth-riding bogies (as opposed to six-wheel 'rattlers', with two wheels at either end and two in the middle), with cosy, panelled compartments, soft lights, upholstered beds and discreet attendants. One of the most famous of the Wagons-Lits Expresses, the Blue Train, was also the longest, and it often conveyed no fewer than twelve sleeping carriages on its nightly trips from Paris to Nice. In 1900, passengers on the P&O shipping line, which was closely associated with Wagons-Lits, were warned not to disturb the boudoir-like aspect of any sleeper trains their journeys might involve. No luggage could be carried into the sleeping cars except a handbag 20 by 12 by 10 inches high. Bundles of rugs could be, and were, taken in.

It seemed strange to find a commercial organisation dedicated to sleeping, and therefore dreaming, and so to mystery in general. On a night train, after all, you might not easily know where you were.

In Vladimir Nabokov's novel, *The Real Life of Sebastian Knight*, one character has a 'strange, almost romantic, passion for sleeping cars and Great European Express Trains ... the soft crackle of polished panels in the blue-shaded night, the long sad sigh of brakes at dimly surmised stations, the upward slide of an embossed leather blind disclosing a platform, a man wheeling luggage, the milky globe of a lamp with a pale moth whirling around it'.

Anything that could get Nabokov going like that must be a good thing, and it turned out that most of the writers I liked as a young man were enthusiasts for the 'grands express internationaux'.

THE SLEEPERS IN LITERATURE AND FILM

In 1931, the young Graham Greene was dependent on selling review copies of novels to Foyle's bookshop. He decided he'd better have a commercial success. As he said in his autobiography, 'for the first and last time in my life I deliberately set out to write a book to please'. The result, Stamboul Train, is set aboard one of the variants of the Orient Express, the Ostend-Vienna Orient Express. Greene could not afford a ticket to Constantinople, so he bought one to Cologne. Therefore, the early lineside scenes are more accurate than the later ones; as he admitted in his memoir, Ways of Escape, 'you may be sure the allotments outside Bruges are just where I placed them'.

His wife made him sandwiches so he could avoid the dining car. In the novel the chorus girl, Coral Musker, also has sandwiches. They enable her to save eight shillings, which is exactly what Greene saved. A chorus girl on a night train outpacing the jurisdictions through which it travels – this was always going to be a risqué novel. Stamboul Train also features a lesbian couple, an opportunist businessman, a revolutionary, a thief on the run. It is highly atmospheric. Here is the quayside at Ostend: 'The wind dropped for ten seconds, and the smoke which had swept backwards and forwards across the quay and the metal acres in the quick gusts stayed for that time in the middle air.'

Greene had feared that international sleeper trains were too popular a subject: 'the film rights seemed at the time an unlikely dream, for before I had completed the book, Marlene Dietrich had appeared in Shanghai Express, the English had made *Rome Express*, and even the Russians had produced their railway film, *Turksib*'. In the event, Greene's career was saved when his novel became a Book Society choice, but it was sent back in disgust by many members.

In the compartment with Myatt (a Jewish currant trader), Coral Musker asks,

> 'What shall I do? Take off all my clothes?'
> He nodded, finding it hard to speak, and saw her rise from the berth and go into a corner and begin to undress slowly and very methodically, folding each garment in turn and laying it neatly on the opposite seat.

This being a Graham Greene novel, the next sentence reads, 'He was conscious as he watched her calm movements of the inadequacy of his body.' The reader is also not surprised that the sex scene is interrupted when the train comes to a sudden stop at a signal. But it wasn't stopped soon enough for Greene's aunt, Miss Helen Greene, who so disapproved of the book that she banished her nephew's photo from her sitting room to her bedroom.

Stamboul Train was filmed as *Orient Express* in 1933. Of the competing productions the best was probably *Rome Express* (1932), a tale of various night train passengers with things to hide. It was the first film to be shot at the Gaumont-British Studios at Lime Grove, Shepherd's Bush – i.e. not on the Rome Express, though a cameraman did travel on the train to capture the moving landscape. The director, Walter Forde, said: 'Even if there wasn't a scene through the window I'd still have the back projection going, because it would throw shadows on the wall and all the stuff. There was always a tag hanging from a piece of luggage; there was always beads on the little table lamps, so that you get movement all the time.'

Sidney Gilliat, who co-wrote *Rome Express*, also co-wrote *The Lady Vanishes* (1938) and *Night Train to Munich* (1940). The former – a sexed-up version of a novel called *The Wheel Spins*, directed by Alfred Hitchcock – is set on board an Orient Express-like train. So Gilliat covered a sizeable part of the Wagons-Lits network.

Greene gave *Rome Express* a good review in *The Spectator*, although he was not usually a fan of British detective films or stories: 'I found them lacking in realism. There were too many suspects and the criminal never belonged to what used to be called the criminal class.' He might have been slighting *Murder on the Orient Express*, published a year after *Stamboul Train*.

Agatha Christie had an affinity for trains. In *An Autobiography* (1977), she wrote, 'Trains have always been one of my favourite things. It is sad nowadays that one no longer has engines that seem to be one's personal friends.' *Murder on the Orient Express* is a refinement of her earlier Wagons-Lits novel, *The Mystery of the Blue Train* (1928), which is far too long and contains an operational implausibility, as we will see.

Christie stood apart from the literary tussle described by Martin Green in his book *Children of the Sun*, which I read in the year of its publication, 1977, when I was in the sixth form. In it Green describes what he calls the 'dandies' of British interwar literature, people like Harold Acton, Cyril Connolly, Evelyn Waugh, Auden, Isherwood and Spender. They were seen as whimsical and decadent by the austere likes of F. R. Leavis and George Orwell. Reacting against Edwardian stolidity and nationalism, the dandies were great travellers, and often wrote travel books. Green cites *Europe in the Looking Glass* by Robert Byron as a 'typical' dandy travel book. Like many of the dandies, Byron was anti-American (except where it came to cocktails and jazz); he wanted to build a 'European consciousness'.

I was already on to the dandies; I had read their work, and it was fun to read *about* them because they lived abroad, giving me the idea – which turns out to be wrong – that the inevitable culmination of a writing life will be the acquisition of a large house in France or Italy. 'The clubs that were most central to the dandies' Oxford,' Green wrote, 'seem to have been the Hypocrites and the Railway.' While the Hypocrites sounds about right, I am surprised at the Railway, which I'd have thought was a collection of trainspotters, but according to Green, 'its members went on railway trips in a specially reserved carriage, all dressed in the height of elegance and eating and drinking luxuriously'. The Oxford University Railway Club was founded in 1923 by John Sutro, who later became a film producer, and died in Monaco. Its activities were recalled by Harold Acton in *Memoirs of an Aesthete*. The first journey was from Oxford to Leicester and back. The members reserved a saloon,

> and devoured a substantial dinner, superior to the usual fare in railway restaurants. The chef had evidently taken a special interest in its preparations, and it was served on spotless napery ... Wine lent a Horation charm to [the] scenery, and the train serenaded us as we discussed the developments of travel since Stephenson's Rocket. On arrival, the station bar greeted us with open arms. For twenty minutes we sipped rare liqueurs, Grand Marnier and green Chartreuse now long extinct, in that hospitable atmosphere.

As to why these Hooray Henrys were so indulged, their practice of handing out silver cigarette boxes to railway staff might have had something to do with it.

One of the 'sonnenkinder' was Henry Green (sorry, by

the way, about all this greenery), the author of *Party Going*, a modernist novel in woozy prose which concerns a group of spoilt, gilded youths frustrated by a London fog in their attempt to travel by European sleeper trains. One of the female characters flags down a taxi somewhere around Mayfair:

'Hurry, hurry.'
'Where to?'
'To the station of course.'
'Which station?'
'For France, stupid.'

The taxi driver takes her to Victoria, but the party become stranded there, in the station hotel overlooking the concourse:

Electric lights had been lit by now, fog still came in by the open end of this station, below that vast green vault of glass roof with every third person smoking it might all have looked to Mr Roberts, ensconced in his office away above, like November sun striking through mist rising off water.

Mr Roberts is the station master, and the only down-to-earth person in the book.

LA COMPAGNIE INTERNATIONALE DES WAGONS-LITS ET DES GRANDS EXPRESS EUROPÉENS

The company that stimulated so many imaginations was conceived in the late 1860s by Georges Nagelmackers, who was Jewish and Belgian, therefore also international. Belgium was, and is, a railway-loving country, and has the densest network in Europe. It is too small for domestic sleepers, so any Belgian interested in long-distance trains would have to look to France and Germany, each of which wanted good relations with Belgium as a counterweight against the other.

It is notoriously difficult – at least, for the British – to name six famous Belgians, but Nagelmackers deserves to make the list. He stands out as an early proponent of European integration. Yes, his trains had to run through border controls, but Wagons-Lits passengers could sleep through the night just as if the Schengen agreement already applied. This was because they entrusted their passports to the train staff, who would hand them over for a nominal inspection at the borders. National barriers were overcome in other ways. For instance, the restaurant cars contained bonded cupboards, meaning spirits served in one country could be locked away when the border was reached, while another lot were taken out of another cupboard. By this method, the company avoided the accusation of exporting spirts – and the duty that would have been payable for doing so. The bills were made out in the currency of whatever country the train was passing through when the meal ended, but any currency was acceptable, and there was an official table of Wagons-Lits exchange rates.

All the staff were multilingual: three was the minimum number of languages they had to command. A man in charge of a sleeping car was called a sleeping car conductor, and he himself did not sleep, although he may have drowsed, as he kept an eye on the compartments from a fold-down seat at the end of the corridor. (How, in that case, could there have been a *Murder on the Orient Express*? This question will be addressed.) The head of the restaurant car was the maître d'hôtel, and crammed inside the kitchen was a brigade de cuisine, with a chef de cuisine in charge (a man often destined, in the first half of the twentieth century, to be headhunted by one of the better European hotels). He supervised an under-chef, a saucier and a plongeur, or washer-up. There would also be a couple of serveurs, or waiters.

The railway systems of Europe differed from country to country – usually deliberately, to deter invasion. Nagelmackers got round this by fitting his carriages with various brake hoses and steam pipes – multi-plugs, in effect. And all standard carriage notices were in French, German, Italian and English. The destinations of the trains were written in blue on white enamel plaques hung waist high on the carriage sides, and these were graciously spelt in the language of the destination, so it was always 'London', always 'Bruxelles' – at least in theory. But when James Bond is about to board the Simplon Orient Express in *From Russia with Love*, he reads 'Istanbul, Thessalonika, Beograd, Venezia, Milan, Lausanne and Paris', wondering 'Why not MILANO?'

In his book about Wagons-Lits, *Sleeping Story* (which, in spite of the title, is only available in French), Jean des Cars described Nagelmackers as a 'magicien' of a 'nouvel art'. But Nagelmackers' vision was inspired by America, a country of *genuinely* united states, where, in the mid-1860s, George Mortimer Pullman had created a sleeper train empire. Pullman ran not just sleepers and diners, but also carriages equipped with hairdressing salons, organs (for church services) and libraries.

In 1873, while establishing his own first sleepers, Nagelmackers formed a brief alliance with an American rival to Pullman. Colonel William Mann was a flamboyant self-declared 'soldier, inventor, editor', who created what would become the standard type of sleeper in Europe and the UK. In

Mann's cars, passengers slept at right angles to the direction of travel, not in line with the train, like a corpse in a hearse, as was the way on the Pullmans. His fellow Americans didn't like the Mann model, which became the European model – and it is possibly *not* a good idea, because when the train goes round a bend, the crosswise sleeper's head is lower than his feet, or vice versa. Presumably, this was what Captain Alfred A. Cunningham was getting at when he wrote, in 1917, in *The Diary of a Marine Flyer in France*, 'Don't like the French Wagon-Lits. The berths are much too narrow and it is not comfortable sleeping crossways of the car.'

Mann's sleepers were in compartments, whereas Pullman sleepers were in open carriages, which suited the less snobbish Americans. Mann said the American arrangement encouraged impropriety. But Mann-type cars had connecting doors, and Mann called them 'boudoir cars', being a racy character himself. (After Nagelmackers bought him out in 1876, it is said that he ran a blackmailing operation from the Langham Hotel in London, based on tip-offs from Lillie Langtry.)

During the 1880s, Nagelmackers established a dozen luxury sleeper trains across Europe. The national railway companies supplied the locomotives, Wagons-Lits the sleepers and diners. The national companies got the ticket revenue, but a supplement was charged, and this went to Wagons-Lits.

In 1883, after negotiations with eight governments, Nagelmackers began running the Orient Express, which groped its way from Paris to Constantinople. In 1889 came the Calais-Mediterranée Express, forerunner of the famous Blue Train. In 1887 came the Sud Express (Paris-Madrid-Lisbon), and in 1890 the Rome Express (Calais-Rome), which went via the Mont Cenis Tunnel connecting France and Italy. The

Simplon Tunnel, connecting Switzerland and Italy, opened in 1906, facilitating the Simplon Express (Calais-Venice). On the eve of the First World War, with the European skies still empty of passenger planes, 120 Wagons-Lits expresses served a territory from Lisbon in the south to St Petersburg in the north.

Two years into the First World War, Germany seized any W-L stock on their territory, and started their own sleeping car company, known by its acronym, MITROPA. On these confiscated cars the brass Wagons-Lits side-crests – showing two lions rampant – were covered up.

***

In the interwar period the Wagons-Lits company reached its numerical peak. By the mid-1930s it had 806 sleeper cars and 661 dining cars. But in *The Lost Pleasures of the Great Trains*, Martin Page argues that quantity had replaced quality: 'It was now to carry larger numbers in less comfort and for less money to holiday resorts nearer home.' People no longer dressed for the dinners, 'which had in any case been reduced to a mere soup, meat and dessert affair'.

That's one way of describing this menu from the Train Bleu in the early 1960s, as quoted by George Behrend in *Grand European Expresses*:

Consommé madrilène
Filets de soles Duclère
Poulets cocotte grand-mère
Petits pois a la française
Salads de saison
Fromages variés
Boule de neige

Corbeille de fruits

True, most of the hotels operated by the company had now closed. The Russian Revolution had forced W-L to relinquish its Russian operations, but they had been marginal anyway. The first scheduled air service between London and Paris began in 1919, but aviation wouldn't dent the W-L business for another twenty years. (One student of the company told me the fatal moment was in 1938, when Neville Chamberlain returned from his meeting with Hitler assuring the world of 'Peace for our time': fatal both because he'd been duped and because he'd travelled by plane rather than W-L express, thereby setting a bad example that thousands would follow after the war.)

In the 1920s and 1930s, the mythology of the Orient Express was created, and much of it was based on the brand-new version, the Simplon Orient Express, which was inaugurated in 1919, and cold-shouldered Germany on its way to Istanbul. It went into Italy via the Simplon, then Venice, Belgrade and Sofia. Whereas W-L normally had to petition governments for leave to run its trains, it was commissioned by the Versailles powers to operate the Simplon Orient. This is partly why its reputation eclipsed that of the original, plain Orient Express, which continued to run, by its more northerly route, from the Gare de l'Est.

By the Versailles settlement the operations of MITROPA had been restricted to Germany and some adjacent countries. The MITROPA carriages were not blue but 'Bordeaux red', and the renewal of Germany's imperial ambitions was symbolised by the new MITROPA logo: a hawk, which doesn't seem right for a sleeper service, and in 1938 MITROPA again seized whatever W-L services lay within reach.

The true watershed was the Second rather than the First

World War. The Iron Curtain came down, impeding W-L services, and its trains began to be diluted. By the early 1960s, Wagons-Lits carriages were referred to as generic 'voiture lits', and might be attached to any old night train. From 1957, the company name was eclipsed by that of a new network of trains operated by a syndicate of Western European railways: these Trans-European Expresses (TEEs) were aimed at businessmen enjoying the integrationist benefits of the new EEC. They were scheduled to allow a full working day at the destination, but were early morning or evening, rather than night, trains. The Cook's timetable described them as 'luxury, air-conditioned services between important European cities'.

There is the Kraftwerk album of 1977, *Trans-Europa Express*. They released a single of the same name, which is not as catchy as their song about roads, 'Autobahn', but has the same suggestion of a somehow dehumanised transportation. *Trans-Europ[no 'e']-Express* is also the title of an experimental thriller of 1966 by Alain Robbe-Grillet, starring Jean-Louis Trintignant and Marie-France Pisier. To quote the blurb on the DVD: 'Trintignant plays a drug courier smuggling a stash of cocaine from Paris to Antwerp on the Trans-Europ-Express. Matters are complicated by surreal encounters with the police ... and erotic fantasy sequences featuring Pisier being bound and subjected to Trintignant's will.' Compared to that last element, it would be of little interest to most purchasers of the film that the TEE train in question was the Étoile du Nord, which had originally been a W-L service, or that W-L did the catering on some of these trains. (The company continued to provide catering services on many European expresses, even as its own famous trains died off.)

Wagons-Lits had sold many of its sleeping cars to the

various national railways, which, from 1971, painted them a more insipid blue, and began operating them under the brands Trans Euro Nuit/Nacht/Notte/Night, according to country, the acronym 'TEN' being formed in each case. The whole consortium was known as TENPOOL, and W-L staff worked on them as required. The sleeper blankets were camel-coloured rather than red, as they had usually been on the old W-L services.

Since 1993, the main brand of European sleepers has been called EuroNight (one word), and there are more than twenty of these services, operated by one or more of fifteen Western European railway companies. When I started working on this book, in early 2015, the second-biggest brands were the French Intercité de Nuit trains, operating almost entirely within France (with occasional spillages over the border, for example to Luxembourg City and Irun in Spain), and the German City Night Line trains, traversing Europe from as far west as Amsterdam to as far east as Warsaw, with Berlin and Rome as the northern and southern extremities. There were about a dozen each of the Intercités and City Night Lines.

If the films and books mentioned above were triggered by the popularity of European sleepers, this book was triggered by their decline, in the face of competition from budget flights, budget coaches, budget hotels and the high-speed trains, which are treacherously killing off their laggardly brethren. European Union transport policy has not helped, as we will be seeing, but the in-built disadvantage of a sleeper is obvious. A full sleeping car might accommodate thirty people. A full carriage on an ordinary train will accommodate eighty.

A *Guardian* article of 13 September 2014 was headed 'The Sleeper Vanishes'. Two City Night Line sleepers – between Brussels and Copenhagen, and Paris and Munich – would be stopped in the coming December. The French-Spanish Elipsos night train from Paris to Barcelona and Madrid had been stopped the previous December, while the joint Italian-French venture, Thello, would no longer be operating its sleeper between Paris and Rome. Other more obscure services had recently been, or would soon be, stopped.

Most of my journeys were undertaken in the second half of 2015 and the first half of 2016, as further death sentences were announced: most of the Intercités de Nuit would cease by October 2016, and all of the Deutsche Bahn City Night Line sleepers would be stopped by December.

The older the British reader of that news, the greater the likelihood of their feeling depressed by it. The youngster, with one experimental Interrail night journey under his or her belt, would be less affected than the ninety-year-old, who might – in childhood – have traversed in Europe in the 1930s, when almost every one of the 300 pages of the *Thomas Cook Continental Timetable* included a footnote designating at least one service on that page as 'Sleeper'. Still other Britons might feel a vague regret at a passing of a world that was vague to them in the first place.

WAGONS-LITS AND THE BRITISH

I imagine that, inside the head of any British person watching *Murder On the Orient Express*, there is a small voice marvelling, 'Never mind this dead body; where did they buy their tickets?' Britain is cut off from the continental railways by the Channel, and our different loading gauge inhibits through working. Originally the European sleepers went out of their way to pick us up from Calais, but from the early 1960s the Calais connections withered. The British, being from an island nation, had taken to the skies. Along with places like Cyprus, we have always been towards the top of lists of nations ranked by propensity to fly.

The basic currency of Wagons-Lits (carriages convertible into sleepers) was also worthless *within* Britain, because by the time the night had ended, any journey on a British sleeper was over – or some time before in the case of the ones that used to run from London to Manchester. Fixed berths have usually sufficed on our sleepers, of which we are down to two: the Caledonian Sleeper from London to Scotland* and the Night Riviera to Cornwall. These have a brighter future than the sleepers on the continent, but they will never emulate the true W-L experience, because passengers are ejected soon after eating their perfunctory breakfast, and the local population speaks the same language (more or less) at the destination as at the starting point. But Britain *nearly* had sleeper trains of true glamour …

I travelled on Eurostar on the second day of its operation. It was November 1994. As I sat next to a rail enthusiast who was timing the journey with a stopwatch and taking processed cheese sandwiches to the gastronomic capital of the world, I picked up a leaflet headlined 'What Next?' which boasted: 'In early 1997 night trains will be introduced, travelling from Scotland, the North West, South Wales and the West into Paris … Passengers can enjoy a good night's rest in comfortable accommodation and arrive refreshed in the morning.'

I like the keenness of that word 'early'. The Nightstars never materialised, although they were built, with both day and night carriages – and a new service depot at Manchester sprouted a billboard reading, 'Le Eurostar habite ici'. But the

---

* For an account of a journey on the Caledonian Sleeper, see my book *Belles & Whistles*.

business case was killed off by the budget airlines, which Eurostar planners failed to foresee. The trains were eventually sold to Canada.

The Nightstars would not only have served the north, they would also have shunned London, or at least central London, because their journey south would have taken them via Stratford in east London, and the only reason Stratford station was built – and the reason it is called Stratford International – was to serve these trains. Today, Stratford must make do with domestic high-speed trains to Kent. Eurostar itself has never stopped there, in spite of intense lobbying *from* Stratford. It would be farcical for a high-speed train to leave St Pancras and stop six minutes later at Stratford. It would be like having a high-speed *tram*.

But if Britain has stood apart from the network of European sleepers, its upper classes were once its main customers. This was because Britain was the richest nation. In the late nineteenth century, most of the passengers on the premier *train de luxe* referred to 'the Orient Express' rather than the 'Express d'Orient', and in 1891 the Anglicised version became the official name. It is odd, therefore, that W-L never became famous in Britain, even when it gained a British chairman, and ran a sumptuous booking office in London – practically an embassy – at Cockspur Street, between Pall Mall and Trafalgar Square. This was because the identity of the company was hidden behind two more stolid brands. Thomas Cook was one; the other was Pullman.

We last heard of George Mortimer Pullman as the founder of an American sleeper train empire. He died in 1897, having failed to establish his sleeper brand in Europe, with the exception of Italy. But the Pullman name would eventually appear throughout the continent, by the following nepotistic route.

In 1903, Georges Nagelmackers' son, René, married the daughter of a British businessman called Davison Dalziel (introducer of motorised taxis to London). Dalziel then joined the W-L board. Three years later, Dalziel purchased the British subsidiary of the American Pullman company. In 1925 he became chairman of Wagons-Lits, and granted it the right to use the Pullman name. So there began to be Wagons-Lits Pullmans, but these were not sleepers. They had armchairs, not beds, and were luxury day cars (either with or without kitchens), used on such W-L trains as ran in daytime only. They never graduated to complete dark blueness, but were – with some exceptions – painted dark blue below the waist, and cream above. These cars were used on such day trains as L'Oiseau Bleu (Antwerp-Paris, 1929), the Flèche d'Or (Calais-Paris, 1926), the Sunshine Pullman Express (Cairo-Luxor, 1929) or the Étoile du Nord (Paris-Amsterdam, 1927).

The Flèche d'Or operated in conjunction with the Golden Arrow (London to Dover), and showed touching solidarity with the Arrow in the following way: its Pullmans were not painted in the usual colour scheme of the continental Pullmans mentioned above, dark blue and cream, but were the same colour as the British Pullmans: chocolate and cream.

This train was a feeder for many of the continental sleepers, and a Fleet Street photographer at a loose end might be sent to Victoria to see which celebrities were boarding the Arrow. But it was rivalled by the other 'British' Wagons-Lits service: the Night Ferry (1936–1980). This had more mystique, being a French train that actually began in London (whereas the Flèche d'Or only picked up the baton passed to it at Dover by the Golden Arrow), and the Night Ferry, as its name suggested, was nocturnal. It too was a Victoria-to-Paris service, but its carriages were loaded onto a train ferry that carried them from Dover to Dunkirk. It was more difficult to see which celebrities were boarding this train, since they did so behind a barricaded-off extension to Platform 2 at Victoria. Yet the attention of ordinary passengers was drawn to this exclusive portal by a high neon sign with the words 'Night Ferry' written in pale blue neon, above a yellow electric moon and a cluster of stars. In effect, this sign said both 'go away' and 'look closer', like a car's tinted windscreen.

I mentioned that the other 'front' for Wagons-Lits in Britain was Thomas Cook. In 1928 Cook's was bought by Wagons-Lits. A network of travel agencies was established, the advertising posters reading 'Wagons Lits-Cook. Partout et toujours à votre service'. A British traveller lost or confused abroad would look for the gold-braided red cap of a 'Cook's man', and I imagine plenty did so in vain after Cook's men ceased to exist. Cook's and W-L went their separate ways after the war, and it had been an odd alliance. On the one hand was Cook's, founded in 1871 by an abstainer who made his first money from temperance excursions; and on the other were Wagons-Lits sleeper cars, with signs all along the corridors pointing towards the bar car. Later, there would be a more emphatic divergence, when Cook's entered the chartered flight business.

PARIS

An article on the Lonely Planet website once described Paris as 'the omphalos' of sleeper trains, which was just the right word I thought (once I'd looked it up), and part of the attraction of the sleepers for me is that they start from my favourite city.

When I go to Paris, I view the selection of reproduction W-L posters displayed in a railway bookshop, La Vie du Rail, at the back of Gare St Lazare. One poster they always have in stock is called 'La Confort Sur Le Rail'. It dates from the 1960s, and shows a woman and a man in a sleeper compartment. He is in his pyjamas, smoking suavely on the top bunk, and I wonder whether the cigarette is pre- or post-coital. She stands in her nightie by the window, indicating to him a nocturnal, Alpine scene. One of the best Wagons-Lits posters was for the above mentioned Étoile du Nord. It was the work of A. M. Cassandre, a Ukrainian-French painter who committed suicide in Paris in 1968, and was the most distinguished graphic artist to work for W-L. The poster shows a tilted star at the end of tracks converging in the far distance. As Henri Mouron wrote in his book *Cassandre*, 'Here the perspective is tipped sharply upward. The horizon is pushed toward the upper reaches of the composition, leaving just enough room for the five-pointed star symbolising the express train. Placed over the vanishing point where the rails converge, the star sheds its luminousness over the entire composition, dissolving the mysterious darkness lingering at the bottom of the composition' – 'darkness' even though the Étoile was a day train.

La Vie du Rail has the intimidating subtitle, written over the door, 'Le Monde du Train et du Voyage Intelligent'. Inside, I once spent – not very intelligently – thirty pounds on a book I couldn't read, my French not being up to it (which is why I look at the posters). *Au bon temps des wagons-restaurants* is written by the interesting-sounding Eve-Marie Zizza-Lalu, and focuses on the Wagons-Lits dining cars. There are photographs of proud chefs and waiters, grouped like so many football teams, the tall ones at the back, the chef in the position of the captain. Also pictured are vast blocks of ice, crates of wine, racks of dangling charcuterie, all being loaded into vans for despatch to the Paris termini from the company's giant pantry at Maison Raoul Dautry, in central Paris. The book has a very French concern with the nuts and bolts of fine dining. There is an engineering drawing showing the ideal dimensions of a Wagons-Lits chocolatier, and a plan of the salle de restaurant and the salon-bar of the Train Bleu in 1928.

While we are in this Parisian locale, I might as well mention a couple of nearby attractions likely to interest the fan of Wagons-Lits. The tracks emerging from Gare St Lazare are straddled by the Pont de L'Europe, which unites intersecting roads, like a great stone star. From here, you can look down on double-decker commuter trains being pulled or pushed by locomotives, like vigorous young men helping old ladies across the road. The French use more locomotives than we do, most of our trains being worm-like multiple units with no separate power car. Locomotives are the alpha males of any rolling stock, and in France they look it, especially the pugilistic B15000s, known as the nez cassé, or 'broken nose class', because of their indented fronts and rears. They resemble squashed letter Z's.

The Pont de L'Europe has often been a vantage point for painters. In 1873 Édouard Manet painted *The Railway*, the composition showing a woman and a small girl in front of some severe black railings. Beyond the railings is large-scale modernity – the bridge, the tracks into St Lazare, the new flats overlooking those tracks – but all is confused by a cloud of steam. The little girl is interested in the scene, but the woman has turned her back on it, apparently in despair. In the late 1870s Claude Monet painted images of the same bridge and station. Both he and Manet followed Zola's injunction to 'find the poetry of stations as their fathers found that of forests and rivers'. But locomotives generated scenes that had something in common with forests and rivers:

a fluid, organic element, arising from the play of light in the shifting steam.

Zola himself made Gare St Lazare the centrepiece of his novel, *La Bête humaine*. This is a hysterical tale of sex and violence, symbolised by the pounding of the engines between St Lazare and Le Havre, with which all the characters are connected. The story culminates on a night train full of drunken soldiers heading for the Franco-Prussian War – or an even earlier demise, since the driver and fireman have fallen to their deaths after an argument over a woman. The cover of the Oxford World's Classics edition is a painting by Gustave Caillebotte called *Le Pont de l'Europe*. It shows a man looking down on the station from the bridge. There is a strolling flâneur, perhaps a depiction of Caillebotte himself. He is possibly eyeing up the man looking down on the station. The woman walking alongside the flâneur has been interpreted as a prostitute. It's unlikely that both interpretations could be true. A dog is heading purposefully over the bridge in the opposite direction, and doubtless it, too, is going off to have sex.

Opposite the *front* of Gare St Lazare, at 40 Rue de l'Arcade, is the Wagons-Lits company's former head office: a neo-Gothic building of 1903. On the corner of the building, at the junction with Rue des Mathurins, is a big clock under a stone canopy, a carved map of the world, and the initials 'WL'. It is now mainly flats. A five-minute walk from here is 3 Place de l'Opéra, which is given in *Baedeker's Paris* for 1903 as 'the principal ticket office of the Compagnie Internationale des Wagons-Lits (sleeping cars)', whereas the travelling public were warned that Rue de l'Arcade was 'administration only'. Number 3 Place de l'Opéra retains a vaguely international flavour in that it now houses the United Colours of Benetton.

Let us now go to Paris.

1

THE BLUE TRAIN

GARE DE LYON

I had boarded the first Eurostar of the day. It had been too early even for breakfast, and I slept for the first hour. Dawn broke soon after Ashford International, but then we were into the Tunnel. When Eurostar services began, the 'transit time' was always given. Now that we have all become more blasé, the announcement is usually dispensed with, and sometimes, on a late-night Eurostar, you only know you're under the sea by the disappearance of the moon.

But in April 2015 the Tunnel had renewed significance, because of the migrants waiting at Calais to get through it. That morning there would have been 5,000 people in the 'Jungle', all in a permanent ticket queue, but with no prospect of the ticket office window ever opening. The Jungle was out of sight for Eurostar passengers, on the other side of town, but as we emerged into a grey French morning, a lonely figure was visible, looking through the high mesh fence that had just been built.

On arrival at nine-thirty, Gare du Nord had been freezing. The greyness of the morning had made it necessary to switch on the lights in their glass globes, but Gare du Nord suits the cold. It is bleak and wintry in a painting of 1908 by Pieter ten Cate, which is on display at the Carnavalet Museum in Paris. In *Les Mémoires de Maigret* (1951) Georges Simenon wrote of Gare du Nord: 'In the morning, the first night trains, arriving from Belgium and Germany, bring the first load of crooks, with faces as hard as the light that falls through the window panes.' This was not the generous spirit that would give rise to the Schengen agreement thirty-four years later, and the banishment of passports within Europe. Nord, like four of the six main Paris stations, is international, and just as the indicator board shows timings of Thalys trains to Belgium and Holland, so the statues on the roof of slightly overweight, toga-clad women represent foreign destinations present and past.

One of the statues represents London, and should there be any doubt about this, the lady stands on a plinth marked 'London'. (The others are Amsterdam, Berlin, Brussels, Cologne, Frankfurt, Vienna and Warsaw.) Nord has always been the point of arrival for the British, and those seeking the sleeper trains then faced the moderate challenge of 'the change at Paris'. It is addressed quite perfunctorily in a leaflet given out to passengers booking trains through SNCF: 'There are seven main train stations in Paris.* The station you need will be clearly marked on your tickets. It sounds obvious, but make sure you are heading for the right station before you set off on the Paris Underground system.'

Travellers are advised to allow at least one hour for the

---

* Most people would say six, but I suppose SNCF would know: they must be including Gare Bercy, which is a sort of spin-off from Gare de Lyon.

change. If you book a through ticket for Eurostar followed by another SNCF train from Paris, you are given two hours. The two stations most likely to be required by a Briton are the nearest one to Gare du Nord, Gare de l'Est, or the one furthest away, Gare de Lyon. A real disaster would have to intervene for the change between Nord and Est to take two hours, since it is a five-minute walk. The trip to Gare de Lyon could take two hours if there were problems on the Métro, but there are seldom problems on the Métro. It presents two difficulties for the changer though: firstly, the map is incomprehensible; secondly, the Métro is mostly just below street level, so there are often staircases where British passengers, with bulky suitcases, would expect an escalator. But a journey on the Métro ought to be, and usually is, a pleasure. The station names are elegantly written in white on dark-blue enamel plates; platform tiles are white, glazed and bevelled, so they sparkle under electric light, and the station names are beautiful. Here is Lawrence Osborne, in *Paris Dreambook*: 'The Métro is above all a system of names, names which are a thousand times more secretive than the places they supposedly denote. Filles du Calvaire, Bel-Air, Crimée, Danube, Pyramides, Campo-Formio, Botzaris, Croix-de-Chavaux, Jasmin, Ourcq ... the mercurial names of the Métro, with the exoticism of the names of extinct birds and buried cities.'

***

The weather at Gare de Lyon always seems better than the weather at Nord. As the Parisian staging post for the Riviera, Gare de Lyon seems to give travellers a preview of the sunlight that awaits them. Today, the stars of the station are the TGV expresses to Italy and the South of France; for much of the twentieth century, the stars were the blue trains of the W-L company going to the same places.

Gare de Lyon was the terminus of the 'Ligne Impériale' – the main line of the old Chemins de fer de Paris à Lyon et à la Méditerranée (henceforth PLM, because I am not typing that again), which was absorbed into SNCF in 1938, when French railways were nationalised. As befits the beauty of the destination, there is a feminine delicacy about the Gare. The ironwork of the roof is green, rather than soot-blackened; there are palm trees in tubs along the platforms. If the station contained an orangery, you wouldn't be surprised, because there is something of the conservatory about it. In his novel *Howards End* (1910), E. M. Forster wrote that, 'In Paddington all Cornwall is latent, and the remoter west.' By the same token, all of the Riviera is latent in Gare de Lyon. The directors of the PLM made quite sure of that, by commissioning the paintings of points south that are seen in the booking hall, and in the gilded Train Bleu restaurant, which is accessed from the concourse by an imperial (that is, two-sided) staircase, an opera set within an opera set. When I first met my wife she lived in Paris, and I used to meet her in the Train Bleu for a glass of wine. Once, we recklessly called for the menu. Surprisingly enough, it seemed that a dinner could be had for about twenty-five pounds, but these turned out to be only the starters. I once began questioning a waiter about the place, and he stalked off without answering, apparently disgusted by my bad French. But he returned with an English-language leaflet:

> The décor of the rooms is almost overwhelming, but the
> overall effect is a harmonious tribute to the distinctive
> style of the 'Belle Époque' period ... The brightly coloured
> paintings in the various rooms are one of the most

distinctive features. They have been carefully preserved, despite the smoke fumes from the steam locomotives of the day and were recently restored to their original state. There are 41 paintings in all, each of which portrays a different scene from the beautiful sites along the old railway network or famous events of the 1900s.

Baedeker's Paris for 1904, the standard guide for British visitors, deals with this sumptuous facility in one short sentence: 'The buffet on the first floor [of the Gare de Lyon] is generously painted and decorated,' which seems churlish, given that this was the year of the Entente Cordiale, and given that this so-called buffet had been opened only three years before by the President of France, Émile Loubet. It's possible that even the French called it 'Le buffet' in those days, because it was not named Le Train Bleu until 1963, in honour of the most famous named train departing from Gare de Lyon. But there is something persistently jaundiced about the Baedeker, perhaps arising from jealousy. Of French trains, it says, 'The carriages are inferior to those in most other parts of Europe ... Before starting, travellers are generally cooped up in the close and dusty waiting rooms.' The generality of Parisian railway restaurants are 'dear and often poor'.

None of this had deterred half a million from Britons travelling to France in 1900, and 'le trafic anglais' was a big payer for the French railway companies. It was the British who had first put the Riviera on the map as a tourist destination, albeit a winter one. In Nice, the 'Promenade des Anglais', the statue of Queen Victoria, and the Anglican church, Holy Trinity, erected in the 1860s, are testament to this. (Holy Trinity has a graveyard, which became the final destination of the many British consumptives who had travelled to Nice for the cleaner air.)

The most famous of the Riviera expresses was the blue train that was actually called the Blue Train, and we are coming to that. Its direct predecessor was another W-L creation, the Calais-Méditerranée Express (CME), which began operations in 1889, running three times a week in the off season, and every day in the high season of December–April. The importance of the British market is shown by the fact that, in its early days, this snubbed Paris altogether. The timetable for 1896 shows the CME leaving London Charing Cross at 11.00, arriving in Calais at 12.49, French time; it next crops up at Amiens, north of Paris, at 02.59. (It arrived at Nice at 11.00 the next morning, terminating in Ventimiglia at 12.36.)

British railway companies were so alarmed at the numbers of wealthy travellers holidaying abroad that in 1892 they had launched an anti-foreign holidays campaign, in the form of a journal called *Travel*. *Travel* promoted holidaying at home: 'Cheap holidays in Scotland ... The new route to the Norfolk Broads.' Readers were stolidly advised to 'Take the Great Northern Railway: The Direct Route to the North-East Coast watering places.' *Travel* mentioned foreign travel to some extent, but the continent was presented as a Wagons-Lits-free zone. Neither the company's trains nor hotels were mentioned, and there was something suspiciously generic about the proffered alternatives. Tickets were bookable from London to Paris by 'special expresses'. 'The South Eastern Railway's Continental Services' were heavily advertised: 'Fast steamers in conjunction with Special Express Trains daily ... Coupe-lits-toilette and Coupe-interior daily between Boulogne and Paris ... This service connects with the continental express trains to Switzerland and Italy.' (It *was* just about possible to circumvent Wagons-Lits on the continent, since it never quite had a monopoly of sleepers. Both Swiss and French railways operated their own, for example, but they were not of Wagons-Lits standards of comfort. Everyone shared a compartment; heating was by hot water in tin trays rather than by hot water pipes as on the W-L.)

Travel advised its readers to buy tickets from men who sounded like British stooges: the London Chatham & Dover Railway's agent in Paris was 'Capt. A. W. Churchward, 30 Bvd des Italiens'. It was all like a version of Europe erected quickly in cardboard. Whereas the Wagons-Lits company hotels had exotic names like (in Nice) the Cimiez Riviera Palace, Travel promoted the Hotel de L'Europe in Milan; in Cairo, the Hotel d'Angleterre; or in Rome the equally unconvincing Grand Hotel de Rome. Particularly suspect was the following: 'Buffet Restaurant, Gare du Nord, Paris. This excellent Restaurant is under the direction of M. Victor Buffetro, and is well appointed in every way.'

Travel was allied to the moralistic idea of travel, to which that British pioneer of package holidays, Thomas Cook, subscribed. According to this, the point of travel was self-improvement. The editor was Henry Simpson Lunn, a muscular Christian and Methodist minister who founded the Lunn Poly travel company and, in 1905, the Public Schools Alpine Sports Club. Under Lunn, Travel – produced in black-and-white – was a worthy affair, advertising stout shoes, travelling rugs (the adverts seem to emphasise the winteriness of 'winter resorts'), trunks and portmanteaus. Other glum objects like Bailey's Surgical Hose, for varicose veins, and Bunter's Nervine ('relieves neuralgia') were advertised, but never alcohol.

There was a culture clash here with the more louche and luxurious world of Wagons-Lits, which responded in 1894 with its own English-language journal, The Continental Traveller. This magazine's pretty covers were all pinks, greens and powder blues, giving an impression of heat haze, much like the paintings in Gare de Lyon. There are many maps – in which the company's sleeping car services are shown as thick red lines – and adverts for things the more epicurean overnight traveller would need, including solid-silver miniature travelling clocks, travelling writing cases, fur-lined coats and whisky. It is full of exciting headings: 'Special Cars for Private Use', 'Buffet Cars on the Riviera', 'Winter Fêtes in Nice', and exciting sentences like 'The train is composed exclusively of sleeping cars, restaurant cars and through baggage cars.' Just as *Travel* never mentioned any foreign railway company by name, so *The Continental Traveller* never mentioned any British one. The approach to that all-important aperture, Calais, is simply by 'trains from Charing Cross' or 'trains from Victoria'.

Whereas *Travel* masqueraded as an independent journal, *The Continental Traveller* made no bones about being 'The Official Journal, Time Book and Guide of the International Sleeping Car & European Express Trains Co.', which is what Wagons-Lits called itself in Britain.

***

The early Calais-Mediterranée Express was not blue. Its sleeper carriages were clad in teak, and were teak-coloured, i.e. brown. After the First World War, the W-L service to the Riviera was relaunched with new sleeper carriages, designated 'S' type. These were made of steel, and they were blue. In 1926, the teak restaurant cars of the service were also replaced with blue, steel ones, and so here was an entirely blue train which, from 1929, ran every day between Paris and the Riviera, with arrangements for gathering up passengers from Calais. It was known to all its users, and to anyone who was interested in railways, as the Blue Train. The only people who did not call it the Blue Train were the Wagons-Lits company, who continued to call it the Calais-Méditerranée Express. The stroke of genius involved in painting the train blue was not followed by what you would have thought was the logical step of officially naming it the Blue Train. W-L, normally so good at publicity, were missing a trick here, because clearly people wanted trains to be blue, hence *Le Train Bleu* ballet of 1924, performed by Diaghilev's Ballets Russes, with music by Darius Milhaud, story by Jean Cocteau, costumes by Coco Chanel and curtain by Pablo Picasso. Hence also the 'Blue Train Races', in which various playboys – particularly Woolf Barnato, chairman of the Bentley company – tested their high-performance cars by racing the train. And hence Agatha Christie's novel of 1928, *The Mystery of the Blue Train*. In 1949, the company would relent, and Train Bleu became the official name. (All that being said, Vladimir Nabokov did not like Wagons-Lits blue. Writing of the Nord Express in *Speak, Memory*, he wrote, 'it was never the same after World War One when its elegant brown became a nouveau-riche blue'.)

For most of its existence until the early 1930s the CME – which from now on I will call the Blue Train – was a service comprising two trains, one leaving from Paris and one from Calais. The financial crash of 1929 ended such operational exuberance, and from now on passengers for the Blue Train who wanted to join the service at Calais could do so, but it was a matter of boarding a different train in the first instance. Usually this different train was the luxury Flèche d'Or (Calais-Paris), the French complement to the luxury British Golden Arrow service (London-Dover), which had begun in 1929. The Arrow was a Pullman train, hence composed of luxurious day cars. The Flèche was also a Pullman, and these were the special Wagons-Lits Pullmans described in the Introduction.

Here is how things worked from the early 1930s to the late 1960s.

The Arrow departed from Victoria at 11am. Having already downed a large breakfast at the Grosvenor Hotel adjacent to the station, passengers would probably do nothing more indulgent before reaching Dover than drink tea, eat a couple of crust-less chicken sandwiches, and drink a quarter bottle of champagne. The Channel crossing was by a particularly elegant steamer called the SS *Canterbury*, which had a palm court and a restaurant 'in the Empire style' that anticipated Parisian brasseries. But most people took lunch on the next stage of the journey, on the Pullman dining car of the Flèche d'Or, which was the most exciting part of that train, with the possible exception of the blue sleeping car that had been attached at Calais for the benefit of those aspiring to the Blue Train. These passengers travelled to Paris through the afternoon, in sleeping accommodation not yet made up for sleeping, but configured as seats.

When the train pulled into the Gare du Nord at about 5.30pm, the sleeping car, which was at the rear, was plucked off by a shunter, and taken to Gare de Lyon via the Petite Ceinture, the smaller of the two orbital railways around Paris. (The other being the Grande Ceinture.) At Gare de Lyon, the sleeper was attached to the ten or eleven carriages of the principal train.

Sometimes Cook's themselves would muddy the waters by changing the way they presented a train. The Blue Train after 1930 started from Paris Gare de Lyon, but had a feeder from Calais. That was the objective fact. But you wouldn't know that from the timetables, which simply gave the time of departure from Calais followed by the time of departure from Gare de Lyon. Starting from the early 1960s, the distinction was made a bit clearer by a footnote corresponding to the Calais departure that said (in effect, although not as comprehensibly as this): 'These are the timings of the Flèche d'Or, and you will be on this train to begin with.' But were you on the Flèche d'Or if you were sitting in a sleeper carriage destined to hook up with the Blue Train? When, in fact, did the Flèche d'Or become the Blue Train? At Calais? At Gare du Nord? At Gare de Lyon? All these questions can also be asked in relation to other W-L services, such as the Rome Express, and the Simplon Orient Express, because sleepers for these might be attached to the Flèche d'Or along with the sleeper for the Blue Train. And there were other, additional methods of getting all of these sleeper cars from Calais to Gare de Lyon.

What each movement had in common was a trip around the Petite Ceinture. So these British passengers of the mid-twentieth century did not have to make the 'change at Paris' themselves; it was done for them while they remained in their seats.

THE REAL MYSTERY OF THE BLUE TRAIN

You might say that these passengers were being treated like freight, because most of the other trains on the Ceinture by the 1930s would have been carrying freight. And from 1943, there were no passenger trains at all on the Ceinture, except for the sleeper carriage transfers, which began to fizzle out in the early 1970s. (The Cook's timetable for 1971 has given up on Calais as far as the Blue Train is concerned: it is unequivocally shown as beginning from Paris-Gare de Lyon.)

This backstage journey around the Ceinture in its twilight years is mysterious, ill-documented, a half-hour disappearance into a smoky limbo, lines with high cuttings governed by obscure signals and operational procedures, which was all very useful for Agatha Christie when she came to write *The Mystery of the Blue Train* – at which point I must introduce a 'proceed at caution', a 'spoiler alert'. Anyone who hasn't read the book, and thinks they might want to read it, should skip the next paragraph.

The fact is that the murderer in that story commits his crime while the carriage for the Blue Train is being taken around the Ceinture from Gare du Nord to Gare de Lyon. This is why the book was originally called *The Mystery of the Blue Carriage*. The killer boards the train on the Ceinture, does the evil deed, then alights. But how does he get on or off the train? This is the true mystery of *The Mystery of the Blue Train*. It is not explained. This is surely a fault of the book, which as a whole is too long, while the exposition is too short.

Two things can be said in Christie's defence. Firstly, she did not like the book herself. In her autobiography, she writes, 'I have always hated *The Mystery of the Blue Train*, but I got it written and sent off to the publishers ... Each time I read it again, I think it commonplace, full of clichés, with an uninteresting plot. Many people, I am sorry to say, like it.' Secondly, there is something admirable about the sheer confidence of an author who can discharge the crucial plot point in eleven words: 'He boarded the train somewhere on its way around the Ceinture.'

The Petite Ceinture was a function of the rail enthusiasm of Napoleon III. It was opened in 1854, and ran around the inside of what was then the city wall, connecting – for military-strategic reasons – the main-line termini, which until then had stood aloof from one another, all serving discrete territories, regional monopolies that nowhere overlapped. The line fell into eclipse from the 1920s, its usefulness undermined by the creation of the Métro, and it dwindled over the subsequent seventy years.

The Ceinture remains, as a ghost railway, without any trains, except for occasional 'special movements' between Parisian termini. In its heyday, the Parisians were proud of the line, and segments of it formed scenic features in two Parisian parks, one to the south and one to the north, the southern one being Parc Montsouris (take RER line B to Cité Universitaire in the south of Paris). Ian Nairn liked the park, and described it in *Nairn's Paris* as having 'a delicious comic-opera flavour ... everything preposterous in the happiest way: lake, hilly slopes, curly lampstandards'.

Parc Montsouris contains a sunken green glade about 500 metres long, concealed behind trees and blocked off by two fences and a couple of warning signs. A rotting railway line emerges from a tunnel at one end and runs into another tunnel at the other end. The sleepers are green with lichen, and the whole thing is asleep. The sides of the cutting are formed by arcaded walls about twenty feet high.

The northerly park, Buttes Chaumont, is accessible from the Métro station of that name. Here, the corresponding cutting of the Ceinture is even more haunting. I know because a couple of weeks before my Blue Train excursion I had gone in search of it. I began by asking after it in the park's café, Café Rosa Bonheur, an oriental-looking pavilion that is itself well hidden behind chestnut trees. It is apparently a meeting place for Parisian lesbians, but a young man stood behind the bar. I asked, in my appalling French, if he knew the location of 'the old railway'. He shook his head, completely baffled. It turned out that the cutting I sought was only twenty seconds away from the café, albeit sunk in the middle of a small wood. It made a dreamy spectacle, with curtains of ivy over the tunnel mouths at either end.

The cutting forms a gloomy complement to a park with macabre overtones, a warped arcadia with its mock Roman temple on top of an artificial cliff. There's a grotto beneath – blasted by explosives out of the remains of a gypsum quarry – through which an artificial waterfall tumbles into an artificial lake. A concrete bridge twenty metres above the lake is known as 'suicide bridge'. It's fitting that this creepy place was the meeting place of the Charlie Hebdo killers, who'd done their murdering a couple of months before my visit to the park.

There were no arcaded walls to this cutting and it was shallower that the one in Parc Montsouris. A middle-aged man with a camera around his neck was approaching. He brazenly scrambled down the bank, climbed over the broken fence, and stepped onto the mildewed sleepers of the track. Should I follow him? Here was a challenge to my courage. I was reminded of the time I first visited New York, in the late 1980s. My guidebook had warned me it was highly dangerous to use the Subway after eight o'clock in the evening, but the first thing I saw, when stepping off the airport bus in downtown Manhattan at half past eight, was a little old lady descending into a Subway station. So I followed the camera man. I tried to ask, in French, 'Is it OK to walk on the tracks?' He actually did give a Gallic shrug before replying in English: 'This is France. You can do what you want.' 'But is it illegal?' I persisted, wimpishly. Another shrug: 'A lot of things are illegal.'

Going by the amount of graffiti on the retaining walls, many people clearly had walked on the tracks. Some was in English, probably post-dating the Charlie Hebdo attacks, which had made this arrondissement notorious: 'I still love my ghetto.' The tunnel was blocked off at the west end, so I scrambled back up to street level, following the route of the old line a little way. After it disappeared under the McDonald's on Rue Manin, I found it again on a blackened viaduct. At intervals there were armed soldiers, who looked as though they were guarding the Ceinture, but they were part of the anti-terrorist force, *L'Opération Sentinelle*. They had more serious crimes on their minds than trespassing on the Petite Ceinture, whose surviving infrastructure – mostly above ground in spite of those tunnels in the parks – is known to attract Parisian cataphiles or troglodytes, a place of timeslip and landslip. Old sleeper carriages have been parked on the line and used as a homeless hostel. It is also celebrated as a pathway for foxes.

To see the line's point of access to the Gare de Lyon, you have to travel about three miles south. Parallel to the traffic jams of the Boulevard Poniatowski, in the 12th arrondissement, are more rotting tracks of the Ceinture. They are at right angles to the great, grey mouth of Gare de Lyon, which lies below. On the south side of the railway gorge that accommodates Gare de Lyon are the remains of the Ceinture station called Gare de La Rapée-Bercy, which closed in 1934, though part of the platform remains. The quickest way to walk from Boulevard Poniatowski to Gare de Lyon itself is to go along Rue de Charenton, which runs parallel to the main line along the north side of the gorge. On Rue de Charenton stands a model railway shop called Le Petit Train Bleu. There is a small layout in the window. A notice reads 'Pour faire démarrer le train, passé la main', and if you do so, you block a beam of light, thereby starting the little train. I would have cause to remember that, towards the end of my Blue Train day.

RUSH HOUR

While Gare de Lyon never had as many workaday commuter trains as Nord and St Lazare (which was estimated to be the busiest station in the world in 1900), it had a rush hour of the blue trains. Between seven and nine-thirty, the Simplon Orient Express, the Rome Express and the Blue Train itself would take their leave, in theatrical style.

Let's look at the Blue Train in the early 1960s. An elderly electric loco would bring the bulk of it to its departure platform from the carriage sidings at nearby Conflans. At the same time, the carriage that had been brought around the Ceinture from the Gare du Nord would be dragged into the station by a giant, wheezing tank engine: a chain-smoking elderly retainer possessing a kind of reverse glamour for being steam-powered in what was by then an electrified station. The sleeper from Nord, which had been at the back of the Flèche d'Or, was now shunted to the front of the Blue Train, while similar manoeuvrings were creating the Rome Express and the Simplon Orient.

The well-heeled passengers now faced a dilemma. Should they have an aperitif in the Blue Train buffet, or wait until the departure of the Blue Train train. Or both? Perhaps dinner itself ought to be taken before departure? In previous decades, they might have bought a 'dinner basket', so they could have a picnic on the train, as Ada Mason does in *The Mystery of the Blue Train*. There would have been time for all these things. To allow for the vagaries of the English Channel, about an hour's latitude was built in between the bringing of the ex-Calais sleepers from the Ceinture and departure of the fully assembled Blue Train (which took place at 20.10 in January 1962). So there would have been meditative, or excited, pacing along the platforms, drawn-out goodbyes and train-watching. Those on the Blue

Train might have been looking at the departing commuters (whose trains at the time were green) with a feeling of 'There but for the grace of God ...' The more particularly gluttonous ones might have been watching the supplies being brought to the restaurant cars. In his book *Grand European Expresses*, George Behrend (1922–2010) described the scene in the early 1960s:

> The Gare de Lyons is at this time a hive of Wagons-Lits activity, alive with blue battery-electric trucks, known in French by the more resounding title of chariots. The charioteers weave their way through the passengers at high speed, bringing the victuals to the various dining cars. They are a band of sinister looking men, yet an essential part of the Company's service. They seem to have a ferocious enthusiasm for their job. The chef can rely on the charioteers to deliver his blocks of ice, his vegetables and his other comestibles without fail.

Incidentally, Behrend was the top British expert on the trains de luxe, and wrote several books about them. 'An authority on Pullman cars,' wrote his obituarist in *The Scotsman*, 'his was a world of Art Deco furnishings, Lalique glass and waiters walking the length of train announcing, "First call for dinner."' He was also an authority on Wagons-Lits, and it is said he knew the numbers of all the sleeping cars off by heart. His short book, *The History of Wagons-Lits (1875–1955)*, more of a pamphlet really, is the nearest thing to a comprehensive English-language history of the company. Behrend was educated at Oxford, and saw much action with the Desert 8th Army in Algiers, Italy and Greece. He was a close friend of Benjamin Britten (whose chauffeur he had once been), and also of Peter Pears, W. H. Auden and

E. M. Forster, and if that all seems to point a certain way, let me cloud the issue by saying that he died at Number 8, Station Road, Findochty, where he'd moved for the sake of his wife's health.

GARE D'AUSTERLITZ

It was easy, amid the happy bustle of the Gare de Lyon in 2015, to imagine the corresponding scene of fifty years before, but it is time to admit that I was in the station, not because the Blue Train goes from there, but because it *used* to go from there. Since 2001, the Blue Train – or the ghostly remnant of it – has left from Gare d'Austerlitz, on the other side of the Seine. So I picked up my bag, and quit the Gare de Lyon. Turning back as I walked away, it looked magnificent, like a great Spanish castle in the blue-green light of dusk.

I reached the river bank. To the right was the Viaduc d'Austerlitz, which carries Line 10 of the Métro. The bridge is single-span, and highly elegant. A train came barrelling up from its tunnel, swept around the fortress-like Institut Médico-Légal (the Paris Morgue) and onto the bridge, firing itself straight into the forehead of the Gare d'Austerlitz. Yes, the Métro station of Gare d'Austerlitz is located in the roof of the main line station, so you have to walk *upstairs* from the Grandes Lignes to reach the supposed underground railway. This section of line is called 'the toboggan', and it seems wrong that a Métro train should be having such fun in the vicinity of the morgue.

A pedestrian heading for Gare d'Austerlitz from the Right Bank must cross the Seine by the Pont d'Austerlitz, as opposed to the viaduct. The station – terminus of the old Paris-Orléans company – dates from 1862. It is solidly neoclassical, and was comprehensively upstaged when the exotic, Moorish Gare de Lyon was built on the opposite bank in 1900. According to Richards and Mackenzie, in *The Railway Station: A Social History*, Austerlitz is notable (along with Paddington, King's Cross and the first Gare Montparnasse) as one of the early 'twin-sided stations, where arrival and departure took place on opposite sides'. Since that method of operation was abandoned early in the twentieth century, this is a fairly slender claim to fame, and Richards and Mackenzie devote more space to Austerlitz's sister station, Gare d'Orsay, two miles along the left bank of the river.

Like Gare de Lyon, Orsay opened in 1900 to coincide with the Paris Exposition. It is in the beaux arts style, like its direct descendant, Grand Central in New York. The painter Édouard Detaille wrote that 'the station is superb and looks like an art gallery', and that's what it became in 1986, after standing idle, a giant haunted house right in the middle of Paris, for forty years. The building features in *Nairn's Paris*, which was written in the mid-1960s when its fate was in the balance. (Corbusier was doing some ominous doodlings, being minded to replace it with one of his monoliths.) 'And this is magnificent,' writes Nairn, 'a great curved shell with the scale of St Pancras – filled now with railway junk, parked cars and a few wee lines that peter off miserably to the *banlieue* from a lower level. See it while you can.'

But for all its grandeur, Orsay was really just an annexe of Austerlitz. You could say it was to Austerlitz what Cannon Street in London is to Charing Cross. When the South Eastern Railway wanted a more central station than Charing Cross, they built Cannon Street; when the Paris-Orléans company wanted a more central foothold than Austerlitz, they built Orsay.

Many people who visit what is today the Musée d'Orsay know it used to be a railway station. The PO initials are carved on to the façade, along with the destinations – in Brittany and the Loire – that duplicate those on the front of Austerlitz; plus there is a giant clock inside, which seems to harry the picture-gazers on the floor below. But I wonder how many people who have made these deductions go on to ask themselves: how did the trains get in? Perhaps the question comes up after they've walked around the outside of the museum, noting that it is bounded to the north by the river, and by buildings older than itself on all other sides. Anyone who saw the children's film *Hugo*, by Martin Scorsese, would have been thrown off the trail. The station in that movie resembles Gare d'Orsay, but is served by steam engines, whereas the Gare d'Orsay was the first ever terminus for electric trains. They came in under-ground from Austerlitz (where the steam locos were taken off and electric ones put on). The tunnel that was used now accommodates part of the subterranean express line called RER C, and is showing its age. It leaks, and must be closed for a few weeks every summer for maintenance.

In his novel of 1925, *Les salles d'attente*, Franc-Nohain described Gare d'Austerlitz as 'adultery's birthplace': 'Like you, monsieur, one comes to wait at Austerlitz for the person who got on the train and who has said their tearful farewells five minutes earlier at Gare d'Orsay. And they continue their journey together from the Gare de Lyon which is very close.' (In fact, then, any of those three stations could have been 'adultery's birthplace'.)

The main entrance to Gare d'Austerlitz is through the cavernous, largely empty space of a booking hall too big for modern purposes. Here, the old, typically poetic French des-ignation of a ticket hall, La Salle des Pas Perdus ('the room of lost footsteps') makes sense. In W. G. Sebald's novel *Auster-litz*, the phrase is used in connection with Antwerp Railway Station, one of several depicted in the book, including Gare d'Austerlitz itself. Austerlitz is the name of the central character, which is implausible, although Fred Astaire began life as Frederick Austerlitz. As a child, the Austerlitz in Sebald's book had been a refugee on a Kindertransport from Czechoslovakia. It is possible he was given the name Austerlitz having passed through the station at some point. This is a strange, inert novel about one neurotic and very long-winded man's search for identity. There are no paragraphs, and the incredibly long sentences are punctuated by the phrase, 'said Austerlitz', which rings like a death knell. (Sometimes this gives way to 'Austerlitz continued', and he certainly does continue.) Here is part of his account of the station:

> That station, said Austerlitz, has always seemed to me the most mysterious of all the railway terminals of Paris. I spent many hours in it during my student days, and even wrote a kind of memorandum on its layout and history. At the time I was particularly fascinated by the way the Métro trains coming from the Bastille, having crossed the Seine, roll over the iron viaduct into the station's upper storey, quite as if the façade were swallowing them up.

He continues about how he felt an 'uneasiness' in the hall behind this façade, which was 'filled with a feeble light and almost entirely empty'.

The information office – a modest, modern affair – is on the concourse, and here a TV screen advertised the 21.22 to Toulon, Les Arcs-Draguignan, Fréjus-St-Raphaël, St-Raphaël-Valescure, Cannes, Antibes, Nice-Ville. This is the heir of the old Blue Train, which for most of its life terminated beyond Nice, at Ventimiglia or San Remo, after its exquisite dawdle along the Riviera. The 21.22 does have a name, but not all to itself. It must share it with a dozen other sleeper trains operating entirely within France and run by SNCF: the Intercités de Nuit, most of which will have been abolished by the time this book appears. At the time of writing, the night train to Nice is scheduled to run for the last time in October 2017.

Most of the surviving sleepers from Paris now start at Austerlitz. It could be said that an outmoded type of train has been concentrated on an outmoded station. In recent years Austerlitz has lost its long-distance intercity services to the TGV Atlantiques, operating from Gare Montparnasse. In 2013, the TGV service from Gare de Lyon made redundant the Trenhotel night train from Austerlitz to Madrid and Barcelona. But Austerlitz is being refurbished, so it will have a bright future eventually, and will be awarded some of its own TGVs. An artist's impression of the new look is shown on posters dotted around the concourse, with the slogan, 'Découvrez Votre Nouvelle Gare, Austerlitz 2020.'

Meanwhile the place was sunk in a Sundayish mood. The lights hanging from the roof of the train shed seemed underpowered. On the concourse, I kept noticing the wrong things: two pigeons having a fight; isolated, garish vending machines; temporary yellow plastic barriers. Austerlitz has a station piano, and one of the few other passengers was playing something mournful and bluesy. Instead of repairing to the Train Bleu brasserie of Gare de Lyon, I bought something called a 'Formule 9.20 Euros' from a snack bar on the Austerlitz concourse: a ham salad baguette, a piece of madeleine and a small can of Heineken. Every so often an SNCF official went past. They were kitted out as though by a chic film director, in bright red jackets and retro white peaked caps, and rode expertly on those two-wheeled scooters called Segways. They might still be operating sleeper trains, but they've left walking behind.

Ought I to enquire about the 21.22? In the buffet of the Eurostar that morning, I'd bumped into a man I knew slightly from York, my native city. On hearing that I would be boarding a sleeper to the South of France, he said, 'First class, I hope? Otherwise you'll be sharing a compartment. Wouldn't fancy that myself.' He had zoned in on my own anxiety. I had a first class ticket – which meant, in the case of the 21.22, a ticket for a four-berth rather than a six-berth couchette – but it was a press ticket, and I didn't know whether it gave exclusive occupation of the compartment ('espace privatif') which can be guaranteed by the payment of sufficient money. I said something of the sort, and my acquaintance responded, 'The French air traffic controllers are on strike today, you know. All those people on the ground who should be up in the air? That's why this train is so crowded. I think your sleeper will be as well.'

The 21.22 *was* in the station, seemingly rather marginalised on Platform 20, the southernmost one. It was *partly* blue, but also partly white, with outbreaks of red, all part of a mongrel assemblage of 1980s carriages. The best colour scheme was that of the electric locomotive: orange and cement grey. At 8.45 both train and platform were empty and unattended. How to kill the time until departure? The one facility Gare d'Austerlitz has that Gare de Lyon lacks is a shower. It is located in Les Toilettes. (Gare de Lyon did have baths in 1931, according to *The Railway Magazine*: they were adjacent to hairdressing and shoe-cleaning salons.) Modern sleeper trains usually include showers, but on the Wagons-Lits services, a full body wash at the compartment sink was the only option, except in the case of the Rome Express and the Simplon Orient Express, whose fourgons, or baggage wagons, included 'bath compartments' which were actually showers with enamel floors, warm towel rails and wash basins. There would certainly be nothing of the kind on the 21.22, so I approached Les Toilettes.

ACCUEIL

The toilettes in Gare d'Austerlitz feature a kind of reception at which a woman awaits. She admits you through a barrier either on the male or the female side, and you pay according to whether you want the loo or the shower *and* the loo. The woman spoke English, but with a patchy vocabulary.

'I'd like a shower,' I said.

She looked at me warily. 'We don't 'ave any ...'

'Towels?' I suggested.

She nodded. 'Towels, yes. And the water is ...'

'Cold?'

'It is not very 'ot.'

The shower was clean, and lukewarm. I dried myself with a spare pair of boxer shorts, which I then threw away, because they would make everything else in my bag soaking wet. (I had neglected to bring a towel, probably because, fifty years ago, the Wagons-Lits company had provided them in all its sleeper compartments.) I was now fit to share a sleeping compartment with strangers, should that be necessary. Those emerging from the showers at Austerlitz have the option of two buttons to press: a scowl or a smile alongside the question, 'Êtes-vous satisfait du relais toilettes?' I pressed the smile, because what the hell? The action reminded me that in France you always have to validate your billet before boarding a train. This is a matter of sticking the ticket into a machine, which stamps it with the date. I walked over to the validating machine on Platform 20 and stamped my ticket. (I once asked a platform guard at Gare de Lyon if it mattered which *end* you stamped, and he was staggered at the question: it did *not* matter.)

To think that in only just over twelve hours, I would be in the South of France! The Riviera! And I'm afraid the real Riviera is in France, and not anywhere accessible from Paddington Station in London, as the Great Western Railway tried to make people believe when, in 1904 – as part of the 'See Your Own Country First' movement that had also given rise to *Travel* magazine – it christened its fastest train to Cornwall the Riviera Express. (The proof of the GWR's failure to transfer any of the Riviera magic to Cornwall lies in the fact that Agatha Christie glamorised her early short story *The Mystery of the Plymouth Express* by turning it into *The Mystery of the Blue Train*, rather than other way around.)

At ten to nine, Platform 20 still looked very quiet, which perhaps ought to be expected. The Intercités de Nuits, I had once read, take up 25 per cent of the budget of the French intercity trains, and carry 3 per cent of the passengers. But now an SNCF man and woman stood at a makeshift stall, on which was written the word 'Accueil'. That means 'Welcome', a word of which I am deeply suspicious, but the pair were smiling broadly as I approached, ticket in hand.

The man took the ticket, and examined it thoughtfully; he passed it to the woman, and they exchanged looks, as if to say, 'Who's going to deal with him, you or me?' It was the man who drew the short straw. 'Your train,' he said, 'has been deleted.'

'Eh?' I said, with great savoir-faire. 'But it's standing there.' And I pointed at the 21.22, all ten carriages of it.

'But there has been a strike,' offered the woman.

'The air traffic control strike, you mean?'

They must have thought this a strange question, but I was wondering whether the train drivers had come out in sympathy with the aviation unions.

'It is a railway strike,' the male half of the pair explained.

'Is that why it's so quiet here?' I asked, bewildered.

'It is quiet,' said the man, 'because it is late.'

'It is late *and* there's a strike,' put in the woman, obviously the more conciliatory of the two.

'But I've been seeing trains leaving Paris all evening,' I said.

'It is only a little strike,' said the woman. And it seemed it affected only the sleeper trains, and the drivers who took them from Paris to the various halfway points, where crew changes took place. They were protesting at new working practices.

'Go to the information office,' said the man, 'and they will arrange you somewhere to sleep.'

It was like that moment at the end of a crime novel when the killer is revealed: the clues had been there to see all along: the overall quietness of the station, the almost total lack of activity on Platform 20 and, come to think of it, the details of the 21.22 had been flashing on the departure monitors. There had also been a longish word flashing underneath that I couldn't understand. As I walked towards the ticket office, I looked up at one of the monitors, and the word was still there: 'Supprimé', which means, I have since discovered, 'cancelled'.

The entrance to the information office was momentarily blocked by male and female SNCF officials kissing each other on the cheeks – apparently a nightly ritual to do with a shift change. The French railways were living up to the way they are caricatured by their British detractors, who elide them with their own wrong idea of old British Rail: complacent, over-subsidised and strike-prone. Certainly they are strike-prone. If only I could move my hand across the beam of light and start the Blue Train, as instructed in the toy shop.

In the information office, I announced myself to the clerk as one of those marooned by the cancellation of the 21.22.

'You can still go to the 21.22,' he said. 'It is a sleeper; you can sleep on it.'

'But it won't be going anywhere?'

He conceded that it would not.

So I returned to Platform 20, and 'Accueil'.

'I've been told I can sleep on this train,' I said.

The man looked at the woman; they exchanged slow nods. The woman reached down behind the panel reading 'Accueil', producing a small cardboard box, which she handed to me. Before I departed, the man asked, 'Do you want a ticket to Nice on the TGV? It leaves from Gare de Lyon,' he added, gesturing towards the river, 'at 07.02 tomorrow.'

'No thanks,' I said. 'I don't want to go to Nice by day.'

This aroused suspicion, and triggered a discussion between the two.

The train consisted of ordinary seating, second-class couchettes (six berths) and two carriages of first-class couchettes (four berths). The only people on board – about half a dozen – were in the same first-class carriage I'd been booked into. It couldn't be that all the people dim enough not to have learnt about the cancellation had booked into the same carriage. It must be that all those reduced to spending the night on the train had been given a first-class couchette in compensation for 'the inconvenience caused'.

The train manager, who was evidently not on strike (but did not speak any English), showed me into my quarters with a bashful smile. Here was a pretty good simulacrum of a prison cell: grey walls, thin purple mattress, a steel ladder to reach the top bunks. (The Y-class Wagons-Lits berths of the late 1930s were the first to have aluminium ladders – rather than wood – but the rungs were carpeted, in honour of people's bare feet.)

As I closed the door, I hoped at least that no one else would come knocking, that I would continue to have the compartment to myself. In a first-class W-L sleeper there was no danger of having to share. In second class you might have to share, which you could avoid by bribing the conductor. You did this by tipping him in advance, rather than at the end of the journey, and as you pressed the money into his hand, you'd say you were *hoping for a good night's sleep*. That would probably do the trick, if he liked you.

In *Murder on the Orient Express*, Poirot finds the train to be almost full up when he boards it at Stamboul to go to Belgrade (where he will be accommodated in the coach from Athens, which will take him through to Calais). The Wagons-Lits conductor explains, 'All the world elects to travel tonight!' He is under pressure to find space for Poirot, however, because Poirot is an old friend of a Monsieur Bouc ('a Belgian, a director of the Compagnie Internationale des Wagons-Lits'), whom he has just bumped into in the Tokatlıyan Hotel in Stamboul. There is one possibility: a Mr Harris has failed to take his place in a second-class (i.e. shared) compartment. Poirot is shown into the compartment, whose sole occupant, a Mr MacQueen, looks disappointed at this development. The W-L conductor explains to MacQueen, 'There is no other berth on the train, Monsieur. The gentleman has to come in here ...' Poirot notices the apology in his tone with amusement: 'Doubtless the man had been promised a good tip if he could keep the compartment for use of the other traveller.' (Poirot, incidentally, had been confident that Harris would be a no-show, and this was because he knew his Dickens. In *Martin Chuzzlewit*, a Mrs Harris is the imaginary friend of Mrs Gamp.)

I glanced at my watch – 21.40 – and then the penny dropped. Nobody *would* come knocking because this train had now officially (even if not in practice) departed. I could lock the door! There were two locks, and a worrying sign: 'For your peace of mind use both closures.' I now had two presents to unwrap: the box I'd been given at 'Accueil', and the sleeper pack that lay on my bunk – which turned out to contain a tissue, a wet wipe, spongy earplugs and beige travel socks. I was about to open the other box when there came a sharp knocking at the door. It was an elderly and agitated man, possibly French. He was speaking in urgent tones about 'Les toilettes'. He took me along the corridor to the WC. He rattled the handle, in order to prove that it wouldn't open; he pointed to the red indicator that showed it was locked, but he gave me to understand that it was not occupied, and that it was the same with every other toilet on the train. The old man's gestures made plain that he'd looked in vain for the chef du train, so I stepped down onto the platform and returned to 'Accueil', where the SNCF couple were packing up to leave. After saying 'Bonsoir' (I had remembered that it was generally best to start with a formal greeting in France, however aggressive you intend to be), I launched in: 'Do you realise that all the toilets on the train are locked?'

The couple looked at each other: who should field this latest outburst? Again, it was the man who took the lead.

'Yes, they are locked,' he said, 'but that is completely normal for when the train is in the station; otherwise the stuff goes on the tracks.'

'But *normally*,' I said, 'the train *leaves* the station.'

He nodded, accepting the contention. 'You can use the toilets over there.' He pointed to the shower block.

'And you don't have to pay,' added the woman.

I relayed the news to the old man, before deciding I'd better use the facilities myself. I was recognised immediately by the woman in the toilettes, who did not seem very surprised to see me again. Returning to my compartment,

I opened the 'Accueil' box, which was marked 'SNCF Assistance', and subtitled 'Falières – Nutrition'. It was a sort of Red Cross parcel, to be handed out in case of a strike. There were four biscuits ('Lait choco') and a yoghurt with a poetic name ('Arlequin de fruits'). There was also a plastic mug containing drinking chocolate that was potentially hot chocolate. There was a canister at the bottom containing calcium oxide. If you shook this and waited three minutes it would heat the contents. I followed the instructions as best as I could, and after three minutes I drank a cup of ... cold hot chocolate.

Now for the bedding, because I would be making my own bed, unlike in W-L days. (Those boarding the Blue Train at Gare de Lyon would find the beds ready made up. Those who had come around on the Ceinture would be invited to step out onto the platform at Gare de Lyon while the job was done.) There was a decent-sized pillow and a sleeping bag of the same indeterminate colour as the travel socks. Both were sealed in plastic wrappers. When I ran my hand over the sleeping bag in the dim compartment, static electricity caused small sparks to fly up. I prepared one of the lower bunks. As I closed the blind, I looked across Platform 20 and saw a man on the second floor of a temporary station office belonging to the contractors refurbishing Gare d'Austerlitz. He stood before the window, stretching and yawning at the end of a long day's work. I lowered the blind, set my alarm for six, and read some of *Nairn's Paris*. Another 'passenger' (possibly the old man) was coughing in his compartment. After a while, he stopped, and I drifted off to sleep.

I was woken up by somebody else's alarm (possibly the old man's) at half past five. I sat up, fantasising that perhaps all the trouble with the unions had been rectified by a late-night negotiation, and I had been whisked to the Riviera after all. But when I opened the blind, Platform 20 was still there, looking just as dark as it had at 10pm, and there was a man in the office across the way, possibly the same one as the night before. He did look similar, and he was stretching and yawning just as the man had the night before, but this was more of a must-shake-off-this tiredness-and-get-down-to-some-work kind of yawn.

Sparrows twittered on a scrubby patch of grey garden next to Platform 20 as I ate the four biscuits from the 'Assistance' parcel. I pulled on my trousers and shirt and opened the compartment door. A young couple were in the corridor, finishing the packing of their bags. They seemed highly amused by the whole experience. They said they were from Hong Kong, and touring Europe. Did they know of the French propensity to strike? 'Yes, we had heard of that!' said the man. Had they slept well? 'Yes,' said the woman, laughing, 'but I need toilet!' And they went off. At six o'clock, the chef du train reappeared, walking along the corridor calling 'Service!' It was unclear what service he was offering, but he, like his colleague of the night before, enquired if I wanted to go to Nice on the 07.02 TGV from Gare de Lyon. Apparently, he was in a position to give me a ticket there and then. He was pushing the TGV quite hard: 'Cinq heures!' he said, as though rubbing in the fact that this train was one of those that are killing off the Blue Train. I was reminded of a remark made to me by one former enthusiast for French railways: 'I boycott French trains these days. They just want to TGV everything – and the TGVs *are* good, they continue to run in the strikes. But the classics and locals are a farce.'

The 07.02 from Gare de Lyon was certainly tempting. I had been on the TGVs to the South of France before. They fulfil the railway fantasy of Adolf Hitler, who dreamt of high-speed double-deckers. It is depressing to think that the niggardly British loading gauge prevents even the operation of double-decker commuter trains, never mind expresses. The seats are so well-padded, the armrests so wide, that the passenger feels resplendent, and if – on a double seat – you lift up the armrest in the middle, you effectively have a sofa. There's no restaurant car, but you can sit on high stools in the buffet cars, which are like space-age cocktail bars. There is such a palpable surge as the train speeds along the Rhône Valley that you keep thinking it's going to take off, but for the run along the Riviera, the trains slow down from their top speed of 200mph. The construction of a high-speed line would wreck that precious landscape, and the relative slowness also allows appreciation of the sea views.

It is also the case that a day train to the Riviera has a Wagons-Lits precedent, in the form of the Côte d'Azur Pullman Express, which coincided with the Blue Train heyday, running between 1929 and 1939. It left Paris at ten to nine in the morning, and arrived at Ventimiglia at midnight. But this book is about night trains, and as I left Gare d'Austerlitz – walking out into drizzling rain at half past seven – it was a case of 'Au revoir', not 'Adieu'.

RETURN TO THE GARE D'AUSTERLITZ

Two weeks later, there had been no noticeable progression in the refurbishment. As before, the place was almost empty of passengers. Instead of the backpacker at the station piano, there was a small boy, and since he was experimenting with a single repeated note, the effect was similarly melancholic.

Yes, the half-blue train awaited at Platform 20, but then it had awaited at Platform 20 before, and it was looking just as neglected as it had done last time. As before, the departure screens showed 21.22, and its list of destinations, but this time the notice was not flashing; the word 'Supprimé' was nowhere to be seen. In the absence of any indication to the contrary, it must be assumed that the 21.22 would be leaving the station, but better to make sure. I flagged down one of the white-capped attendants passing by on his Segway, and asked, 'Le train pour Nice – c'est d'accord?' He answered, as the French tend to do when I speak to them, in English, 'Of course it is, of course.' Having already eaten dinner, I bought a can of Heineken, then drifted towards the information office. According to a female clerk, the 21.22 is 'still called the Blue Train by "older" [she made the quotation mark gesture] people, but I've never called it that myself'.

By now, a couple of dozen people with rucksacks and suitcases were flowing towards Platform 20. Alarmingly, another pair of male and female officials had set up a little booth bearing the dreaded word, 'Accueil', but they were only checking tickets, and they wished me 'Bonsoir' as they pointed me towards the first-class couchettes, where it seemed that quite a lot of people were already in their beds and asleep.

I located my four-berth compartment. My bunk was one of the two lower ones. There was no one else in the compartment, but a backpack lay on one of the top bunks. Its owner must be the youngish bloke loitering in the doorway while eating a long baguette sandwich. In response to my 'Bonsoir,' he nodded vaguely. He then came into the compartment and took another sandwich out of the backpack. He resumed his position in the doorway to eat this one. Did he know that the originator of this train, the Wagons-Lits company, was famous for its five-course cordon bleu dinners? He had now jammed his sandwich between his knees in order to start swigging from a litre bottle of mineral water.

The window blind was about a quarter of the way down. As the whistle blew for departure, I opened it fully and perched on my bunk, glad to see Gare d'Austerlitz finally recede. I fished the can of Heineken out of my rucksack, and spread my railway map over my knees. We began to wriggle through the suburbs of Paris, over suburban lines mainly used by Line D of the RER. We would be crossing the Seine at Melun, about twenty-five miles to the south-east, prior to linking up with the old PLM main line (the one we should have been on all along from the historic-romantic point of view) emanating from Gare de Lyon.

Today, the PLM line forms the slow – or, as SNCF cleverly call it, the 'classic' – line south. It dates from the 1850s. The modern, high-speed route to the South of France was opened in 1981. They both go via Lyons, albeit via different stations, but the classic line bulges out east to Dijon en route. TGV trains are not confined to the TGV lines: they are equipped with two electrification systems, which is why you can catch a TGV train from Paris to Dijon, even though Dijon is not yet on a TGV line. But we would be stopping at neither Dijon nor Lyons. In deference to a good night's sleep, our first stop would not be until Toulon, at 06.39.

A well-preserved Frenchman, aged about sixty-five, now entered the compartment. He put a bag on the lower berth and heaved another bag onto the upper one. An elegant woman of similar age was hovering behind him, so it was clearly going to be a full house. She smiled at me, and he said something in French, which I took to be a greeting. I wheeled out my 'Bonsoir,' which caused him to say, in English, what he had probably just said in French: 'We close the blind, OK?' I did so. The Seine crossing at Melun would have to be taken on trust.

I picked up my beer for a walk along the corridors. The

scenes in the compartments – such as still had their doors open – were reminiscent of footage of soldiers relaxing during downtime in the trenches of the First World War: some people were reading, some slept, while others just sat on their bunks and stared into space. There was no restaurant or bar car, but there was a leaflet on the floor that promised breakfast with a picture of a hot chocolate and a croissant.

I felt like a street drinker, having nowhere to put my beer down. On the old Blue Train there would have been the Voiture Salon Bar, which was customised from a Pullman day car, and adjoined the Voiture Restaurant. In the bar car, as in the restaurant, the soft pink table lights would have been glowing on the marquetry. One could sit at a table (and you could eat your dinner in the bar car, since it was used as overspill for the restaurant) or on one of the stools by the bar itself. The wine list was extensive; the main attractions of Paris or Nice were listed in pages at the back, and could be quickly found by means of a thumb-index.

All the most interesting people on the train would have congregated in the bar car. (Since this was an entirely nocturnal service, there was no day car.) In the 1950s, for example, one might have seen Evelyn Waugh, Charlie Chaplin, Somerset Maugham and our own George Behrend. In restaurant, bar, and all along the corridors of the train, the carpet – probably of light blue – would have had a deep pile, so the erratic footfall of passengers returning to their berths late after dinner would not wake those already asleep.

Sometimes, a space was cleared for dancing to a gramophone in the bar car. In *Charles Dickens: A Life*, Claire Tomalin relates that Dickens once taught his business associate George Dolby how to dance the can-can on a moving train. That was in the 1860s. In the 1960s, there was a sleeper service from Calais to Innsbruck called the Snow Sun Express. It was aimed at young British skiers, and had un-switch-off-able piped music in all the compartments. There was dancing – all night – to the twist in the bar car. In 1962, ITN made a short film about the train. The presenter was Michael Barsley, who would go on to write a book on the Orient Express. He did a grumpy old man act, professing to find it all very regrettable. Today, there is the Mixery Melt! train, which carries 600 revellers every summer from Cologne to the Melt! Festival of electronic music, which is held at Ferropolis, an open-air museum of vast industrial machines. The train is a sleeper, theoretically. 'But with decks set up in the club carriage,' I read in *The Guardian*, 'and DJs from Dekmantel Soundsystem on board to run them, this is not rail travel for those who like to doze off while reading a book.'

Back in the compartment, the sandwich-eater was already fast asleep, like a corpse, on his top bunk. The French couple were making up their beds. The woman was on the top bunk. Remembering that the man spoke English, I said, 'Are you a regular on this train?'

He frowned, not understanding. I tried something less colloquial: 'You know this train?' But that was clearly *too* simple, because he replied, with a note of sarcasm, 'I know this train.'

I went to the WC. There was a toilet going straight onto the tracks and a sink about as big as a shoe box. There was a single tap; the eau was non-potable. I had a wash, which necessarily involved spraying water everywhere, then tried to pee away every last drop of Heineken from my bladder.

In the compartment, the French couple were now eating their dinner: she above, he below. Each had a paper plate on which were neatly arranged crackers, cheese, pâté and garnish. Well, it was no worse than sharing a compartment with someone who'd bought a dinner basket at Gare de Lyon. I made up my own bed, then riffled through my bag looking for the paperback I'd brought: *My Friend Maigret* (1949), by Georges Simenon.

Inspector Maigret is travelling from Paris to the South of France to investigate a murder. He is accompanied by the earnest Inspector Pyke, who has come from Scotland Yard to study Maigret's methods, but the trouble is, Maigret has no methods. At about 8pm they arrive at the Gare de Lyon, and Maigret wonders which train to take:

Alone, he would have been content with a couchette. At the Gare de Lyons he hesitated. Then at the last moment he took two wagon-lit places ... It was sumptuous. In the corridor they found *de luxe* travellers, with impressive-looking luggage. An elegant crowd, laden with flowers, was seeing a film star on to the train.

'It's the Blue Train,' Maigret mumbled, as if to excuse himself.

An hour later, Maigret is sitting fully clothed on his bunk, smoking his pipe. Inspector Pyke, impeccable in dressing gown and pyjamas, asks:

'Do you sleep well on trains?'
'I sleep well anywhere.'
'The train doesn't help you think?'
'I think so little, you know!'

The entente cordiale was also under strain in my own compartment. The male half of the French couple was eating a bag of crisps, or 'chips' as the French call them, and every so often he'd hand a few of these up to his wife, which was irritating: why didn't she have her own bag of chips?

After half an hour of Maigret, I turned off my personal reading light. The Frenchwoman did the same with hers soon after. Now the only light left on was the Frenchman's. He would presumably be turning his off soon, and we could all try to join the upper-bunk sandwich-eater in the land of nod. But the Frenchman now produced his own book from under his pillow. It was by somebody called Russell Banks (an American whose novels concern 'detailed accounts of domestic strife and the daily struggles of often marginalised characters'). Judging by the methodical regularity of his page-turning, the Frenchman was lapping up the struggles of the marginal. But at the exact moment I realised I needed to go to the loo again, he briskly locked both locks on the door, and turned out his light.

So I did not go to the loo. I fantasised instead about 'espace privatif' – sole occupancy. That would have been guaranteed in the sleeping accommodation most closely associated with the Blue Train, namely the Lx10-class, introduced in 1928, and the most luxurious that Wagons-Lits ever made. These had the most elaborate marquetry and the widest beds, and the sink was in a wooden bay that was almost like an en-suite bathroom, with a big mirror to one side. Each compartment had only one bed, and there were only ten compartments to a carriage. A couple would – or could, if they were getting along – book two adjacent compartments and open the intervening door. After the Wall Street Crash there were fewer takers for this sort of extravagance, and from 1931, the Lx began to be modified. Extra berths were added to four of the ten compartments so two people might share. In 1942, some of the cars were further modified, so that *every* compartment could house two people. What had been Lx10s therefore became Lx20s. You could have one of these to yourself, but you'd have to pay twice as much as someone wiling to share.

Further bathos was in store for the Lx, in that, from the early 1950s, the maple panelling was replaced with Formica, the art deco lights by fluorescent strips. In that same decade the 'P' type car – so called because it was designed by M. Louis Pillepich, Engineer-in-Chief of Wagons-Lits – was introduced to the Blue Train alongside the Lx. The 'P' type cars were for 'the atomic age', and had skins of unpainted ribbed steel. So they were not blue, and there was nowhere to hang the company crest. They were designed for sole – if cramped – occupancy. The larger berths were like an inverted 'L'. There was standing room in the vertical part of the 'L', and a raised bunk was slotted into the horizontal part. But what of the void beneath? That was given over to a berth euphemistically designated 'Special', wherein you could only stand up immediately inside the door, after which it became coffin-like; this berth would be called a 'pod' today. The P's had plywood panelling, held by aluminium strips. This was all part of the democratisation of the Blue Train, a spur to which had come in 1945, when the beginning of a regular air service between Paris and Nice took away many of the wealthier clients. Another milestone, or gravestone, was reached in the early 1980s, when SNCF couchettes began to replace the sleeper carriages, a demotion reflecting the fact that the daytime TGVs were reducing the journey time from Paris to Nice from twenty hours to five.

At what turned out to be about 2am I was woken up (therefore I must have gone to sleep) by the very proximate barking of a dog. But that couldn't be right, since the train was still moving; we couldn't be near any dog on any station platform. Surely it was a mishearing or a dream. (In 1864,

Gustave Flaubert wrote to a friend, 'I get so bored on the train that I am about to howl with tedium after five minutes of it. One might think it's a dog someone has forgotten in the compartment; not at all, it is M. Flaubert, groaning.' In spite, or perhaps because of, the boredom, he could not sleep on night trains unless he stayed up throughout the previous night.)

Just over an hour later, the train had stopped moving, and was being bashed about by a heavy shunting manoeuvre. We had reached Valence Ville, not to be confused with Valence TGV, which exists in the parallel world of the fast trains. The 21.22 has a portion for Briançon in south-east France, and this is detached at Valence Ville at about 3.30am.

THE CURIOUS INCIDENT

I woke for a third time and groped for my mobile phone. It was 06.16, a permissible time to get up, and there was enough light filtering in to see the locks on the door, which I opened as quietly as possible. Further light spilled in from the corridor, revealing something grey and furry on the opposite upper bunk. A dog? But it might easily have been a grey furry coat or wrap, especially since it seemed to be completely motionless. The corridor was deserted. We were passing hills and trees that resembled either church spires or lollipops. The sea would be on the other side. In the vestibule at the carriage end, the window of the door was largely obscured by a label reading 'Voiture 16', but there was the sea, looking rather grey beneath a pale blue-and-white sky.

Fifteen minutes later, we rattled through a tiny station: a pretty little pink temple almost overwhelmed by two big bushes of red bougainvillea – and illuminated by bright sunshine. All the travails of the journey were instantly worth it.

The station was Cassis, about ten miles east along the coast from Marseilles. The Old Blue Train would have called at either Marseilles St Charles or Marseilles Blancarde, but we had cut the corner, avoiding central Marseilles by means of the by-pass called Raccordement des Chartreux. (Only the French can make an avoiding line sound beautiful.)

The backpacker had also emerged from the compartment, and he was standing in the corridor, his bag neatly packed. He gave me the same minimal nod of the night before. His mobile phone was charging in what had been intended as a shaver socket. Here is George Behrend, from *Grand European Expresses*:

> As you carefully adjust your electric razor to the 110 volts of the Wagons-Lits supply, perhaps you think of all the many journeys made before that wonderful new system was fitted, when you struggled with a safety razor and pondered how an earlier generation, armed only with a cut-throat, could appear sleek at the breakfast table, with chins unornamented with cotton wool. The answer? They made full use of any stops.

(Behrend regretted the gradual replacement of multilingual notices explaining about the shaver sockets, in favour of a small stylised drawing of a man shaving.)

The window in the door now disclosed swimming pools with water slides, palm trees, an industrial estate and a freight yard. Even the graffiti on the wagons in the freight yard was starting to look picturesque. At 06.42 we called at Toulon, and the backpacker walked away along the platform. As we departed – now heading away from the sea – I saw another leaflet on the carriage floor promising breakfast. I began walking along the train until I came to a recessed booth in the next couchette carriage. It was billed as 'Point Information', and a uniformed official was standing in it, looking through the window on the landward side. I held up the leaflet, and asked in my broken French about breakfast. He answered courteously: 'I am sorry but I am not the train manager. There are two ladies. I think they are that way.' He pointed west, so I began walking that way until I came to the end of the train. There had been no two ladies, with or without breakfast. On the other hand, here was an end-door with a window looking directly onto the receding tracks.

The dining car – as it had become chic in the 1920s to call the Voiture Restaurant – disappeared from the Paris-Nice night train in 2007, and with it went the doggedly English Blue Train breakfast: eggs, bacon and tomato, cooked on an open, coal-fired range.

In *My Friend Maigret*, the Inspector accompanies the Englishman, Pyke, to the restaurant car, observing him warily: 'A slight contraction of the nostrils on the arrival of the bacon and eggs, which were indisputably not as good as in his own country.' The waiter, who knows Maigret, comes up and asks an embarrassing question 'in an insinuating voice': 'Something to drink, as usual?'

At Fréjus-St-Raphaël we rejoined the sea, running past the pretty, but deserted, beach at Agay. If anyone had been standing on that beach, they could have watched the train crossing the Viaduc d'Anthéor, which is depicted in a famous Wagons-Lits poster captioned 'Summer on the French Riviera by the Blue Train'. On the beach are candy-striped parasols; the sea is dotted with white sails. The Blue Train itself is impossibly elevated, as small in the sky as an aeroplane.

A few minutes later, we pulled into Cannes. In the early 1960s George Behrend had observed 'a galaxy of gold-braided officials and porters' at Cannes. In 2015, there were no officials at all to be seen. Amongst those alighting were the French couple. They each pulled a big, wheeled suitcase along the platform, but ... no dog. As the train eased away, I darted back into the compartment, which was now empty except for my things. The couple had left their beds neatly made up, but the top bunk was covered with grey hairs. So there presumably had been a dog, but why had they not been walking it along the platform? Perhaps they had given it to someone at or before the previous station, Les Arcs, and that other person had carried it off the train? But as far as I could tell, the French couple hadn't emerged from their compartment until Cannes. Or perhaps the dog had been put in one of the wheeled suitcases, which begs the question of how it could breathe ... The episode goes down as 'The Curious Incident of the Dog on the Night Train', and it would have been even more imponderable in Wagons-Lits days. According to one student of the company: 'I know of no regulations concerning dogs. Probably you could bring one if you bribed the conductor, but remember that many of the passengers in the early days were British, and dogs had to go into quarantine if they were taken from the continent back into Britain.' In *Orient Express*, Michael Barsley quotes an article by Joseph Wechsberg in the *New Yorker* of 22 April 1950, relating how 'one Katharina Schratt, actress at Vienna's Burg-theater and a favourite of the Emperor Franz Joseph, would have her dogs with her on the train, and the chef in the wagon-restaurant would make special dishes for them; their favourite was schnitzel.'*

---

*When I returned home, I phoned SNCF and asked the policy on dogs: 'Generally speaking, they have to have a ticket and the owners must have sole occupancy of the compartment; otherwise the dog is classed as an illicit passenger.'

Juan-les-Pins was approaching, with a countdown of trackside palm trees and the sparkling sea beyond. Then we went inland again, by-passing the Cap d'Antibes, on which stands one of the world's most luxurious hotels, the Hôtel du Cap-Eden-Roc. It's a heavenly chateau with a kind of annexe on a cliff overlooking the sea. In 1923, Gerald and Sara Murphy, American socialites, held a season of parties at what was then the Hôtel du Cap, which they persuaded to stay open in what was considered the 'off season': summer. This was a staging post on the way to Nice becoming a summer resort. Another was Coco Chanel's proud flaunting of her suntan, making the look acceptable in fashionable society. (The glamorous Dick and Nicole Diver, the neurotic principals of F. Scott Fitzgerald's terrific novel *Tender is the Night*, are based on the Murphys.)

As we approached Nice, the only passengers remaining in the carriage were two young men from Cambodia. They were both eating raw carrots, but this was only a snack, because, as one of them explained, 'We will have breakfast in Nice, then we transit to Monaco.' What had he made of the trip? 'In Cambodia, everybody drives, so this has a very, like, old feeling. And we had to take pills to get to sleep, but we saved 800 dollars by not flying from Nice to Monaco.'

We arrived in Nice dead on time at 08.37. The guard's parting announcement wished us, not a 'bonne journée', but a '*belle* journée', which train guards on the Riviera are entitled to do with some confidence.

From the station, I walked for five minutes to a big block of flats called, according to the notice on the gatepost, Number 2 Boulevard de Cimiez. If I had been a wealthy traveller before the First World War, I might have been staying here, because it used to be the Cimiez Riviera Palace Hotel, built by Georges Nagelmackers in 1891 and opened in 1895

(*The Continental Traveller* reported that 'it had been wisely left to dry before being opened to the public'). Some of the more exuberant art nouveau flourishes have been lopped off since then, but it's still a vast white wedding cake of a building, albeit one that seems slightly dismayed by the incessant roar of traffic along the Boulevard de Cimiez.

The first foreign visitors to Nice – the English – didn't come for the beach and the sea, but for such humble requirements as the absence of damp. Cimiez, on an upland above the town, was the favoured spot, and Queen Victoria had her villa there. Nice must have been a melancholic place, full of frail people demanding of the town that it make them better. A consumptive called the Rev. Henry Lyte went there in fruitless search of better health, and he was in Nice when he wrote the hymn 'Abide With Me', whose second verse contains the line 'Change and decay in all around I see'. (I had always assumed that was written in some dark, satanic British mill town.)

The railway connection to Paris came in the 1860s, and gradually turned Nice into the kind of place Queen Victoria didn't like. The same had happened with Brighton, which she had initially favoured, but she found the railway brought in people who were 'very indiscreet and troublesome'. Modern Nice is reminiscent of Brighton: the beach is stony, the dome of the Hotel Negresco is like the dome of the Pavilion, and Nice is rackety like Brighton. At ten o'clock in the morning the cafés of the Promenade des Anglais feature plenty of peroxide blondes having champagne with their breakfast croissants, often with a palpitating lap dog (which also seems to be a peroxide blonde) slumped under the seat. Some of them are Russian.

The Russians have enjoyed coming to Nice since pre-Revolutionary times. The Russian Orthodox church behind the station is a reminder of this. Nagelmackers catered to the Russian market with the St Petersburg-Vienna-Nice-Cannes Express, which first ran on 15 November 1898. At 18.00 on Sundays it left St Petersburg for Warsaw, to meet the Vienna-Nice Express. It left Warsaw for Vienna at 17.50 on the Monday. On arrival at Vienna, it was shunted from the Nordbahnhof to the Südbahnhof. The train arrived in Nice at 14.19 on the Wednesday. It was known for its formality, being one of the last on which passengers dressed for dinner.

In 2010, another sleeper train began running between Moscow and Nice via Warsaw. The Nice Express is operated by Russian Railways, RZD; it provides the longest continuous train journey available in Europe, and runs only in summer. The second longest is also provided by RZD: from Paris Gare de l'Est to Moscow, which runs all year round, and started in 2011. Russia has a broad gauge, and both trains switch gauges at Brest, so these are heroic enterprises, in the Wagons-Lits mould, with luxurious sleeping accommodation. At the time of writing the plan is for a couple of the sleepers from the Moscow-Nice service to be attached to the Paris-Nice Intercité de Nuit, for travel at premium rates. Passengers in these carriages will be loaned tablets, on which they can download entertainment, as happens on the Russian sleepers. This scheme offers a small prospect of a reprieve to the descendant of the Blue Train.

2

THE NORDLAND RAILWAY

THE NIGHTCAP

Ten o'clock on a late June evening in Trondheim, halfway up the coast of Norway. I was sitting in the penthouse bar of my hotel, looking down on a rainswept marshalling yard ten storeys below. A shunter was pushing some flatbed wagons about, some of them carrying green containers marked 'BRING'. That morning, I'd had a tour of Trondheim, and the guide had apologised for the marshalling yard. 'We're thinking of moving that,' she'd said, 'it's such an eyesore.' But you can't just shift a marshalling yard. You need a railway line to feed it, for one thing, and this particular marshalling needed to be by the sea, or rather the Trondheim Fjord – indistinguishable from the open sea – whose container vessels it serves.

The shunter had its headlights switched on, which perhaps helped with visibility in the rain, but darkness had not fallen, and would *not* be falling because this was midsummer, the time of the midnight sun. The sky had merely turned violet, with lingering hints of orange, while the heavy rain generally blurred the issue. I was feeling disoriented and slightly drunk. This was my third glass of Riesling, in spite of the fact that each glass had cost about ten pounds. The Norwegian state does not trust its citizens not to drink to excess, and so taxes alcohol heavily. Other disapproved-of commodities, such as cosmetics and cars, are also heavily taxed. On the other hand, social services are well funded, so that Norway scores high on quality of life indexes, and the British visitor has the impression of being in a more sensible country than his homeland.

I was in Norway because of a conversation at a funeral. My father, a lifelong railwayman, died in June 2015, a fortnight after I returned from my trip on the remnant of the Blue Train, and the story of my misadventures en route to the Riviera had caused him to nod politely in his hospital bed, rather than laugh, as I had been hoping. As we drove away from the crematorium, one of his friends – also ex-BR and a former member of the British Railwaymen's Touring Club – recommended a trip on the Nordland Railway in Norway. 'You can see half the country in ten hours, and we've nothing over here to compare. I've been on the West Highland Line, Settle-Carlisle Railway, the Cornish Main Line – they're London-to-Croydon in comparison with the Nordland.' He knew about my interest in sleepers, and he explained that there were both day and night trains along the Nordland, with the condition that there was no 'night' in north Norway in midsummer.

I had not planned on going to Norway, but it was certainly within my chosen area – which is to say that it was shown on the badge of the British Railwaymen's Touring Club – and the full extent of the Nordland Line was there on my European Railway Map, albeit on the separate Scandinavian pull-out. But surely Norway was not a very fertile railway territory? With its 2,580 miles of track, it takes up four pages of the European Railway Timetable. Britain, with its 9,188 miles, takes up 128 pages, yet Norway is almost twice as big as Britain.

Railways came late to Scandinavia. Denmark started track-laying in 1847, Norway in 1854, Sweden two years after that. As Christian Wolmar writes in Blood, Iron & Gold, 'The reason for their tardiness was obvious. These were poor and sparsely populated countries with a harsh climate that was not conducive to railway construction. Norway, for example, had just 2 million people in the middle of the nineteenth century, spread over a vast country eking out a living from agriculture, timber and fishing.'

But the terrain that made the railways difficult to build also made them beautiful. An English-language booklet issued by the national operator, NSB, is confidently entitled 'Enjoy Norway by Train'. The west-east Bergen-Oslo Railway is billed as 'Perhaps the most spectacular scenic experience in Europe'. In 2010, a branch line off it, the Flam Railway, 'was named one of Europe's 10 most scenic train journeys by the National Geographic Traveller Magazine', while the Rauma Railway (Åndalsnes-Dombås) 'stands at the top of Lonely Planet's awards for Europe's most beautiful railway journeys'. The Nordland does not miss out: 'Lonely Planet has named this line as one of the world's most beautiful night train journeys.' Night trains also operate on the Bergen-Oslo, Oslo-Trondheim and Oslo-Kristiansand-Stavanger routes, and all of these sleepers operate under the banner of NSB Sove ('sove' meaning sleep).

The four night trains of Norway appear to have a secure future, just as the two in Britain do. This is nothing to do with being at arm's length from the European Union, but rather because the trains all operate within a single territory. In Britain this arises from the country being an island, and Norway might as well be an island because it only has a railway connection to one other country, Sweden, and while there is one 'international' sleeper between the two, it is a Swedish train. The more countries that are involved in running a sleeper service, the greater the chance of it being stopped, because one of them might pull the plug, sleepers being inherently uneconomical. But as Chris Jackson, editor of the *Railway Gazette International*, puts it, 'If there's only one national operator involved, they might decide to take the hit, either for social or patriotic reasons.' But does the healthy condition of Norwegian sleepers owe anything to a Wagons-Lits heritage? Had there ever been a 'Norwegian Blue', so to speak?

It turns out that Wagons-Lits did once have a fingertip in Norway. The Norway connection was a spin-off from the Nord Express, a particularly ambitious project even by Nagelmackers' standards. The Nord Express began running in 1896, as a Paris-St Petersburg service. The aim was to join it to the Sud Express – which, as we will see, ran from Paris to Lisbon – to create a vertical counterpart to the horizontal Orient Express. But the Nord was at the mercy of politics to a much greater extent than the remarkably constant Sud Express. After the First World War and the Russian Revolution, Warsaw became the northerly terminus of the Nord, and by the 1950s it had become a train from Paris to various places in Scandinavia. After rereading a certain paragraph about this late-period Nord Express about six times – it was written by George Behrend, always much clearer about railway dinners than railway routes – I divined that it had gone into Norway from 9 June 1953. 'This lasted until May 26th 1962,' Behrend wrote, before suddenly, and characteristically, lobbing away the fine brush and picking up the broad one, 'when Wagons-Lits ceased to run in Norway.' Why did it cease to run? He does not say, but presumably aeroplanes had something to do with it.

The Nord Express had entered Denmark via Jutland, rather than by the Baltic Sea. It then crossed the bridge at Fredericia, gaining Funen (the central island of Denmark) where it called at Odense. The train was then put onto the Nyborg-Korsør train ferry across the Grand Belt to Zealand, the island on which Copenhagen is situated. Most of the carriages would continue from Copenhagen to Malmö (and then Stockholm) by means of the train ferry between Helsingør on Zealand and Helsingborg in Sweden, a service now replaced by the Øresund Bridge, which we will be returning to in the chapter on the Berlin Night Express. But one sleeping car went from Copenhagen to Oslo via the same train ferry. At the preserved Nene Valley Railway near Peterborough, which accommodates vehicles with foreign loading gauges, they are restoring one of the Wagons-Lits sleeping cars that had sometimes gone to Oslo. Generally referred to by the volunteers as 'Number 3916', it is fading from light to dark blue under its tarpaulin as a campaign proceeds to raise the funds for refurbishment.

So the blue coaches did reach Oslo, but they certainly never reached Trondheim, which is over 300 miles north of Oslo. Still less did they reach Bodø, terminus of the Nordland, which is nearly 450 miles from Trondheim. But there was an elemental appeal about the trip.

Bodø is a pleasingly emphatic terminus. When the Nordland reached that town in 1962, that was the completion of the Norwegian network. Another 600 miles of Norway lie beyond Bodø, but terrain, weather and lack of demand conspired against any extension of the line. The idea of going to Bodø on the day train and coming back on the night train was also appealing: the symmetry of it. Admittedly, this would be complicated by travelling in midsummer. Instead of comparing day with night, I would be comparing day with the witchy twilight of the midnight sun. But how often does one have the chance to make a night train journey in the light?

KOMFORT CLASS

After the night-that-never-was, the rain still fell. At 6.50am, I set off from my hotel for Trondheim Central Station, with a slight feeling of guilt at being about to leave the place after only half a day.

The centre of Trondheim is built along two waterways: a canal and the river Nid, both of which are lined with old warehouses painted in a strangely harmonious palette of faded browns, dull greens, rust reds, mustard yellows. The buildings are rather wavy and bulging, like their own reflections in the water. Trondheim suffered from repeated fires, and in 1681 it was apparently 'turned to ashes' ... which is hard to credit, Trondheim seeming to be such a watery place, what with the rain that had been falling since my arrival, and the proximity of the great, grey fjord.

The tour guide had been full of civic pride, and armed with plenty of facts, some of which she would transcribe in my notebook. Trondheim, she had explained, was the most northerly city (as opposed to town) in the country; it was also the second oldest and the third largest. She seemed reluctant to discuss my intended destination on the Nordland Railway – Bodø – except to say that it takes twenty-one hours to get there on a ferry, forty-five minutes on a plane, or ten hours on the train. The train, she implied, was the poor relation.

In a country with over 50,000 miles of coastline, boats and ships were always the main mode, inhibiting railway-building. The development of the roads then had the same effect, and the Nordland Railway shadows the Arctic Highway rather than the other way around.

The guide's relentless focus was Trondheim itself, or its rural hinterland, Trøndelag. Had I considered going sightseeing on a hired bike? Or a bus could take me into those beautiful wooded hills to the south in half an hour. Did I know that the Gulf Stream keeps the fjord ice-free? On Saturday, there would be a farmers' market. She pointed out the Trondheim Town Hall, the Trondheim flag flying from its roof, and the Royal residence where the king lives, sometimes. (It was an elegant late-eighteenth-century house, with vagrants sleeping in the garden, which seemed admirably democratic.)

***

Trondheim Central Station is elegant and pastel-coloured, like most of the city. The main building is Italianate, and pale yellow. It is a fulcrum of the railways in this vertically long country, in that it forms the terminus of the Dovre Line, running south to Oslo, and the Nordland, running north to Bodø. (There is also a commuter line that heads east across Norway and into Sweden.) The Dovre is electrified, the Nordland is not. In the absence of any *Lonely Planet* superlatives for the Dovre, NSB offer the following: 'The landscape along the Dovre railway is very varied in both topography and vegetation, which is not unexpected for a route with a height difference of 960 metres and a high point of 1,025 metres above sea level.' (Height above sea level is an obsession with NSB, as we will see.)

The Nordland train awaited: six red carriages and a red Di 4 diesel locomotive. A diesel loco is the exception rather than the norm in Norway, where more than half the lines are electrified, and there are plans to electrify the Nordland.

In *Norway, Changing and Changeless* (1939), Agnes Rothery wrote, of Norwegian railway carriages:

> These are built in compartments and are so similar to the English model that one is a little surprised to be warned that 'sigaretter' and 'sigarer' are not to be 'kast ut' of the 'vinduet' ... Not only does the 'konduktor' speak better English than the cockney Englishman ... but the passengers with their zipper bags and spectacles look entirely familiar, as do the people waiting on the platforms, lapping ice cream cones or sucking soft drinks through a straw out of a bottle.

But in summer 2015, many cultural differences were evident at Trondheim. In the station shop, commuters had apples or raw peeled carrots along with their newspapers, rather than grab bags of crisps and coffee, which is the English way. The train was being boarded by a few executive types, who didn't look as though they were intending to cross the Arctic Circle, but also by people who looked as if they would be taking that landmark in their stride: literally, in the case of a party of retirees, all coming along the platform in expensive-looking quilted jackets, while walking with two sticks, like cross-country skiers. I was half irritated, half jealous of this prosperous, apparently happy nation, where even the nights are not dark for some of the year.

My ticket was for a seat in 'Komfort' Class, denoting an open carriage that was grey, very clean, and if anything slightly too spacious (the tables were too far away from the seats). The carriage windows were also exceptionally big. I took out my iPad to test the free Wi-Fi. 'Have a good trip,' said the message that immediately popped up. 'You are logged in.' And it was telling the truth, whereas when you get that message on a British train, you are usually not logged in, despite having yielded up all your personal details.

As we pulled away from Trondheim – at 07.38 – I looked for another seat, because I was sitting with my back to the engine. I moved into a window seat facing the direction of travel, but this turned out to have been booked by a late-boarding executive, a completely grey, silent man who stood over me until I vacated the seat. While I returned to my original place, he sat down and began typing on his laptop, never once glancing through the window. Perhaps he had become blasé through living in a country with such scenic railways, just as the Parisians never look up from their newspapers when they cross the Seine on the Métro bridges.

The Nordland would be stopping twenty-seven times, but it passes through more stations than it stops at, including – twenty miles north of Trondheim – the one called Hell, which is probably the most famous and widely photographed small station in the world. Hell means 'cave' in Old Norse and tourists like to be photographed under the sign reading 'Hell Gods-Expedition', which means 'freight service' or 'cargo handling'. As we passed the station, some young people on the platform had the temerity to be laughing, even though they were in Hell. The next station, and the first stop, was Trondheim Airport. ('The fourth busiest in Norway,' the meticulous tour guide had informed me.)

We now entered deep countryside. The chalet-like houses and station buildings were usually either maroon or mustard yellow. Under the grey sky, the lush farmland of Trøndelag was a vivid green that put British grass to shame. Sometimes the train, on its single track, seemed to be threading through farmyards; there were never any fences, Norway being such a civilised and trusting place. (The many bikes, on the passing station platforms, tended to have been left unlocked.) And there were hardly any people. The Norwegian flag often flew from the farmhouse roofs, as though the lonely occupants wanted to remind themselves who they were. The engine periodically whistled, as though trying to raise the dead. I was enjoying the journey, in the melancholic way described by W. N. P. Barbellion in *The Journal of a Disappointed Man* (1919):

> A journey on a railway train makes me sentimental. If I
> enter the compartment a robust-minded, cheerful youth,
> fresh and whistling from a walk by the sea, yet, as soon as
> I am settled down in one corner and the train is rattling
> along past fields, woods, towns, and painted stations, I
> find myself indulging in a saccharine sadness – very
> toothsome and jolly.

As we approached any given station, there would be a quiet, relaxed automatic announcement in Norwegian, followed by the translation: 'We will be arriving at [whatever the next station might be] in five or six minutes.' At each arrival, the time and the outside temperature would be displayed on the dot matrix screen at the end of the carriage, together with another figure, to be discussed shortly.

Some stations were at the head of branch lines leading to ports, because the Nordland begins by skirting a fjord. There is the same thrilling proximity of rail and sea that you get on the Cornish main line at Dawlish, but that's over after five minutes, whereas this lasts for a hundred miles. I asked the middle-aged Norwegian man in the next seat (he was drinking something probably very healthy from a high-spec flask) what this fjord was called. 'Trondheim Fjord,' he said. He took pleasure in leaning across to me twice more in the next hour, and saying, 'Still Trondheim Fjord,' and pointing through the window. His name was Larry, and he was dressed for the great outdoors in neatly pressed lumberjack shirt and combat trousers.

On the eastern side appeared the beginnings of what was to become a vertiginous gorge. 'Namsen river,' explained Larry, who was now eating a fascinatingly well-organised lunch from a green Perspex lunchbox that had separate compartments for cold meat, cheese, berries, yoghurt. His bike was in the baggage van, he explained, and he would be 'touring the Bodø district, as I do every year'.

I walked to the buffet through a crowded family carriage that was bathed – for some doubtless very good reason – in orange light. There was a kind of romper room in the corner, with a climbing frame, a padded floor and an indestructible-looking TV looping cartoons. The class status of the family carriage was unclear, but the next one along was definitely a 'second' or 'økonomi'. It was the same as 'Komfort' but with smaller seats. The European Timetable says of Norway, 'All trains convey second-class accommodation. Many trains also convey NSB Komfort accommodation.' In other words, not all trains have first class.

The buffet was spacious and ultra-clean, with red leather transverse benches. The female attendant recommended a Norwegian pork stew called lapskaus that was both traditional and gluten free. It was also delicious, although it came on a rather bendy paper plate. I bought a coffee and took it back to my carriage, whereupon Larry looked up from the map he was perusing on his tablet and enquired, 'You bought that?' Pointing to a vending machine, he said, 'No need. Coffee is free in Komfort Class.' (There were also free newspapers on a rack by the coffee machine, but they were in Norwegian.)

The forested hills became snow-capped mountains. The station buildings now had a plainer, more austere look, having been built by the occupying Germans in 1940, whereas the previous ones had been built by Norwegians in the early twentieth century. The story of how the Nordland developed after the 1930s is salutary, and makes the traveller feel slightly ashamed at being in Komfort Class ...

***

An article about Norway appearing in *Railway Wonders of the World* in 1935, gives a jolly survey of engineering difficulties overcome in ways likely to be appreciated by the schoolboy reader. After a long survey of the Rauma Railway, the Nordland merits only a paragraph, since it was, at the time, mainly a projected railway. The line north from Trondheim had reached Hell by 1881; by 1929 it was at Grong, a hundred miles north of Trondheim:

> Work is proceeding [wrote the anonymous author] at the time of writing on a further extension which will carry the Nordland still further north to Bodø, a town within the Arctic Circle. Here, the fisheries of the Lofoten Islands – where all the major part of the Norwegian cod and herring fishing is carried on – will greatly benefit from being able to put their catches on rail as near to the islands as Bodø, and the transport of fish southwards will be greatly expedited.

But it would be the occupying Nazis who would push the

line northwards, and not for the benefit of the fishermen of Bodø. The Luftwaffe would have other plans for Bodø, as we will see, and the line would not reach there until 1962 in any case. The Germans extended the line to Dunderland, thirty miles short of the Arctic Circle, as part of the infrastructure necessary to create 'Fortress Norway'. Hitler believed that the Norwegian coast, especially the north coast, was the 'zone of destiny', and the defence of it against an Allied attack was prioritised even over the defence of the German coast. The Germans used slave labour to build the line: 20,000 prisoners of war, mainly Russians, Yugoslavs and Poles. At least 10 per cent died of exposure, overwork or starvation, and these men were buried at the lineside.

Our train started to climb, until we were at an angle more usually associated with Swiss railways. The trees became thinner, then disappeared entirely. All was grey rock and snow, our train moving silently, like some lunar vehicle. There came an announcement, not automatic, and more urgent than the laid-back ones hitherto: 'Your attention please! We are about to cross the Arctic Circle.' Stone pyramids on either side of the track marked the spot.

Approaching Røkland, greenery reappeared, but with much greyness persisting, in the form of rocky cliffs and a grey eagle flying lazily over some raging rapids. At Fauske, the majority of those left on the train got off. Larry, who had been listening to music on expensive headphones, briefly removed them (classical music seeping out) in order to explain, 'Quarrying town.' No more than a couple of dozen remained for the Bodø termination, including Larry, who took my picture on the platform.

The railway void north of Bodø is perhaps to be considered precious. In their book, The Northern Utopia, Peter Fjågesund and Ruth A. Symes quote Lady Wilde, Oscar Wilde's mother, who visited Norway on her honeymoon in 1852: 'owing to the nature of this country, railways can never be universal, and this is fortunate, as Norway must remain sacred to nature, and the picturesque, and the poet'.

BODØ

It is possible to progress north from Bodø by bus. As the European Rail Timetable explains, a bus runs to Narvik, nearly 200 miles north, but you wouldn't hop on it casually, because the footnote also reads: 'Journey time: four and a half hours.' You *can* take a train to Narvik, but for that you must first go to Sweden. A sleeper from Stockholm departs at 17.55. It is apparently a very comfortable one, and reindeer stew is a dinner option. Arrival at Narvik is at 14.18 the next day, and if this sounds like a chance for a long lie-in, the time-table warns passengers they may be ejected from their beds to travel in seated accommodation some three hours before Narvik, at Kiruna. The mines at Kiruna are the reason the line exists: to carry iron ore from there to Narvik, which is ice-free all year round because of the Gulf Stream. In 1935, *Railway Wonders of the World* said of the line from Vassijaure (on the Swedish border) to Narvik, 'It is curious to reflect that on a line like this signal lights and engine headlamps never need to be lighted for a considerable period in the summer, and can never be extinguished for an equal period in the winter.'

I had asked Larry what I ought to do with the evening and day I would have in Bodø before boarding the night train back. 'It's a great base to explore the country!' he had said. The booklet advertising NSB Sove services had been similarly evasive: 'The location is an excellent base for glacier hiking in Norway's largest glacier, Svartisen, or for a trip to the portentous Saltstraumen, the world's most powerful tidal stream. Bodø is also the ideal stopover for a trip by ferry over to the majestic Lofoten archipelago.'

But what of Bodø itself?

Walking away from the station, passing 1960s buildings of the kind you tend to see in the outskirts of English towns like Hull, I kept thinking I would soon be in the pretty, historic heart of Bodø.

It soon became obvious that no such quaintness would be appearing. This is because old Bodø was flattened by the Luftwaffe on 27 May 1940, by way of punishment for harbouring a force of British fighters, and an airstrip used by the Allies. The close presence of the sea is a compensation, along with the beautiful snow-capped islands and mountains that seem to be encroaching from all directions, and which look somehow incongruously romantic, like scenery wheeled on from a different play.

I checked into my hotel, built in the 1970s, with all the architectural charm that implies, but the staff were very pleasant. I then walked around town in a gentle drizzle. Fishing and tourism are the main industries. Bodø, it is fair to say, is obsessed with fish, and there is a tourist attraction called the Salmon Centre, which prompted thoughts of the late Peter Cook, who would occasionally amuse himself (and others) by phoning up a London radio station in the guise of Sven from Swiss Cottage, a lovelorn fisherman originally from Norway. 'In Norway,' Sven explained on air, 'the phone-ins is mainly devoted to subject like, you know, fish, when people ring up for one hour, and the gist of it is, "A carp is very big ... Is a tench very big?" and on and on all night.' I dined on a well-cooked halibut in a restaurant in a shopping mall, where a half bottle of white wine was only about eighteen pounds, then went early to bed.

The next morning, I walked to the Nordlands Museum,

which stands opposite the austere 1950s cathedral. Here, a film shown on a loop in a darkened room tells the story of Bodø, and how a charming-looking fishing village (although it apparently did stink of fish) was flattened in ten minutes by that bombing raid. It is remarkable that only fifteen people died out of a population of 6,000. The film was heartbreaking in its absence of self-pity: '*Some* people say the new architecture is boring ...', but the jaunty voice-over begged to differ, boasting of how Bodø cracked the problem of shopping in bad weather. It built shopping arcades under glass roofs: shopping malls! There was also touching footage of the celebrations surrounding the coming of the railway.

With this in mind, Bodø Station appeared in a different light that evening: less a bland, municipal-looking edifice, and more like the precious connection between Bodø and the world. On one of the platforms is a plaque commemorating the opening of the station on 7 June 1962, and the little garden alongside it is well tended. The actual railway *line* had arrived a year earlier, and many photographs of both events are displayed in a permanent exhibition inside the station building.

THE CONTINUATION OF THE DAY

At 8.30pm, the station booking hall was closed, but the waiting area was filling up. There were two extremely beautiful young women, one stretched out on a bench, the other reading to her from a Kindle. There was an elderly American couple: both wore baggy white trousers, multi-pocketed waistcoats and white bush hats with dangling flaps that made them look like a pair of beekeepers. They were both intently studying their iPhones, and it was hard to believe the content of the one phone differed much from the other. As on the Blue Train I had a press ticket, and had not wanted to look a gift horse in the mouth by asking if I would be sharing. I knew I would not likely be sharing with the beekeepers, as they were surely travelling together, and the one thing I knew about the accommodation on the Nordland night train was that it was a proper sleeper, so the compartments held two berths each, as on the Wagons-Lits trains, rather than four or six, as in couchette carriages.

I began watching a man eating beans cold from a can. He wore very short shorts, sandals and an army shirt. At least he was not committing the solecism of wearing socks with his sandals, I thought, but then I saw his socks (black, ankle-length) drying out on a heating pipe behind him. Ominously – yet perfectly understandably – he was travelling alone, and he went down as the person I most particularly did not want to share with.

The train – due to depart at 21.10 – was already at the platform, under a drizzling rain. There were seven carriages, including two sleepers. It would be stopping at most, but not quite all, of the stations the day train had stopped at. A small Norwegian man, carrying an old-fashioned canvas rucksack, was also walking along the platform. What follows is a literal transcription of our conversation. I am the first speaker:

'You are taking this train?'

'Of course it is.'

'Do you often take it?'

'Of course; it is my home.'

'Where are you going?

'I don't know.' But after a while he said, 'Steinkjer.'

'You live there?'

'In the morning.'

At nine o'clock, the doors of the train were unlocked, and we passengers were admitted. Signs on the doors to the sleeping compartments read, 'Entrance to the berth is by keycard. Please collect your card from the conductor in the restaurant car', and moreover the conductor *was* waiting, as billed, in the restaurant car. So it was obvious that here was a well-organised and secure sleeper service. Taking the keycard, I asked the conductor whether I'd be sharing. He seemed shocked by this unprogressive idea: 'If you are travelling alone, you always have the right to sleep alone.'

The berth did not disappoint. It was cosy, orangey-brown; two bunks were made up and, as in a good hotel, there was a chocolate on the pillow. It was a good pillow too, and there was a proper mattress and excellent starched linen – and a decent-sized, fluffy towel. The rungs of the steel ladder were carpeted, as on the 'Y' class Wagons-Lits sleepers. There was a leaflet on the bed: 'Taking the night train is a one-of-a-kind experience. Awake refreshed, and with a great rail experience behind you.'

There was a sink in the corner. The eau was non-potable, but this was gracefully couched: 'Please use the bottled water.' A cup dispenser said 'Cup'. A panel of light switches read 'Lights', with the sub-headings, 'Assistance', 'Reading' and 'Ceiling'. There was no little hook on which to hang your wristwatch, as on the Wagons-Lits, but there was a slot marked 'Keycard', in which to put your keycard.

The neighbours were very wholesome: a family of four, who inhabited two compartments, the door between them having been unlocked. Just at that moment, they were singing 'Happy Birthday' in Norwegian. When they had finished, the chef du train (and it was as though he had *waited* for them to finish) announced himself over the tannoy. He said something in Norwegian, followed by, 'Welcome to our train. It will bring you to Trondheim. The café will be open all night.'

I walked along to the café, partly because I couldn't bear

to muss the beautifully made-up bunks. After Fauske, the quarry town, where we stopped at 21.50, the light seemed to be growing stronger rather than fading. We had left the rain behind, and the sky was a deep gold above bright-green fields. Some horses ran away from the train; cattle looked up. Did they know it was night? It was as though time had stopped. Maybe that's what happens when a country stays outside the European Union. Lights twinkled from the windows of the occasional houses we passed, but these were like the lights on a model railway layout – apparently switched on as a kind of special effect rather than because they were necessary. We stopped at Valnesfjord, a request stop on the water's edge. One man got off, with a backpack, and he looked like he would be needing it, because he walked straight off the platform into the woods. The dot matrix display at the end of the car gave the time. It also read '3m OH'. As the female train guard was coming along, I asked her what this meant. 'It shows how high we are. As you can see, Valnesfjord is very nearly in the sea. Our maximum point is Stødi, just inside the Arctic Circle, in the Saltfjellet Mountains. It is 680 metres above sea level.'

An hour later, during which I had eaten a ham-and-cheese sandwich and drunk a Diet Coke (a quarter bottle of Chardonnay being twelve pounds), the sky had turned violet, and we were entering the moonscape again. We rolled past a small station: Stødi, the highest point. That meant the Arctic Circle was imminent. The guard was passing again, and I asked whether she would be making an announcement. 'No announcement,' she said, smiling. 'Of course, because people are sleeping.'

There was only one other passenger in the dining car: a heavily made-up woman in leopard-skin tights. She had invested in an entire bottle of red wine, which must have cost fifty pounds, and it was fuelling some pretty frenetic texting. Having passed the Arctic Circle, we were descending steeply; trees were reappearing, but they were unhealthy specimens, and some had toppled into the arms of others, like fallen comrades. Fast streams of white water hurtled towards the tracks at right angles from either side, as though with malicious intent, but at the last minute, they were diverted into stone channels going beneath the line.

The texter's phone now rang. I had assumed she was Norwegian, but she answered speaking English in an Australian accent, and the conversation was surprisingly laid-back. 'We've just passed the Arctic Circle,' she said casually, almost yawning. 'No,' she went on, 'it's not the Northern Lights, it's just northern light ... Do you want to meet me at the station? It's up to you. You don't have to. I get in at 07.17.' But then things did start to get a bit heavy. 'Look,' she said, quite loudly, 'you're talking to me as if I'm a healthy girl when you know perfectly well I'm not!'

At 00.20, we came to Mo i Rana, a wide, low town – the second largest in Nordland, after Bodø – illuminated by orange lights. In the mid-1950s, a big steel industry was developed here on the basis of local iron ore, and what had been a village of a thousand people became a town of 20,000. The importance of the railway to this process is shown by the existence of a Mo i Rana freight terminal, and a siding serving an industrial park, where things are now more 'diversified', with new service industries. In 1951, the Norwegian government planned to disinter from the vicinity of Mo (as the place is known) the corpses of Russian prisoners of war, who had died during the building of the railway, but the project was abandoned after a mass protest by 800 Norwegians. Some or all of this sadness is expressed in an Antony Gormley artwork, erected in 1994, in the shallows of the Ranfjord on which Mo i Rana stands: *Havmann* (meaning 'man from the sea') is eleven metres high – therefore visible for a long time from the train – and shows every sign of wanting to wade out to his death. The melancholia is compounded by the fact that Gormley had wanted to make the statue from steel, but the steelworks had just closed down.

That protest at Mo should be seen as part of a wider picture. In 1951, 8,000 other Russian corpses were collected from ninety graves along the northern part of the Nordland, and 'reassembled' in a central cemetery in Helgeland, Nordland, as part of 'Operation Asphalt'. The expressed rationale was that the graves could be better looked after in a central location, but Operation Asphalt owed something to Cold War animosities.

At one o'clock, I walked back to my bunk, which meant walking through the carriage for seated sleeping. The NSB Sove literature says, 'If you choose to travel in an ordinary seat on the night trains, we offer you a special package containing a pillow, travel blanket, eye mask and ear plugs. You are welcome to take the package home with you. If not, the blankets are donated to charity.' Whereas everyone in that carriage was asleep (including the socks-and-sandals man) I spent the next hour and a half lying awake on my bunk, watching the landscape and the light. I dozed a little from about half past three, thereby missing our stop at Namsskogan, where we crossed with the night train going in the opposite direction, and here – with Norwegian rationality – the crews apparently swapped over, to avoid being taken too far from their homes.

At 4.55am, I was woken by a rapid rattle on the line. Looking at my map, I saw that the rattle might have been made by our going over a steel bridge at a place called Jørstadelva. The Norwegian Resistance repeatedly attacked the

Nordland Railway when the Germans took it over, and the most spectacular act of sabotage, Operation Woodlark, was carried out in January 1945 at Jørstadelva Bridge. The National Military Museum, located in a courtyard behind Trondheim Cathedral, shows how it was done, with displays of detonators and fuses. The target was a troop train heading south, and two Norwegians were killed (the driver and the fireman), together with seventy-eight German soldiers, and 200 horses. The current bridge at Jørstadelva must therefore post-date 1945. Incidentally, while the National Military Museum details acts of sabotage by the Resistance, it makes no attempt to finesse the extent of Norwegian collaboration: 'Many Norwegians served in the German armed forces. Between 15,000 and 20,000 volunteered but only 6,000 were accepted. The majority served in the Waffen SS on the eastern front, or in Finland. After the war they were tried and convicted as traitors.'

Returning to the buffet, I ordered a coffee and a snack that turned out to be sugary bread and cinnamon – just what was needed. The Australian woman had departed, but possibly not long since, because the bottle of red had not been cleared from her table, and there was a quarter bottle of the same next to it. At 5.40am, at Steinkjer, the strange, small man from Bodø got off. I waved vigorously through the window at him, but he didn't look my way. The golden light was now entirely magical; a man was rowing a small boat across the completely flat, pinkish waters of the Trondheim Fjord. Not including people at railway stations, he was about the sixth human being I'd seen from the Nordland Railway day and night trains combined. (And two of those six had waved at the train.) We had now begun threading through the farmsteads again, perhaps serving as an alarm clock to the inhabitants.

We arrived at Trondheim on the dot of 07.17 and the small

crowd disembarking from the train soon dispersed, including the Australian woman. (A Goth on a bicycle had been politic enough to turn up and meet her.) Stepping from the station, I seemed to have the city to myself. It was Sunday morning, but too early for church bells. The canal water might have been blue glass; traffic lights changed irrelevantly. I was armed with a brochure that had been placed in my compartment, advising me that, on production of my train ticket, the Best Western Hotel would provide me with a cheap breakfast.

The lobby of the hotel was made to seem dark by the brightness of the morning. I asked the young man at reception, 'Do you do breakfast for train people?'

'Sure!' he said, after a brief pause, and rather in the tone of someone saying, 'Why the hell not?'

It was an excellent breakfast in any case.

HELL REVISITED

At Trondheim Airport, with three hours to kill before my flight back to London, I recalled the closeness of the airport to the village of Hell. So I stepped out of the terminal.

After a few minutes of walking through an anonymous terrain of light industry, a forested bank appeared. Within the trees were tall white letters, slightly askew like their Hollywood equivalent, spelling 'HELL'. The railway track was beneath, with a river adjacent. A rough road of white stone led towards Hell Station.

The name seemed highly inappropriate – indeed, ironic – because Hell has all the features one would like to find in a railway station. The station clock works. There is extensive free parking and a well-designed and secure lock-up facility for bikes – not that there can be much crime in Hell.

The station, bathed just then in bright afternoon sunlight, serves half a dozen large, attractive, timber-framed houses, peacefully arranged around a small green. A positively angelic-looking child creaked backwards and forwards on a swing located in the centre of this green, and she watched with interest as I approached the main station building, which is painted a pretty mustard colour. A sign helpfully pointed out that Hell is 3.9 metres above sea level. The station building itself was locked and shuttered, but one dusty window disclosed the first hint of self-consciousness about the name: a plastic devil mask, together with a devil's trident and a 'Ghostface' mask associated with the film *Scream*. It was like looking into the rummage room of a fancy-dress supplier.

The waiting for trains no longer takes place in this building, but in a nearby structure similar to a bus shelter. Two sleepy-looking teenage boys sat on the bench inside, meditatively prodding at their smartphones. Here was my opportunity to join an honourable tradition of British travel ...

'North of Trondheim,' somebody wrote in *Railway Wonders of the World* in 1935, 'there is a small junction known as Hell – to which the facetious Englishman, alas, has a fondness for buying a ticket, so that he may display it to his friends on the return home.'

Obviously one has to move with the times, and the modern equivalent of a ticket in one's railway scrapbook is an image on one's electronic device. I would ask these boys to photograph me in front of the station sign, which would enable me to put the photo online, over an amusing caption such as: 'Here's me in Hell!' or, 'They told me to go to hell, so I did!'

The boys turned out to be the first Norwegians I'd met who did not speak fluent English. It was possible they had almost *no* English, but one of the two got the message that I wanted my photograph taken, so I took up a position directly adjacent to the station name, and handed over my iPad. I posed; the boy frowned, indicating that I should step forward a little way. He pressed the button, and I thanked him as he handed back the iPad. He returned to the bus shelter, and I inspected the photograph. It was quite a good one of me (for once) but the boy had not included the station sign. I was obliged to summon him again. When he emerged, somewhat reluctantly, from the bus shelter, I explained in slow English that I had been hoping he would picture me alongside the word 'Hell'. 'It's a joke, you see?' I urged. He frowned – he was turning out to be rather good at frowning. But he agreed to take another shot, and this time I indicated that he should not return to the bus shelter until I had inspected the result ... which was excellent, in that it looked like all the other thousands of pictures taken at this place. The boy rejoined his companion, giving a brief, baffled shake of the head. A train was now approaching – it was not loco hauled, like the star turn of the line, the Nordland, but rather a perfunctory two-car diesel multiple unit.

I walked away as it drew up to the platform, and no doubt my departure from the station just as the train arrived would have merited another shake of the head between the two boys. But I did not turn around to check. I had a plane – not a train – to catch, and my very satisfactory engagement with the Nordland Railway was ended.

3

PARIS-VENICE

TRAVELLING TO THE BATTLEFIELDS?

As I waited for the night train to Venice, the Gare de Lyon – that outpost of the Riviera – was not its usual exuberant self. The station was cold on this November evening, and darkness seemed to seep in from outside. Armed soldiers in camouflage gear stood around on the concourse and platforms; the crowd below the departure screens was wary and quiet, and the screen was not giving much away: usually, the words 'à l'heure' appeared where I expected a departure time, including in the case of the 19.13 to Venice, operated by a company called Thello.

On the previous Friday, supporters of Islamic State had murdered 130 people on the streets of Paris, including 89 at the Bataclan nightclub. A state of emergency was in operation, and the entire city was subdued. There'd been no trouble getting a seat on the Métro all day, and at lunchtime, the giant Bateaux Mouches had been sliding under the Pont Neuf, with only half a dozen people on board.

During the misty, quiet afternoon, I had walked along

the Viaduc des Arts, just north of the station. This is now a walkway and linear garden, with many exotic plants, and quite a few rats. Until 1969 – when it lost its passenger traffic to RER Line A – the viaduct carried a suburban railway from Vincennes and the suburbs of eastern Paris to Gare de la Bastille, the smallest and most obscure Parisian terminus, which was at its busiest in the 1930s. After years of decline, the station was earmarked for a railway museum, but it was demolished in 1984 to make way for the Bastille Opera House. But the locale of Bastille was more operatic during the lifetime of the station, which – besides its hordes of commuters, alighting from double-decker steam trains – received exotic cargoes, originally in the form of wine from the vineyards of the Marne Valley, and then – when the wine growers saw more profit in flowers – from roses. In the summer of 1897 a nocturnal Train des Roses carried a million blooms every night to the Gare de la Bastille.

***

I had bought the euros for my trip from the Eurostar terminal at St Pancras International three days after the Paris attack. That station too was full of armed police, and my visit coincided with a minute's silence for the victims. A notice had been pasted onto the window of the ticket office: 'Travelling to the Battlefields? If you are planning to visit the World War One sites in France or Belgium, please ask a Eurostar staff member for some very important information before you travel.' Alongside the notice was a picture of a bomb with a red line through it, and this was all to do with the dangers of picking up old and possibly unexploded shells from muddy fields, but it seemed that all Eurostar passengers would be travelling to the battlefields.

The booking of my ticket, a month before, had also been a glum affair. I had gone to the elegant Voyages SNCF premises on Piccadilly. ('Your experts in High-Speed European Rail, Eurostar, Overnight Trains, Interrail and European Passes, Ski Trains and Auto Trains.') It occupies no. 157, which used to be known as French Railways House, and has long been the London home of SNCF. The place was empty, so there was no need to take a numbered ticket and wait for a consultant: one was immediately available.

I explained that I wanted to go from Paris to Venice on the Thello night train, and gave the date. The woman asked if that was the only date I was interested in. 'Yes,' I said, 'because it's the full moon.' She looked at me suspiciously. 'It's for the views as we go through the Alps,' I said. She began making the booking on her own tablet rather than using the PC on the desk. She said something about how she was not making the booking through the usual channels of the Voyages SNCF office, because the office was about to close down. This was a shame, because there ought to be a railway travel agency on such a grand, cosmopolitan street as Piccadilly. Thomas Cook used to have one of its offices there.

I thought of all the places where I had formerly bought international railway tickets that had now closed: my local travel agent in North London; the offices of a Belgian company called Wasteels in Victoria Station; a little office of South Eastern Trains behind Cannon Street Station – and that must have been a long time ago, because I remember one woman looking up from her typewriter when I walked in.

The one I would most sorely have missed, though, had I ever used it, was the Wagons-Lits company's London headquarters in Cockspur Street, SW1. *The Continental Traveller* magazine gives the company's London HQ as 14 Cockspur

Street, with additional booking offices at 36 Leadenhall Street, 'inside the Hotel Cecil', and Charing Cross and Victoria Stations. That was in the 1890s. The 14 Cockspur Street of today is a different building, worth a digression as indicating the nature of the street, which in London terms is an anonymous, if stately, conduit between Pall Mall and Trafalgar Square, but whose true significance is international.

The present day no. 14 was built in 1906 for the Hamburg-America Line, a German shipping company. In the early twentieth century, their ship, the *Deutschland*, won the Blue Riband on three occasions for the fastest Atlantic crossing. The building is decorated with two carved figures holding what appear to be model ships, and these are believed to be *Deutschland*, and another of the company's ships, *Amerika* (hence the eagle standing next to the figure). The fall of Icarus is also depicted – a bit of scaremongering directed at anyone who might think that aeroplanes would soon be the way to go. After the First World War, the building was seized by the British government from the Hamburg-America Line, for reparations, after which the shipping line P&O moved in. New decorations were added, including caryatids on either side of the main entrance, one representing Britain, the other 'The East'. On his architectural website *Ornamental Passions*, Chris Partridge writes, 'I love the way that Britannia stands in a strong, confident but no-nonsense stance, whereas the dusky oriental lovely has a slight but sensuous swing to the hips.' Above the door is the P&O motto: *Quis Separabit?* ('Who will separate us?'). If my decoding of the Edwardian Post Office Directory for London is correct, Wagons-Lits, billed as 'Sleeping Car Company (International)', moved to the only slightly less grand, and rather Gothic, 20 Cockspur Street in 1906, where it flourished – presumably, since no. 20 was built especially for it – alongside its globalised Cockspur neighbours, such as the White Star Line, the Cunard Steamship Company, the Royal Mail Steam Packet Company, the Oceanic Steamship Company of San Francisco, Henry Martin Snow (Passenger Agent), the Great Northern Railway of America and the Union Pacific Railway. In 1929, Wagons-Lits moved again to 20 St James's Street, a much-messed-about block that today houses some gents' outfitters and gives no clue to its former identity. When Wagons-Lits acquired Thomas Cook in 1928, the joint HQ was established in Berkeley Street, Mayfair. In 1973, 14 Cockspur Street was listed Grade II, at which time it had become a bank. In 2012, it became the Brazilian Embassy. After W-L moved, no. 20 Cockspur Street was taken over by the Grand Trunk Railway System of Canada, whose name adorns the top of the building, on the side facing Trafalgar Square. Today, the lower floors are occupied by a snare for tourists retailing Union Jack coffee mugs and the like.

The Voyages SNCF consultant told me the telephone booking service would continue for a few more months, then it too would end. She then turned to the complicated Thello booking system, which she suggested might be regarded as a sort of bet. If you booked a place in a compartment assigned to three passengers, there was a chance you'd have to share with two other people. If you booked a two berth, there was a chance you'd have to share with another one. But if the trains proved to be undersubscribed, the risk of sharing was reduced, with the three berths being filled before the more expensive two berths.

My three berth option cost £90.50. Taken together with a Eurostar ticket to Paris, the total cost was £170 for the one-way journey, more than twice as much as the cost of a return flight to Venice, which no doubt helps explain the closure of the Voyages SNCF office. 'We've heard that Jamie

Oliver's bought the building,' said the consultant. That figured. Never mind about trains, the modern Briton is like a snail: moves about on his stomach.*

***

Tired of waiting for 'l'heure' on the freezing concourse of the Gare de Lyon, I repaired to the Train Bleu buffet, which was mentioned in the chapter about the train of that name. The main space is called the Gold Room, just in case anybody should think they might be able to buy a cheap snack. Oddly enough, there is something of the waiting room about it – in the bench-like seats of studded leather, surmounted by luggage racks (which are, admittedly, gold plated).

I headed for the back room, where drinks are served. This used to look more railway-ish than it does today, having once been subdivided into compartment-like booths separated by heavy purple curtains. But the area has recently been refurbished in beige, and the effect has been created along one wall of a Moorish screen, which does tie in with the architecture of the station, especially the clock tower. Mindful of a review I'd once read in *Time Out* ('a few reasonably priced wines would be welcome') I ordered what appeared to be the cheapest and smallest option: a Chardonnay for eight euros. The Train Bleu cat – a ginger tabby – did me the honour of sitting down by my seat to lick its paws. The people around me were quietly engaged with their smartphones or laptops. I looked through the window towards the dark rooftops of the 12th arrondissement. The most striking feature was the green neon sign of a pharmacy. This always seems an anonymous district, as though intimidated by the

---

* At the time of writing the premises remain empty.

overbearing glamour of the station, whose high white clock seems to replace the moon over this part of Paris.

THELLO

A scruffy-looking rake of carriages waited on Platform A, and I approached it warily. This night train to Venice gets mixed reviews. Mark Smith, who heroically keeps Britons in touch with European trains via his admirable *Man in Seat 61* website, says, 'I so want to like Thello, but they don't make it easy ...'

The livery is a jumble of white, blue, green and red. Perhaps it's meant to combine the colours of the French and Italian flags, since the train is operated by Trenitalia (the Italian national operator) and a French private firm called Transdev, under the name Thello. It is branded a EuroNight service, and it is one of the few privately operated passenger trains to run through France. There is also the Venice-Simplon Orient Express (VSOE), a tourist train from Paris to Venice, with beautifully restored Wagons-Lits carriages of the Lx-class. The VSOE trades on the history of the Simplon Orient Express, which – running to Istanbul via the Simplon Tunnel and southern Europe – became the primary route of the Orient Express in the interwar period, overshadowing the plain Orient Express of 1883 vintage that continued to run from Gare de l'Est.

The Thello train was interesting because it echoed the first part of that Simplon journey. It also echoes another Wagons-Lits service, the Rome Express. This began life in 1883 as the Calais-Nice-Rome Express, which went to Rome along the Riviera. A quicker route would have taken it through the Mont Cenis Tunnel, between Modane in France and Bardonecchia in Italy. That was open for business from

1871, but not to the Wagon-Lits company, because the Upper Italian Railway had struck an agreement with the American Pullman Palace Car Company whereby only Pullman sleepers could run through the tunnel. (As mentioned in the Introduction, the only European country in which the American Pullman company had established its sleepers in those early days was Italy.)

In 1889, Wagons-Lits gained access to the tunnel, and the Rome Express began running in 1890. It went via Aix-les-Bains, Turin, Genoa, Pisa and Florence. According to George Behrend, writing in *Grand European Expresses*, 'The direct Orient Express is mysterious, the Blue Train is chic, the Sud Express is dignified, but the Rome Express is majestic.' It certainly gives rise to one of his most majestic passages of prose, concerning the passengers of the late nineteenth century:

> They had enormous wardrobe trunks in the fourgon, and they stayed for months in Italy, sketching in Florence, or wintering unnoticed in Alessandria, masculine ladies with wispy hair, or mothers with grown-up daughters going for a protracted stay in Rome. The regulars were often known personally to the station interpreters, long-suffering men, whose life seemed akin to the retriever's: lost trunks, lost people ...

Behrend also mentions that the Rome Express luncheon of the late 1890s included – alongside the Côtelettes de Mouton à la Mont Cenis – Petits Pois à l'Anglaise. 'The fresh peas in November were possible by buying them in Brindisi from Corfu shippers and sending them specially to Calais on the Indian Mail.'

A journey on the Rome Express was the object of many of

the passengers on the smugly named Club Trains which ran from London to Dover between 1889 and 1893. One of these was run from Victoria by the London, Chatham & Dover Railway, over its main line via Chatham (which was known amongst railwaymen as 'going up Chatham'). The other was run from Charing Cross by the South Eastern Railway over its main line, which went via Ashford. The first of these was a contracted operation with Wagons-Lits. The second was a spoiler. They both departed from London at 16.15, and they crossed en route to the coast at Chislehurst. Passengers from both trains boarded the same Channel steamer, and it was said that bored fishermen on Admiralty Pier at Dover would place bets on which would arrive first.

The Rome Express was renamed the Palatino Express in 1969, by which time it was no longer a Wagons-Lits train, but operating as part of the TENPOOL. From 1995 the Palatino was operated by the Artesia Railway Company, a joint project of Trenitalia and SNCF. Artesia, and the train, ceased to exist in late 2011. It was briefly revived by Thello between December 2012 and December 2013, but today there is no sleeper to Rome. In fact, there are no direct trains from Paris to Rome at all. Even the high-speed services require a change at Milan or Turin. Nor is there any direct train from Paris to Venice, except the surviving Thello.

The loco on the front was fitted with tri-current voltage, enabling it to run on the electrified lines of France, Switzerland and Italy. But this can-do engine is put to shame by the feeble extent of European rail integration of the 'classic' lines. Each country requires a different in-cab safety system, so we would be changing locos – probably at Vallorbe, after entering Switzerland through the Mont d'Or Tunnel, and at Domodossola, on entering Italy after the Simplon. An observer of the European railways told me, only half jokingly, that the national operators felt they might not get their engines back if they let them go into another country. Even though aviation causes ten times more pollution than conventional rail, the EU and its predecessors have done more to encourage aviation than railways, beginning with the deregulation of European air travel in 1997, which ushered in the budget airline boom. The aim of the EU has been to integrate its most far-flung populations, and places like Dublin and Stockholm can be more easily brought into the fold by cheap flights than cheap trains.

It can now be assumed that a flight between any two countries will be cheaper than taking the train, whereas the opposite was once the case. The high-speed trains are particularly expensive. The slower trains, such as the sleepers, ought to be able to compete with the planes, but they are hampered by EU legislation, specifically Railway Directive 95/19 of 1995, which required a split between the train operators and the infrastructure providers. By this, the former must pay 'track access charges' to the latter. It seems an unnatural distinction to some. 'All initial definitions of the railroad,' wrote Wolfgang Schivelbusch in *The Railway Journey*, 'unanimously describe it as a machine consisting of the rails *and* the vehicles running on them.' In countries attached to the traditional, monolithic idea of railway nationalisation, such as France, the split is observed more by way of an accounting convention than a matter of having genuinely separate organisations. Even so, the measure shines a spotlight on the most heavily loss-making services – such as the sleepers – begging the question: 'Are they worth paying the charges?' But we British can't blame the EU for the directive, because it represents the implementation of the British railway privatisation model, and it was the former Labour leader, Neil Kinnock, who, as Transport Commissioner, was behind the policy.

Stepping aboard the Thello train, I was greeted by a friendly sleeping car conductor, who was either French or Italian, but spoke excellent English, and seemed to have a lot of time on his hands to talk to me. He agreed that business was slack; there had been many cancellations. 'It's because of what happened last week.' I asked where we would be stopping, and after telling me 'Dijon, Milan, Verona, Padua, Venice' he ruefully added, 'We should put up a notice because people often ask.' He politely requested to see my ticket. 'You are entitled to a free drink in the bar,' he said, handing it back. 'Also a free breakfast, because you are in first class.' By this, he meant I was in a sleeper rather than a couchette. I wondered whether I would be having the compartment to myself. 'I think so,' he said, 'unless someone gets on at Dijon.' (But surely he must *know* whether somebody would be getting on at Dijon?)

He asked for my passport – and it seemed he intended to keep it. That was always the way it worked in the heyday of Wagons-Lits, but its trains predated the Schengen agreement, whereas the countries we would be passing through – France, Switzerland and Italy – were all Schengen, so why did the conductor need my passport? 'There have always been special arrangements for this train,' he said, leaving open the possibility that additional special arrangements had been required in light of the current situation.

The compartment looked washed out, with pale wood veneer and bright fluorescent light, like the hospital my father had recently died in, but there was a certain solidity about it. After all, here was a Wagons-Lits berth. It was an MU-class, the last generation of Wagon-Lits sleepers, commenced in the late 1960s, with production continued in the 1970s by SNCF. 'MU' meant Modern Universal, and there was a note of desperation in the name, welcoming all comers to compartments that could be configured as single berth (for the thrusting Eurocrat), double (for the moneyed couple) or as a 'three' for students on a jolly. Chris Jackson, editor of the *Railway Gazette International*, told me that the trouble with the modern sleeper trains was that 'They've lost the middle classes.' The travellers are either nostalgists of a certain age, or young backpackers, and it has been this way for a while. Michael Barsley wrote in *Orient Express* (1966) that the train 'should be preserved for two types: the student, for whom it is cheap, and the sentimentalist, for whom it is fun'.

The MUs inherited by Thello have been refitted. According to Mark Smith, the Man in Seat 61, 'the refurb removed the civilised carpet and classy varnished-wood panelling decor, replacing it with grey synthetic flooring & off-white fascia that shows the dirt'. There was space for three bunks on one side, and only the top one had been made up, leaving room below for me to sit on the bench-like seat that would make up the bottom bunk if necessary. In the corner was a cabinet, harbouring a tiny sink, from the plug hole of which arose a ghostly roar. On the three racks above the sink were three small towels and soap bags corresponding to each of the possible bunks. The toilet bag was quite stylish: plastic, transparent and decorated with multiple Zs, suggesting deep slumber. Inside were a Thello toilet seat cover, a Thello handkerchief and not only Thello soap but also Thello liquid hand cleaner ('No water or towel required'). There were Thello slippers – white towelling ones, like the kind you get in a good hotel – and a toothbrush and miniature toothpaste, about the size of a tube of Airfix glue. Scrutinising this, I was reminded of Cary Grant's bemusement at picking up Eva Marie Saint's tiny razor ('No good for shaving a *face*') in the sleeping car he is sharing with her in *North by Northwest*.

I closed the cabinet door to banish the roaring, and now

the compartment seemed sinisterly quiet. On the window was a symbol of a bottle with a red line through it – a warning not to throw bottles out of the window. The window was unopenable to the ordinary passenger in any case, the carriage being air-conditioned. (But it could have been opened by the use of one of those European railway master keys called a Berne key, introduced after a railway conference in that city in 1886, to permit host countries to access international trains passing through their territories.) Wagons-Lits carriages had a more verbose prohibition. 'Travellers are reminded that Railway Officials and employees ON DUTY ON THE PERMANENT WAY are often seriously injured through different articles, such as bottles, glasses, empty tins, etc. being thrown out of the windows.' In *Our Iron Roads*, published in 1883, F. S. Williams wondered which was the greater problem on British railways: passengers throwing bottles out of windows, or boys throwing stones at trains.

We pulled into the grey railway gorge that serves Gare de Lyon. We were the only train on the twenty or so tracks, and so the loneliness of my compartment – and seemingly of the entire carriage – was compounded. After only a few minutes, there was nothing beyond the window but pure blackness, with no sign of the full moon that had been billed to appear.

***

Time for the dining car. The conductor had offered to lock my compartment when I went for dinner, but there was nothing worth stealing if I took my wallet with me. I also took my book, *The Passenger from Calais*, by Major Arthur Griffiths, not that anyone would want to steal that.

Arthur George Frederick Griffiths was a (fairly) enlight-
ened prison administrator, who wrote the *Encyclopaedia
Britannica* entry on 'Criminology', but his later works on the
subject, such as *Criminals I Have Known* (1895), were sensa-
tional, and on the cusp of fiction. He wrote more than sixty
books, and *The Passenger from Calais* (1905) was the last of his
novels. It begins with the protagonist, Lieutenant Colonel
Basil Annesley, boarding the 'Lucerne wagon-lit' of the
'Engadine express'. Griffiths is rather grudging with his
capital letters, but from the mid-1890s the Wagons-Lits
company did run an Engadine Express from Calais to various
places in Switzerland, including Lucerne and Chur. Colonel
Annesley becomes intrigued by an apparent 'adventuress'
riding on the train. Being a purposeful man ('I closed my
Bradshaw with a bang, replaced it in my bag, drank up my
coffee and started for the telegraph office'), he decides to
pursue her through various baffling changes of train and
tram on the Swiss-French border.

At first the Colonel regrets his interest in the woman: 'She
was presumably an adventuress, clever, designing, desirous
of turning me round her finger.' Fortunately, 'she was also
a pretty woman', and he realises she is in trouble in some
way, which brings out the chivalrous side of his nature.
He recruits the aid of a Swiss sleeping car attendant called
l'Echelle, who is only too happy to become one of several
'confidential agents' flitting about in this labyrinthine tale.
The attendant declares, 'I fancy I have fallen into a snug
berth, a soft job, better than making beds in a wagon-lit and
being shaken to death in express trains.' It is a very bad book
indeed. Perfectly – or at least fairly – reasonable statements
will be followed by, 'he shouted with scornful laughter'.

In 1896, Griffiths had written another 'wagon-lit' story,
The Rome Express, which is the first of several fictions to be

set aboard that Wagons-Lits train. In spite of featuring the sentence (if it is a sentence) 'It was murder! murder most foul!' this is a much better book, with a neat mystery at its heart concerning who was in what compartment when. But it seems an opportunity missed in that there isn't much of either 'Rome' or the 'Express' in the book. The murder happens on the train's approach to Paris, and most of the action takes place as the shrewd French detective questions the suspects in his bureau at what Griffiths calls – in the old-fashioned British manner – Gare de Lyons, with an 's'. (An even more fuddy-duddy British spelling was 'Lions'.) In the copy I took from the London Library, some reader who evidently combined the qualities of pedant and vandal had crossed out every single superfluous 's'. It wouldn't be surprising to learn that Agatha Christie had read this book, and drawn the conclusion, 'There needs to be more action on board the train.'

DINING CAR

The dining car was light blue: it consisted of a bar and seating space, with fixed chairs, like an American diner. The lambency of a Wagons-Lits diner (mellow marquetry, warm-hued armchairs and carpet) had been entirely banished. The only W-L element that had been retained was in the form of the good-quality white linen tablecloths. But it could not be said that I was doing much to uphold the formality of earlier days, because I had removed my shoes in the compartment, and come to the diner in the Thello slippers. In *The Lost Pleasures of the Great Trains*, Martin Page writes:

Another Englishman travelling on the continent, Lord Russell, was acclaimed for putting a native with whom he was sharing a compartment in his place. As the train drew out of the station the foreigner proceeded to open his carpet-bag, take out a pair of slippers and untie the laces of his shoes.

'If you do that, sir,' proclaimed the great Victorian jurist, 'I shall throw your shoes out of the window.'

The foreigner remarked that he had the right to do as he wished in his own country, so long as he did not inconvenience others. Lord Russell demurred. The man took off his shoes, and Lord Russell threw them out of the window.

A female maître d'hôtel stepped out from behind the bar, and showed me to a seat. At my mention of the free drink, she said, 'Yes, you can háve one. You could have beer or champagne.'

'I'll have the champagne please,' I said, trying not to sound too excited.

'Well,' she said, 'it's like champagne except it's not champagne.'

It was sparkling wine to be exact, and not bad at all, even if served in a rather small plastic glass. From three hot options on the menu, I ordered seafood risotto.

The only other customers in the dining car were an American couple with their two sons. They were from Texas, and were regulars on European night trains. 'We use them,' the man said, 'because we can't do this sort of thing in America.'

'But America invented sleeper trains,' I said.

'I know,' the man replied, with a sigh.

And did they like the Thello train?

'Yes,' the man eventually replied, but his wife refined the point: 'We like it because we have low expectations.'

They had been from France to Italy on the Palatino Express

shortly before it expired. 'It was on its last legs,' said the man.

'There were no sheets on the beds until midnight,' said the woman, 'because of a strike.'

On the question of whether they'd been put off by the terrorist attack in Paris, the woman replied, 'Our friends said "Don't go, not with the kids",' then she shrugged.

My risotto arrived, on a paper plate, along with plastic cutlery and a paper napkin wrapped together in cellophane. It looked a prostrate, dead thing compared to the linen napery on the Wagons-Lits, which was customarily folded in the shape of a vertical conch shell. And everything looked mute: nothing tinkled. On a train, cutlery, crockery and glass should tinkle musically. On the W-L services, there was also the tinkling of the little bell – described by Eve-Marie Zizza-Lalu, in *Au bon temps des wagons-restaurants*, as 'la mythique clochette' – carried by the maître d', who walked along the corridors announcing the service of dinner.

The microwaved risotto was not bad, if a bit congealed. At least I was not being intimidated by what George Behrend called the 'gastrology' of the night trains. The British film of 1948, *Sleeping Car to Trieste* (which is more or less a remake of *Rome Express*) satirises the philistinism of the British when confronted with sophisticated railway catering. At the outset of the journey the on-board chef – French, of course – makes a regal entrance to the kitchen car, being 'the top chef of the Wagons-Lits company'. Throughout the film, he engages in a dialogue with a crass Englishman who 'is thinking of going into the catering racket', and wants a few tips. The chef tells him how to cook a fillet of white fish, involving white wine, shallots, herbs. The Englishman counters by commending the British method – lower it into a pan of hot water and boil it – as being both simpler and quicker. 'But there is no sauce!' exclaims the chef, appalled. 'Oh, there's usually a bottle of sauce lying around somewhere,' says the Englishman. He then offers the chef a recipe for roly-poly pudding.

There's a strain of Francophobia in that, and W-L, head-quartered in Paris, *was* seen as a French company, even though it was Belgian. It did not therefore benefit from the British admiration for 'plucky little Belgium'. If it really was true that the sleeping car conductors were fluent in three languages and conversant in half a dozen, then the average Englishman, fluent in one (and not even that after a few drinks), might easily feel intimidated. It might be thought that *Sleeping Car to Trieste* had been written by some gauche person who'd suffered social embarrassments on the Wag-ons-Lits, but the scriptwriter was William Douglas-Home, an old Etonian who'd also attended Sandhurst and Oxford and whose older brother, Alec Douglas-Home, became Prime Minister in 1963.

Dinner eaten, the choice was between the bleakness of the dining car (because the Texans had left and no one else had come) and the bleakness of my compartment. I ordered half a bottle of white wine to 'take away', and asked for the bill, which came to a reasonable twenty-five euros. Asked whether she took cards, the maître d' said, 'All except American Express and Visa Debit.' The first part of that was not surprising (*nobody* takes American Express, as far as I can see), but it's more unusual to meet a block on Visa Debit. I looked in my wallet, and saw about 120 euros, so I paid in cash and left a tip on the table. I also left something else, by accident, which we will come to.

THE COLONEL

In the compartment, the sleeping car conductor had now created the bunk below the top one, by a process that eliminated the back rest of the bottom seat. So now two beds were made up, but only the top one was made up for sleeping, with a pillow and a duvet of good clean linen. Surely this indicated that nobody would be getting on at Dijon. But then *why* was the second bunk made up?

At 10.10, we arrived at Dijon. This was the main junction of the old PLM network; but nothing happened. For five minutes, I had a good view of the depressing neon sign of a nearby restaurant: 'Chic 'n' Food'. We started again. It was too early for bed, so I decided to read, whereupon I realised I had left Major Arthur Griffiths in the dining car. I couldn't be bothered to go back for him, and decided I would collect him in the morning at breakfast. I had a wash and climbed into bed with the half bottle of wine and my second book.

This was an autobiographical volume called *Venices*, by Paul Morand, author of fiction and travel books, who was described in an essay of 1987, written for the *New Criterion* by Renee Winegarten, as 'the typical "haunted traveller" of the inter-war years'. Morand was such a regular on the sleepers that he described himself as a 'horizontal nomad', and he is one of the best writers on international trains, but he was not an easy man to love, being a dandified racist, anti-Semite and believer in the need for strong men to save Europe from excessive democracy. Winegarten sums him up as 'a Proustian snob and salon Nietzschean'. In *Venices*, Morand described himself as being 'homesick for every country!', but Venice was his favourite destination. In his early twenties, he would get there by taking advantage of the low fares designed to attract passengers to trains running through the newly opened Simplon Tunnel.

Here he is, going to Venice and beyond, riding the Simplon-Orient Express, as it 'dragged its tri-weekly public' eastward from Paris through the new tunnel:

> The train shook the loose glass of Gothic Swiss railway stations. For twenty-nine minutes the Simplon offered its large iron symphony. Then the banked roads and rice fields of Piedmont. Then a station leading off into nothing, a great cistern of silence and shadows that was Venice. In the morning a zinc-coloured north wind overbent the Croatian corn in the plains. Pigs, striped black and white as with racing colours, betrayed the presence of Serbia; they were apparently devouring the corpse, or rather the wheels and an alarm signal, of a car which lay derailed in a ditch. After rivers came yet other rivers that we crossed on rickety trestles beside the ruined piers of older bridges which had been destroyed in retreats. At Vinkovci we got rid of the velvet Rumanians ...

At about midnight we stopped. A station sign read Vallorbe, which is on the French-Swiss border, at the south-eastern end of the tunnel under Mont d'Or. There was a white station building and white swirling snow. Muffled men walked up and down, and the train jerked about. They were changing the engine. About half an hour later we stopped again. Lausanne: a Swiss clock, flurries of snowflakes rushing across the face. As we pulled away, my conscience was afflicted by thoughts of Major Griffiths. *The Passenger from Calais* was a London Library book, long out of print, and would be expensive to replace. In the old days, I would have rung for the sleeping car conductor, and asked him to get it for me, or I would have asked him by simply opening my door and calling along the corridor – because the conductor would have been on his fold-down seat at the end, possibly dozing beneath a light-blue blanket (the staff blankets were always light blue, and never red like those of the passengers).

These were not the old days, however. So I put on my trousers, and the Thello slippers, and quit the compartment, almost immediately colliding with a bulky man in a leather jacket. He smelt strongly of cigarette smoke. I apologised, and he made no reply. I continued along the deserted corridors. The slippers were completely inadequate against the freezing cold of the jostling metal plates that formed the bridge between carriages. In W-L days, I could have warmed them, and myself, by the coke stoves at the ends of the corridors.

In the dining car, the book was on the table where I'd left it. The car was empty except for two people: the chef du train was talking to the woman behind the bar. He was a friendly chap, probably French, in a blue quilted jacket, and we discussed the train for a bit. I then returned to my compartment and locked the door.

What happened next is confused in my mind. I intermittently slept and looked through the window. It was at about half past two in the morning, on the approach to the Simplon Tunnel, that the scenery became stunning. The full moon suddenly seemed to have been switched on, or maybe it was the luminosity of the snow on the mountainsides, revealing deep gorges, pine trees, a fast-flowing river by the side of the tracks. I recall the stop at Brig that preceded our run through the 'iron symphony' of the Simplon, and – more vaguely – working out that the next stop we made, after emerging from the Tunnel, must have been at Domodossola, in Italy. At about 3.30am I went to sleep for a couple of hours, and awoke when we stopped at Milan Central. The grandeur of that station, a vanity project by Mussolini (who was 'committed to a surprisingly advanced modernism,' according to Steven Parissien in Station to Station), is undetectable from a train that has been swallowed by it. All I really noticed was one bleary-looking commuter checking his mobile phone. I did the same; it was 5.50am.

We reversed out of Milan, which is a terminus, and were quickly into frosted fields, with mountains in the distance. Was it too early to claim my free breakfast? I knew I wouldn't get back to sleep, so I got dressed and put on my jacket, checking in the pockets for my wallet. I then opened my wallet. All my credit and debit cards were present, but where I expected to see about a hundred euros in cash, there was a solitary English five-pound note.

I hunted through the compartment for the missing money. After ten minutes the verdict was in for certain: I had been robbed in the night. I could clearly recall that the nasty shock of the dining car not accepting my Visa Debit had been mitigated by the fact that I'd had the necessary euros in my wallet. I walked along the train, and found the sleeping car conductor on my way back to the dining car. He was as friendly as he had been the night before, and his face fell when I said I'd been robbed. He showed me into the dining car, where I re-encountered the chef du train. He sat down opposite me at a table, and as I was served with my free breakfast – coffee, fruit juice, yoghurt and croissant – we reviewed the various scenarios. I told him about my visit to the dining car to eat, before Dijon. I admitted I had not asked the sleeping car conductor to lock my door, but then I had been carrying all my valuables with me. The chef du train then reminded me that he had seen me in the dining car later on. Feeling like a fool, I admitted that on that occasion, I had neither asked for the door to be locked, nor carried my wallet with me. It had remained in my jacket pocket, which

1. Anhalter Station, Berlin, towards the end of the Second World War. The most famous Wagons-Lits dining car, number 2419, was stabled nearby, having been stolen by Hitler from Paris in 1940.

2. Gare de Lyon in the modern day. As if the station were not exciting enough, the palm tree gives promise of the Riviera, lying in wait at the end of the PLM main line.

3. A Wagons-Lits dining car, as burnished to perfection for the Venice Simplon Orient Express. Note the lamp shades, interestingly suggestive of French knickers.

4. The cosy buffet at Budapest Keleti station (complete with Christmas decorations in February). Here the author drank two glasses of decent, cheap white wine with characteristic speed, whilst regretting he did not have time to order 'mozzarella cheese grilled on lava stone'.

5. The bar car of the Blue Train, a promising chat-up venue, even for the rapidly balding. The year is 1950.

6. The Train Bleu restaurant in Gare de Lyon. Francophobes like to say, 'Oh, you mean station the buffet?'

7. There was never much sleeper train action at Gare Montparnasse, which will always be associated with this accident, caused by a brake failure on 22 October 1895 (even though the station was called Gare de l'Ouest at the time).

8. Lisbon Oriente station, as photographed by the author at 07.20am, after a sleepless night on the Sud Express.

9. Passengers at Calais Maritime in 1951, about to exchange the pampered luxury of the Golden Arrow for the pampered luxury of the Fleche d'Or. Unfortunately, a little walking was required.

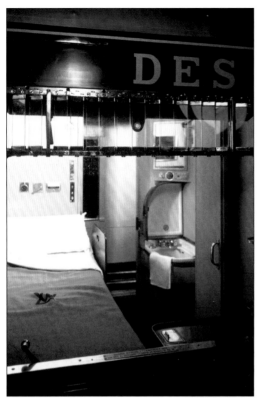

10. A cabin of the Night Ferry, the sleeper train that was put onto a boat. Somewhere in there is a lifejacket.

11. The author's quarters on what is left of the Blue Train. On the seat are SNCF emergency rations, including four biscuits, a yoghurt and a drink that was potentially (if instructions were correctly followed) hot chocolate.

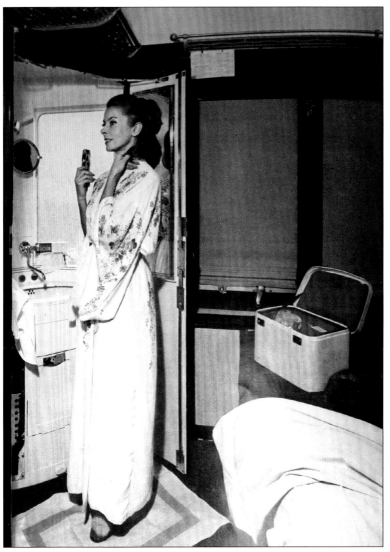

12. A Wagons-Lits sleeper of the Lx type, pictured in 1955. These offered ample facilities for one's *toilette*. The actual toilet, however, was at the end of the corridor.

13. The Wagons-Lits company's exotic magazine, *The Continental Traveller*,
exciting counterpart to the dour (and monochrome) British publication,
Travel, which tried to pretend that Wagons-Lits did not exist.

14. The badge of the British Railwaymen's Touring
club, as sported by the author's father on his
summer blazers, at the start of family excursions
by sleeper in the 1970s. These badges, symbolising
an excitement rarely surpassed in the author's
subsequent life, can be bought on eBay for about £3.

had been hung up just inside the door. This was just after Lausanne, at about 12.45am.

The chef du train then had an admission of his own to make. There had been other thefts on the train in recent months: 'There is a man who ... I don't know the English word – we call him "the stealer".'

'The word is "thief",' I said.

'Yes, that's it, he is a thief.'

In the past, the chef du train explained, the thief had furtively boarded the train during the 'technical stop' at Lausanne. 'Lausanne to Brig can be the danger,' he said. 'We have a security guard – a detective. He was on the train last night, but he didn't get on until Brig. That is always how it works, because he says he is not authorised to work in Switzerland.'

'But Brig is in Switzerland,' I said.

'Yes,' said the train manager, 'so it is contradictory.'

He then explained that the detective had got off the train at Domodossola, and looked along the platform. He had glimpsed the thief on the platform but he (the thief) did not get on the train.

'So,' I said, 'as far as the detective was concerned, the thief was not on the train last night?'

'That's right,' said the train guard, rather doubtfully.

'Was it possible,' I suggested, 'that when the detective saw the thief at Domodossola, the thief did not need to get on the train, because he'd just got off it, having robbed me?'

'It's possible,' said the train manager.

The detective had left the train at Milan, so he was unavailable. I asked the train manager why the thief, if he was known to be the thief, could not be arrested. 'Because there is no proof,' he said with a sad shake of the head.

I mentioned the man I had bumped into while walking

towards the dining car to collect Major Griffiths, after Lausanne and before Brig – right in the danger zone.

'We think the thief is a Moroccan guy,' said the train
manager. 'Did he look Moroccan?'

'He could have been Moroccan, yes, but it was dark, and
...'

We seemed to have become enveloped in a clichéd detective story. But if this had been fiction, the crime would have
occurred *after* Brig – as the train sped through the Simplon
Tunnel. Atavistic suspicions surround deep and long tunnels:
they are unnatural. When the Mont Cenis Tunnel was being
excavated one English paper warned that the contractors
shouldn't be tampering with 'the bosom of the mighty fortress'. (Paradoxically, this tunnel, through which sleepers
like the Rome Express would run, was excavated using so
noisy a new invention as the pneumatic drill.) A subterranean transition from one place to another is too simple,
fate-provokingly glib. Somehow-disturbing photographs
exist of trains with snow on the carriage roofs – picked up
on one side of an Alpine tunnel – running under bright sunshine on the other side. The presumption of people entering
tunnels is likely to be challenged. When I was going through
the Simplon as a boy in the 1970s, the explosives by which
the Italians and the Swiss proposed to blow it up during the
war were still in place. They were not removed until 2001.

In an essay of 1979, 'Tunnels Through the Alps', Paul
Sharp writes, 'Tunnels have always held a deep fascination
for man. The legends of ancient times are full of references
– the myths of the Labyrinth, Persephone, the Styx ... and the
early SF of Jules Verne and Edgar Rice Burroughs with their
tales of journeys to the centre of the earth ... All this combined with Freud knows what makes a strange and sombre
contrast to the wide vistas above ground.' He adds that while

the signalling of the Simplon was now automated, there used to be 'a signal box in the heart of the mountain, manned in shifts'. It was located in one of the galleries between the two bores of the tunnel.

In fiction, a railway passenger entering a tunnel may not emerge. In *From Russia with Love*, the Simplon is where the fraudulent 'Englishman', Grant, plans to shoot Bond as he returns from Istanbul on the Simplon Orient Express. (Bond suspects he is not English because in the dining car he orders red wine with fish.) In *The Venice Train*, one of Simenon's novels not featuring Inspector Maigret, a down-trodden French family man called Calmar is returning to Paris from a holiday in Venice. He is intending to change trains at Lausanne, and will have a three-hour wait for his connection. He mentions this to a stranger sitting opposite, whose own connection will allow him only a few minutes at Lausanne. He therefore asks if Calmar will take a bag from a left luggage office in Lausanne to a certain address in the city. Unwisely (and, I contend, implausibly) Calmar agrees, and he goes through with the commission even after the stranger steps out of the compartment as the train goes through the Simplon, and fails to reappear.

The chef du train asked if I wanted to make a formal report of the crime, which could then be handed on to the police. I said I would think about it. I then speculated that perhaps the thief had not entered the compartment when I'd left it, but had done so later on, while I was asleep. 'But your door was locked,' the train manager reminded me.

'But perhaps they had a master key?' I suggested, thinking of the Berne key. 'Perhaps they were able to unlock the door, steal the money, then lock it again from outside?'

The chef du train heard me out politely, then we walked back to my compartment (passing the Texans, on their way to the dining car, who cheerily hoped that I'd slept well). The chef du train wanted to demonstrate a security feature. He invited me to step into the compartment and lock the door. He then attempted to open the door from the corridor with his master key, and it only opened a couple of inches, being retained by a steel fixture triggered by the locking of the door. The logic was that the door opened far enough to see whether it would be necessary to override this retainer by force – which would involve making a lot of noise. His point was that nobody, even equipped with a master key, could get into the compartment undetected if the compartment was locked. So the thief could only have done his work when I returned to the dining car to collect Major Griffiths.

In Wagons-Lits days he could not have done it even then, because the sleeping car conductor would have been sitting on his fold-down seat at the end of the corridor. The only way around this would have been to involve him in the crime, as with Pierre Michel, the conductor in *Murder on the Orient Express*, whose complicity (Poirot decides) explains the whole reason for committing the murder on the train in the first place.

After cleaning my teeth and packing my things, I decided I would ask the chef du train to make an official report of the theft, but not to involve the police. It didn't seem worth it for a sum equivalent to about sixty pounds.

As we traversed the causeway between Venice Mestre and Venice Santa Lucia stations, I ought to have been paying attention to the promising brightness of the day and the sparkling water. Instead, I was back in the dining car with my bag beside me, and making a statement to the chef du train, who wrote in French, beginning, 'Le client déclare avoir découvert à environ 5h du matin ...' It was a waste of time, just as the empty water alongside us seemed a waste of space, a necessary penance before the beauty of Venice. He finished writing as we were approaching Venice Santa Lucia, which involves running parallel to the vineyard of the Carmelite monastery that is part of the Church of St Mary of Nazareth.

Inviting me to sign the statement, the chef du train said, 'I don't know what happened, but I'm sorry for what happened,' and I believed him.

VENICE

Construction of the Venice Santa Lucia Station was started in the 1930s and finished in the 1950s. It is low, wide and austere, a function of Mussolini's surprising Modernism and rail enthusiasm. In *Blood, Iron & Gold*, Christian Wolmar addresses the question of whether Mussolini really did 'make the trains run on time'. He begins by pointing out that 'Italy emerged from the inter-war period with the greatest proportion of electrified lines among European countries. The driving force was the dictatorship of Benito Mussolini, who saw electric trains as epitomizing the modernizing image to boost Italy's standing in the world.' Mussolini certainly invested heavily in railways, but his reputation for making them run on time

was based on a special press trip staged in July 1939, days before the outbreak of war. A three-car electric unit travelled from Florence to Milan at an average of 102 mph for the near 200-mile trip, despite a long section through the Apennines, a world record that would stand until the launch of the Japanese high speed train a quarter of a century later.

Venice is about other things than railways, and even accounts of the Simplon Orient Express (the most famous train to call there) pass over it pretty quickly. But it was the favourite railway destination of Paul Morand, who preferred the original Santa Lucia, erected on the site of a church whose name the station inherited in 1861, and which 'consisted of three arcades which had turned green from the damp and had been blackened by the coal smoke'. The modern station, like the old one, is right on the Grand Canal – a reminder that all arriving trains have to reverse out to proceed – and on this suddenly very sunny morning, the conjunction was uplifting, like that of a luxury hotel and its pool.

On the station steps, a dozen men of Middle Eastern appearance were holding a demonstration, but more in sorrow than anger. Their placards showed white and black hands intertwined, and a slogan that translated as 'We are Italians too.' This must relate to the Paris attacks. A few metres away, a Jewish man dressed in Hasidic black was being accosted by a street trader offering brightly coloured selfie sticks: 'Do you have one in black?' the Jewish man asked. (Morand wrote of the tourists of Venice: 'Those Leicas, these Zeiss; do people no longer have eyes?')

I began walking through the Venetian labyrinth to my hotel, following the stencilled street-corner directions marked either 'Per St Marco' or 'Per Rialto'. The guidance is given rather grudgingly, appearing only on every third or fourth corner, but the elegance of the lettering and the prettiness of the crumbling walls on which it appears is disarming. Those walls are ochre-coloured or yellow; the house windows tended to feature potted plants of an ultra-vivid green. I seemed to be walking through a hand-tinted postcard.

It would be necessary to cross St Mark's Square to reach

my hotel, but all the possible alleyways leading to the square were blocked by policemen who didn't speak English, and a line of tape. I then heard, from the direction of the square, a band striking up 'La Marseillaise'. A woman standing outside an antique shop smiled sadly at me, as if to say, 'Now do you understand?' Looking towards the square, I glimpsed – through the gap between two churches – a coffin, carried on the shoulders of six gondoliers. Of *course*: a young Venetian woman had been killed in the Paris attacks.

All through a day of golden winter sun, that funeral stayed with me. Morand quotes ran through my mind: 'The privately owned gondolas at their moorings nod their iron prows sadly as we pass by; we disturb their slumber.' Also, 'The cats are the vultures of Venice', and 'A person's life frequently resembles those palazzi on the Grand Canal where the lower floors were begun with an array of stones carved in the shapes of diamonds, and whose upper floors were hastily completed with dried mud.'

After checking into my hotel, I took a vaporetto to the Lido, where I had the beach and, apparently, the Mediterranean Sea to myself. I thought about my father, who had taken my sister and me to Venice, and the Lido, as an excursion from one of our stays in Lido di Jesolo. I cannot now remember how we got from one place to the other, but I do remember my dad at early evening on the Lido in full holiday rig: not only the holiday cravat, but a cotton jumper over his shoulders. He had reverted to the way he looked in the opening pages of our family photo album, in the pictures taken before he met my mother. The Venice Lido was a kind of benchmark of glamour to him: I think because a typical British visitor – without benefit of belonging to the British Railwaymen's Touring Club – might not know about it.

As the boat took me back, the sky was turning pink as the

sun descended into the waters of the lagoon, and the clank-
ing church bells combined somehow harmoniously with
the growling of the boat's engine. I saw, ahead of us, some
more gondoliers removed from their usual habitat: half a
dozen of them, in their straw boaters and stripy shirts, were
standing and rowing an outsized, seagoing gondola across
the choppy waters of the lagoon while shouting rhythmic-
ally in unison. Was this a self-improvement exercise for the
oarsmen? A chap might easily become complacent and soft
if always confined to the sleepy canals. Or maybe it was an
affirmation of the proud Venetian identity in difficult times.

EASYJET

At the bus garage, where I waited for the shuttle to the airport, I kept seeing double-deckers with 'Lido di Jesolo' on the
front, which was slightly depressing, putting that Shangri La
of my boyhood on a level with Camberwell or Sydenham. But
those buses did solve the mystery of how we'd travelled from
one lido to the other on our family holidays.

I flew back to London on easyJet, with the usual rail-enthusiast's feeling of fraternising with the enemy. Even though
the aeroplane has been the 'traditional' method by which
the British have accessed Europe since the mid-1950s (when
British European Airways began offering cheap flights to
European capitals), it has never become romantic, except to
a tiny number of connoisseurs. Nobody goes 'interplaneing'
on their gap year.

Stowing my bag in the overhead locker, I wondered to
what extent the unlikelihood of anyone being able to raid
my wallet on the plane compensated for the blandness of
the experience. Certainly, as I write this, I have forgotten all
but the barest details of the flight, whereas I have recounted

my night train journey to Venice with hardly a glance at my notebook.

POSTSCRIPT

As I was finishing this book, I learnt that Transdev was relinquishing its holding in Thello, the business having 'not grown as much as we were hoping'. The Paris terrorist attacks of November 2015 were mentioned as a contributory factor. Where this leaves the overnight service from Paris to Venice is unclear at the time of writing.

4

THE 'ORIENT EXPRESS'

WHICH ORIENT EXPRESS DO YOU WANT?

On that morning's Eurostar from London to Paris, I had been reminded of Wagons-Lits: by the livery of the new Eurostar carriages, the excitingly named e320 class. The predominantly cream colour of the old trains has been succeeded by mid-blue with a yellow stripe, which is nearly the midnight blue and gold of W-L, although apparently no homage is intended. I had then made 'the change at Paris' in its easiest and shortest form, walking from Gare du Nord to Gare de l'Est, which takes five minutes, and you really can't go wrong if you follow the Rue des Deux Gares. In *Nairn's Paris*, Ian Nairn recommends this pedestrian approach to Gare de l'Est: 'platform roofs almost as far as the eye can see, a human meat market beyond the dreams of Smithfield'. He rated it 'the best of the Parisian train sheds', but the distinction of the station is traditionally found elsewhere. In *The Railway Station: A Social History*, Richards and MacKenzie write that Est has been 'long regarded as the finest station in the world', because it is 'the model head station'. The dominant feature of the head station is the 'head building' running at right angles to the tracks, as opposed to the hump of the train shed. The head station is focused on the people rather than the trains. Passengers mingle in the head building, or filter through it on their way to the platforms, and there is a great sense of lateral freedom on the concourse at Gare de l'Est, which was doubled in length in the 1930s. But this long, wide building has been filled up with shops and cafés, so that it now resembles a generic shopping mall.

Gare de l'Est is neither compellingly gloomy, like Gare du Nord, nor upbeat like Gare de Lyon. It seems caught between two moods. On the one hand, troops departed from the station in 1870, 1914 and 1939, which explains why Georges Simenon had found 'a heavy feeling' in the Gare. The concourse is dominated by Albert Herter's painting showing troops entraining in 1914. It was painted in memory of his son, Everit-Albert Herter, who had fallen in action in 1918. Richards and Mackenzie write: 'A platform is seen, with the troops boarding a train, and elderly parents seeing off their sons, young children their fathers and grieving wives their husbands ... The prevailing mood is sombre. There is none of the jubilation and euphoria that really attended the outbreak of war.' The other famous Gare de l'Est leave-taking – the first ever departure of the Orient Express – was a happy event, even in retrospect, and I would be keeping it in mind during my own journey, which would involve more than one 'magic carpet to the east,' as Nagelmackers shamelessly called his own train.

***

After a long expiration, the Orient Express disappeared from the European Timetables in 2009, but I wanted to duplicate the experience as far as possible. Ffestiniog Travel, being railway specialists, did not flinch when I set out my aim, but the consultant asked, 'Which Orient Express do you have in mind?'

The one usually invoked is the Simplon Orient Express, which became the fashionable route after the First World War, when Germany was shunned. It ran to Constantinople from Paris Gare de Lyon via Switzerland, Venice, Trieste, Belgrade and Sofia. But the Simplon did not appeal as a model, firstly because it involved too much of the Balkans and the Balkans give me a headache. Secondly, I'd already covered the first part of that route in my journey aboard the Thello train, and the Simplon is overexposed in literature. It is the setting, for example, of both *Murder on the Orient Express* and *From Russia with Love*. Another consideration was that the Gare de Lyon has never displaced Gare de l'Est in my mind as the definitive starting point of the Orient Express.

On 4 October 1883, the first Express d'Orient – as the train was known until 1891, when its name was changed to the Orient Express, in acknowledgement that the British and Americans were its main customers – departed from Gare de l'Est (or the Gare de Strasbourg, as it was then known). This very first trip was over a special, provisional route. It went Strasbourg-Munich-Vienna-Budapest-Bucharest, then to Giurgiu on the Danube in Romania. Passengers would cross the Danube by ferry to Rustchuk in Bulgaria, where they took a train to Varna on the Black Sea ('the sea capital of Bulgaria'). From there they would begin a fourteen-hour voyage to Constantinople, and if that sounds a bit watery, well, this *was* called the Maritime Route. Owing to local times not being synchronised, the journey took 81 hours 40 minutes eastbound, and 77 hours 49 minutes the other way. For the next six years, the route was slightly different, but still involved a boat. The railway connection between Paris and Constantinople would not be completed until 1889. This would take the train from Budapest to Belgrade to Niš, in Serbia. It would then go through Bulgaria, via Sofia and Svilengrad, entering Turkey at Edirne. The train called daily at Vienna. Twice a week, the train terminated at Bucharest. The big production number, the run to Constantinople, happened three times a week. The Constantinople approach of this – the plain Orient Express – was combined with that of the Simplon Orient between Belgrade and Constantinople when the Simplon was inaugurated after the First World War.

But let us revert to October 1883, and the Maritime Route. The inaugural journey was staged as a publicity stunt by Georges Nagelmackers. Crowds streamed along the Boulevard de Magenta for the big send-off, just as if they personally knew the people who were travelling, or as if this were a rocket launch rather than the departure of the 18.00 for Constantinople. The Gare de l'Est was newly illuminated by electric lights. The Orient Express was not yet blue, but its varnished teak carriages compared favourably to some worn-out green 'Boudoir Cars' of the Colonel Mann era that Nagelmackers had arranged to be marshalled on the next platform to show how he had progressed since his association with that dubious American. Nagelmackers himself would be travelling, as would various of his top-hatted sponsors, as well as a few French and Belgian government ministers and the Paris chargé d'affaires of the Ottoman Empire. And there was a party of journalists for this most momentous of freebies, principally two fat dandies. The first was Edmond About, a bestselling French novelist and bon viveur. (His account of the trip, *De Pontoise à Stamboul*, has never been available in English.) There was also Henri Opper de Blowtiz ('Ce nom!' exclaimed Jean des Cars in *Sleeping Story*). Opper de Blowtiz was a literal Bohemian by birth, and Paris correspondent of *The Times*.

Behind the engine was a fourgon, carrying mail, to help the train pay its way, after which came two sleeping cars of an unnamed type (W-L had not yet embarked on its series of standard cars). There was also a restaurant car and another fourgon crammed with such essentials as wine, champagne, brandies, cigars and (a railway first) ice. One thinks of the Orient Express as a long train, because it went a long way, but it seldom involved more than half a dozen carriages. The train was meant to depart at six o'clock, but was impeded by the press of well-wishers on the platform. It left at twenty past; other trains on the main line to Strasbourg were held back on branches.

Edmond About was impressed by his accommodation, as E. H. Cookridge wrote in his book, *Orient Express*:

In his account he extolled the teak and mahogany panelling with inlaid marquetry of the compartment walls and car doors, the deep armchairs covered in soft Spanish leather embossed in gold patterning, the spring loaded roller blinds ... augmented by the flowered-damask drapes held back when not in use by silk cords and tassels of gold thread. When the seats were converted to beds for the night, they were covered with silk sheets, the finest wool blankets, and counterpanes filled with the lightest of eiderdown. He pressed the bell, which immediately brought the attendant ...

TO MUNICH

My own departure would be by TGV: the 15.25 to Munich.
I regretted that my itinerary did not allow a later train. The
old Orient Express was always an evening departure, with
dinner a more or less immediate treat at what Wagons-
Lits would call, in later publicity for their catering service,
'L'Heure Agréable'. The Russians have the right idea. The
three-times-a-week RZD sleeper to Moscow leaves Gare de
l'Est at 18.58. It was no consolation to think that I could have
started out on a night train as recently as December 2014,
when the City Night Line sleeper from Paris to Munich ran
for the last time.

The TGV Est was a plush duplex with a joint French-
German crew. The Ligne à Grande Vitesse Est, over which
it would be running towards Strasbourg, is considered the
first stage of a European Union project called the Main Line
for Europe, which will provide high-speed services between
Paris and Bratislava, with a branch to Bucharest. It is scheduled to be completed in 2020, and has been likened to a
modern version of the Orient Express route – but there will
be no sleeper trains on it.

The TGV was half full. My only complaint was that the
second class (which I was in) was pale blue, whereas first
class was seductive, bordello-like reds and purples. On the
new Eurostars, too, standard class is a cold colour, with
pale-blue carpets, whereas business premier is a warmer
colour, with a red carpet. It seems unfair that standard class
travellers should be gratuitously penalised in this way.

My booked seat turned out to be alongside a middle-aged
man who spoke continuously to himself in German. He
didn't seem at all dangerous. In fact, he wore a duffle coat
with a badge showing the dove of peace, with an olive branch
in its beak. Even so, I moved pretty sharply to an empty seat,

about which I began to feel guilty when the German started showing signs of normality – muttering less, and reading the sports section of an English newspaper (*The Times*).

A certain jumpiness might have been permissible. My destination, Turkey, was suffering shockwaves from the Syrian war. On the day I'd booked my tickets, 17 February 2016, there had been a terrorist attack on the capital, Ankara. In January, a party of tourists had been killed in Istanbul itself, and the Foreign Office was urging British visitors to 'exercise caution'. When I suggested to the native Turk who runs my local news agent that it was an 'interesting' time to be going, he said, 'Not really ... but you should be OK if you stay in your hotel room.'

The room rate at that hotel, the Pera Palace, built by Nagelmackers and famed for its Orient Express connections, had proved disturbingly cheap (and well down on what it had been a few months before). The cost of a British Airways return flight was also unexpectedly low, which was just as well because on the day before I bought my euros, Boris Johnson had announced (possibly having flipped a coin) that he favoured Brexit, so sterling had slumped.

I took out my tickets and my European Railway Map. I had a second class ticket on this TGV to Munich. I then had a ticket for the Hungarian-operated EuroNight train from Munich to Budapest. I would be spending most of the day in Budapest before taking the Romanian EuroNight train to Bucharest, for which I also had a ticket.

The prospect beyond Bucharest looked a bit hazy for me, as it had to the earliest travellers on the Orient Express. (They had not been told by Nagelmackers that boats would be involved; they thought they were going the whole way by train.) According to Ffestiniog Travel, computer booking from Britain did not stretch beyond Bucharest. For that leg, I didn't have a ticket, only an itinerary. This showed the timings of a night train from Bucharest to Istanbul, for which I would have to buy the ticket in Bucharest. Some photos on the *Man in Seat 61* website suggested that this train not only existed, but had a name: Bosfor. But even if I caught it, I expected bother on the final approach. Disruption caused by the digging of the Marmaray Tunnel under the Bosphorus meant that bus replacements were likely.

I was undoubtedly doing something quite silly. For my Ffestiniog tickets alone I had paid £500, with the Eurostar fare and hotel bills on top. A century and a quarter after the running of the first Orient Express, my train journey was bound to take longer than the original eighty-one hours, there no longer being any through service. A flight to Istanbul would have cost about £100 – a journey that would have taken five hours in total, half of which would have been spent reading a paper on the Tube to Heathrow. But part of the appeal of this trip was the proof it offered that history can run backwards. And the Orient Express was always a bizarre train, a lure to the romantic, or to those diplomatic couriers with diplomatic luggage that must be hand-carried and yet was too bulky to be taken onto an aeroplane. In the early days, a steamer from Venice was a more relaxed way of getting to Istanbul, and from 1947 there was a scheduled air service there from Paris.

What we might call The Murder *of* the Orient Express began after the Second World War, but the train is like one of those ham actors who, when shot in a play, milks the death, writhing about, apparently expiring only to revive for further histrionics.

After the war, Wagons-Lits resumed its various Orient Expresses, but its sleepers operating wholly within the Eastern Bloc countries were gradually taken over by the communist governments. On one of her immediately post-war journeys on the Simplon Orient, Agatha Christie was attacked by bedbugs when heading between Venice and Paris. In 1948, she planned a visit to Iraq with her archaeologist husband Max. 'No Orient Express this time, alas!' she wrote in her autobiography. 'It was no longer the cheapest way ... This time we flew – the beginning of that dull routine, travelling by air.'

In 1962, the Simplon Orient Express was withdrawn and replaced by a slower train mendaciously called the Direct Orient Express, with fewer weekly services all the way to Istanbul. On 20 May 1977 the Direct Orient Express ran for the last time. When I first opened my second-hand copy of *Sleeping Story* by Jean des Cars, a small newspaper cutting – I think from the personal columns of *The Times* – dropped out. It read: 'In affectionate remembrance of the Direct Orient Express which passed away quietly in Paris last night. Deeply lamented by a large circle of friends and acquaintances at the Raleigh Club. Ride on! Ride on in majesty! In lowly pomp ride on to die.' (The quote is from a hymn, written in 1820 by Henry Hart Milman, and the Raleigh Club was a travel-cum-dining club, connected to the Royal Geographical Society.)

So now there was no through train from Paris to Istanbul. Was that the end of the Orient Express? Not quite, because the plain, original Orient Express continued to run from Gare de l'Est to Budapest and Bucharest.

In 1991 the Orient Express lost its sleeper to Bucharest. Surely that was the end? But no, because the Bucharest sleeper was restored between 1998 and 2001, and even after 2001 there was still an Orient Express, even if it was hardly at all oriental, running from Paris to Vienna via Strasbourg, where most of the passengers got off. With the opening of the TGV Est line in 2007, the Orient Express suffered its final demotion, running Strasbourg-Vienna as an Austrian Railways EuroNight train. This was listed as the Orient Express in the European Timetable ending 12 December 2009. It was absent from the one starting 13 December.

***

We were now about a hundred miles from Paris. If we had been on the 'classic' route to Strasbourg, which the Orient Express took, as opposed to the Ligne à Grande Vitesse Est, we would now have been running through a station called Châlons, and until the Second World War the Orient Express stopped at Châlons to pick up the British, who therefore wouldn't necessarily have to bother with that Parisian walk along Rue des Deux Gares. Here was the equivalent of being taken around the Petite Ceinture from Gare du Nord to Gare de Lyon to connect up with the Blue Train. But in the case of the Orient Express connection, Paris was avoided in a wider arc. At 2pm passengers would have boarded the 'Continental Express' at Victoria for Dover. At Calais they would have boarded a blue W-L sleeping car attached to an ordinary French express heading for Châlons. *Railway Wonders of the World* magazine described the journey in the mid-1930s:

Through Northern France, the train crosses some of the most fought-over country in Europe, though it looks smiling enough in the gathering dusk. During the past hundred years, it has seen the Franco-Prussian War and the Great War, though but for place names which are familiar, one would never know it. Rheims, in the evening dusk, looks as peaceful as ever, although it was nearly shelled to pieces barely twenty years ago. On the plains of Châlons, over which the train runs late in the evening, the advance of Attila the Hun, with his Asiatic hordes, was finally stemmed centuries ago.

Châlons Station remains, on the classic route. The station used to be called Gare Châlons-sur-Marne, because that's what the town was called, but in 1998, the town went upmarket, becoming Châlons-en-Champagne, which is what the station is now called. It is served by high-speed trains even if they don't go at high speed, because it is on the LGV Est *network*, even if not actually on the fast line.

The next station east on the classic line is Vitry-le-François. Here, on 16 November 1929, the Orient Express crashed into a freight train. The driver, fireman and one conductor were killed. A photograph of the wreckage was turned into a postcard – which it would have been cruel to send with the message 'Wish you were here.' (In June 1961 there was another railway disaster at Vitry-le-François. A passenger train was derailed by a bomb planted by the OAS, French far-right dissidents opposed to the independence of Algeria; twenty-eight people died.) While on the subject of OE disasters ... In December 1901, the Ostend-Vienna Orient Express (1894–1993) jumped the tracks and entered the station restaurant in Frankfurt. In his book *The Orient Express*, Anthony Burton writes, 'It was an establishment made for serious eating, the sort of place where one would not expect anything more disastrous than a corked bottle of wine.' Nobody was killed.

As we whirled through wide dark fields, punctuated occasionally by enormous farmhouses, I myself began to feel hungry. Dinner on the original journey was served an hour and a half after departure – at 8pm. The restaurant car incorporated a gentlemen's smoking salon with all the European newspapers, and there was further expensive marquetry, with scrollwork, cornices and gilded metal flowers protruding, and 'rather garish' (according to E. H. Cookridge) paintings. The lighting was by gigantic – yet mellow – gas chandeliers. The meal involved nine courses: soup, lobster, oysters, caviar, fish, game, cakes, sorbets and cheeses. Afterwards, Edmond About walked through to the kitchen to shake the hand of the Burgundian chef.

In the buffet of the duplex TGV from Paris to Munich – with night falling rapidly over the countryside of the Champagne region – I myself bought a tuna sandwich. Glancing down at the receipt I saw the words 'Newrest Wagonslits', which gave me a jolt, until I remembered that one corporate remnant of Wagons-Lits, Newrest, is still in the railway catering business, and is allowed to use the hallowed W-L name by Wagons-Lits Diffusion, which controls the brand. Contemplating the receipt, I imagined, materialising before me, an early W-L waiter, in a uniform comprising frock coat, knickerbockers, white tights and Prince Charming slippers. Admittedly, this rig-out was for special occasions only, not for normal dinners, such as this, taken from an Orient Express menu dated 6 December 1884:

Potage tapioca
Olives et beurre
Bar sauce hollandaise
Pommes au naturel
Gigot de mouton à la Bretonne
Poulet du Mans au cresson
Épinards au sucre
Fromages
Tarte aux fruits

***

The truly high-speed phase of the LGV had stopped at Baudricourt, a hundred miles short of Strasbourg. (The second phase, reaching that city, would be opening shortly, having been delayed by the derailment of a test train – killing eleven people – in November 2015.) Now, the countryside seemed to have become slower as well, with muddy woodlands appearing, the farmsteads becoming more picturesque. On arrival at Strasbourg, there was much cheek-kissing between French people on the platform, as though to affirm the Gallic identity of a place so close to Germany. Half of our train was detached and then we pulled away, past the illuminated sign of a Restaurant A l'Abattoir. Things were becoming subtly more foreign. As we passed though Kehl there was a 'Diamond Casino' on the platform.

Five minutes after our departure, an unshaven, urchin-like man came and sat opposite me. He looked too scruffy to be on a TGV, even in second class. He was watching me as I looked at my map. 'Your plan, Signore – I look?' Seeing my hesitation, he smiled. 'Quick look? How about it?' I passed it over, and he began scrutinising it like a general planning a campaign. He seemed mainly concerned with Italy: 'Venezia, Venezia, Venezia,' he muttered, then 'Roma, Roma, Roma.' After a few minutes, he looked up, smiling again. 'Cigarette, Signore? One cigarette? How about it?'

'You can't smoke on the train,' I said, trying not to sound too priggish.

He nodded, then changed tack. 'A coffee?' he suggested. 'One coffee, signore? How about it?' I fished in my pocket and gave him the only coin I found there – a single euro. He eyed it ruefully. 'Ah,' he said, '*almost!*', and he returned to his study of the map. I was paying the price for having moved from the seat next to the undoubtedly less-nutty German. But when we pulled into Stuttgart, the Italian neatly folded up the map and returned it to me, saying, 'Grazie, Signore.' He got off the train, and I watched through the window as he inspected the tracks on the opposite side of the platform, possibly looking for discarded fags. I was relieved that he'd got off; all I needed now was for him to *stay* off, but our TGV was lingering in the station. Finally, as we pulled away, he disappeared from view. If he did get back on the train, I never saw him again.

Karlsruhe Station was dominated by a giant neon sign reading 'Karlsruhe', and snow was falling beyond the platform canopy. We began heading south-east towards Stuttgart and at Augsburg the snow was coming down thickly enough for me to envisage the cancellation of the train. Nevertheless, we pulled into Munich Hauptbahnhof on time at 21.36.

On that original journey, the train stopped at Munich to take on German journalists and a replacement dining car, something having gone wrong with the original. According to Martin Page in *The Lost Pleasures of the Great Trains*, the French journalist, Edmond About, soured the international-ist mood of the junket by noting 'somewhat bitterly that the new station in Munich had been built out of French repa-rations after the war of 1870'. (About had lost his home in Alsace as a result of the Franco-Prussian War.) The present station represents a rebuild of 1960. Hitler had planned a massive new station for Munich based on St Peter's Basilica in Rome but – naturally – six times bigger. It was meant to be completed in 1950, but only the foundations were laid.

I had two hours to kill before my sleeper. A bell – like a church bell – was tolling in the station. It created an air of tension. The main concourse was full of food courts, inhab-ited by weary-looking people who might or might not be about to catch trains. I scoured the departure board, veri-fying that EN 463 to Budapest was listed. (It's also known

as Kálmán Imre, after a Hungarian composer of operettas.)
I then approached the exit by walking through a shopping
mall. Red plastic buckets collected melted snow dripping
from cracks in the roof. Most of the shops were closed, but
a well-stocked tobacconist was open for business directly
beneath a banner proclaiming 'Welcome to Munich Station:
Smoke Free Zone'. But nicotine had the last laugh, because,
emerging from the station, I ran a multicultural gauntlet of
shifty-looking characters who were all smoking, and most of
them were drinking as well. They were what the Edwardian
railway police of Britain used to call 'station loungers.'

Heavy snow fell onto the square in front of the station. As
I stepped over some tramlines, my suede shoes – suitable
for padding along carpeted railway carriages – immediately
started to leak.

I trudged through the snow towards the welcoming lights
of what turned out to be a strip club. Next door to it was a
place called Sport Café Schiller, which was crammed with
boxing memorabilia and big German blokes. Middlesbrough
vs. Wolverhampton Wanderers was on the widescreen TV.
You have to go a lot further than Munich to escape even sec-
ond-tier English football. I ordered a beer, and 'Noodles and
ham'.

'Enjoy the evening, and the town,' said the waiter (probably an ex-boxer) as I was about to leave.

'I'm afraid I'm only going back to the station.'

'Yes,' he said regretfully, 'and that is not at all pleasant.'

Inside the station, a shouting match was taking place in
one of the food courts between a waiter and a man of Middle-
Eastern appearance. A small crowd looked on, half amused,
half nervous. As far as I could tell, the waiter was inviting the
man to leave, but the man was refusing to do so, or at least
not until he'd finished the plate of food before him.

I drifted over to a deli counter, contemplating the purchase of half a bottle of wine for the train. A young German man came up to me. He looked like an overgrown schoolboy, with short blonde hair and glasses. 'You can get cheap Berliners after 11 o'clock, you know,' he said, in excellent English. By way of explanation, he pointed to a display of cakes, and I recalled that a Berliner was a jelly doughnut.

Quite a crowd was gathering around this cake counter, and the young German explained that the prices would be dramatically reduced in five minutes' time, at eleven o'clock. As we waited, he said, 'You are on a tour of Bavaria?' Before I could deny it, he said, 'Then may I recommend a visit to Berchtesgaden? That's Berchtesgaden near Salzburg, famous as a base of Mr Adolf Hitler and later the American Army. When I say "Mr" Adolf Hitler, that does not mean I approve of him. You take a Deutsche Bahn bus – not a train – from Salzburg. For the first person it is twenty-three euros, for the next one in the party, it is five, and at night it's two. So you can get people there without telling the police.' I didn't quite see how this last remark followed, but there was no opportunity to say so. 'All of Bavaria is very beautiful, and safe,' the young man continued. 'It is Conservative. In Germany, politics is governed by population density. Low density is Conservative; high density is Social Democrat. As a city, Munich is Social Democrat, but it is also safe. You can have 5,000 euros in an open pocket, and no one will touch it, because everyone has money. But we have a problem with immigrants, because they do not have money.'

'But Germany welcomes the migrants,' I said, thinking of the images from Munich Station in September 2015, six months previously, when Syrian refugees, alighting from trains from Budapest, had been greeted with hugs.

'Mrs Merkel welcomes them,' the young German man

corrected me. 'She has been very direct about that, and it is a courageous policy.'

'But you don't agree with it?'

'No.'

The Berliners were now available at the knock-down price. 'Can I recommend the apple ones?' he said. I offered to buy him one.

'It is not necessary,' he said, but then he changed his mind. 'Thank you,' he said, 'I will take two. They are thirty cents each.'

As I carried my wine towards the platform for EN 463, the food court argument was approaching its climax, with two policemen attempting to mediate. It was resolved as I passed by: the man who'd been invited to leave *did* leave, but while carrying his yet-to-be-eaten plate of food.

About thirty people were waiting on the platform for EN 463: backpackers, a couple of family groups, careworn businessmen. All types were represented except the rich. The entrance to my sleeping car was guarded by a Hungarian official in a blue Puffa jacket and peaked cap. He asked very politely for my ticket, and I couldn't find it. After two minutes of fumbling through my pockets, I asked if I could look for my ticket on the train. He shook his head regretfully: 'A ticket is a must,' he said. I found it at last, but in the confusion failed to see that the blue-and-white carriage was marked 'Voiture Couchette' and not 'Voiture Lits', which would have denoted a proper sleeper, which is what I had booked. And I was only able to glance fleetingly at the window label, which would have read, had I had time:

Salzburg 01.18
Linz 04.51
St Pölten 05.44

Vienna Westbahnhof 06.10
Hegyeshalom 07.12
Győr 07.36
Budapest Keleti 09.05

Only a couple of other sleeping compartments besides my own were occupied. A menu in the corridor advertised 'Tea, coffee, alcoholic drinks.'

'Not available,' said the Hungarian guard, who was following me.

'But is there a service of breakfast?'

'A small breakfast,' he said, with an apologetic smile.

The compartment was brown, cream and yellow, and had one lower bunk made up and no sink. An announcement came over the tannoy: 'I am Martin, your German train manager. We will be calling at Salzburg at 01.18, where our train will split into three. One part to Zagreb, one part to Venezia, and the third part to Budapest. There will be no further loudspeaker announcements.'

Five minutes later, I encountered Martin while strolling along the train. He was in the next carriage along, which was far more luxurious than mine. The corridor was thickly carpeted. Wood-panelled sleeping compartments were set at an angle, to allow them to be longer. The corner of each protruded into the corridor, but these protrusions had been rounded off, creating a sinuous effect, like vertical waves. 'This car is German,' Martin explained. 'Yours, along there,' he added, with a slight note of disparagement, 'is Hungarian, and unfortunately there were no sleepers available tonight, so you are in a couchette.' A woman was emerging from one of the compartments, revealing a stylish wood-framed bed and a rich-blue carpet. 'There's no problem at all about sleeping in these,' she said, smugly, before heading off to the loo.

Our train seemed to be entangled with other trains. 'That is because it is three trains in one,' Martin said, in his trenchant way. 'It is a EuroNight train to Budapest, also two City Night Line trains: one to Venice, one to Zagreb.'

City Night Line, incidentally, used to be spelt in the same annoying way as EuroNight, with no gap between the words. That was when it was a joint operation between German, Swiss and Austrian national railways, a collaboration beginning in 1995. From 2007 it became a subsidiary of Deutsche Bahn (DB) alone. For the last three or four years, DB has been paring back any sleepers that competed with its high-speed trains, including services running between France and Germany, Holland and Germany, and Berlin and Munich. As already mentioned, the entire DB sleeper service will have stopped by the time this book is published, unless a petition has managed to save it. But the plan is for some of the German sleepers to be taken over by the Austrian national railway, ÖBB.

A German campaigner for Friends of the Earth had told me that while this cutback of sleepers was undoubtedly a bad thing, he was pleased it will not be accompanied by any great expansion of German high-speed rail. In fact, Germany is scaling back on that too. High-speed rail is less environmentally friendly than conventional rail, even if it is not as bad as aeroplanes, but this is not why DB is scaling back on it. The motivation, according to the Friends of the Earth man, is that DB 'has huge financial problems'.

After ablutions in the WC (which was clean, although the sink was so small there was no room to put down my soap bag), I went to bed and to sleep. But the shunting at Salzburg woke me up, and I went to the loo again, passing the Hungarian sleeping conductor, who was not sleeping, but making notes in a ledger on a high, Dickensian desk in his cubicle at the end of the corridor. This was almost as reassuring as if he'd been on one of the folding seats occupied through the night by Wagons-Lits conductors.

Salzburg has a baleful place in Orient Express history. While the train carried many people worth killing (Michael Barsley lists 'King's Messengers and couriers ... crowned heads and princelings with their retinues, and gentlemen on important diplomatic missions') only one murder seems to have occurred on the train – or perhaps the word is 'from' the train. In February 1950 the battered body of Eugene Karpe, a US Naval Attaché in Bucharest, was found by the side of the line near Salzburg. The previous week, a friend of his, a businessman named Robert Vogeler, had been sentenced in Budapest to fifteen years in prison for spying. Karpe was travelling to Paris on the Orient Express having visited Mrs Vogeler in Vienna – so his was a life strung out along the Orient Express route. The Austrian authorities declared his death the result of foul play, but no arrest was ever made.

Waking again at quarter to six, I raised the blind. We were at St Pölten in eastern Austria. About an hour later, I dozed through arrival at Vienna. On that original press trip, the train had arrived at Vienna late on the second day. A tour of the city had been arranged, so that the party could see the new electric lighting. Edmond About and Opper de Blowitz declined this tour – they had already seen the new electric lighting at Gare de l'Est and Strasbourg, after all. They were more interested in the two women who boarded at Vienna – the very first female passengers. These were Mme von Scala, wife of the Vice-Minister of Transport, and her sister, Mlle Leonie Pohl. Being French, Edmond About was a connoisseur of women as well as food, and he preferred Mme von Scala: 'She is somewhat of the type of a great English lady, but more animated and with Viennese features that make her even more alluring.' E. H. Cookridge observes that, in the 1880s, 'for a woman to travel by night on a train was regarded by most Europeans as unconventional if not actually dangerous'. At night, women could lock themselves in their sleeping cars, but a short night could descend at any minute, when the train went through a tunnel, and women in day cars were advised to keep hatpins and long needles handy. But erotic danger was good for business – for Nagelmackers, and others.

In Paris, from 1898, a musical called *The Orient Express* ran at the Ancien Élysée Montmartre, 'departing' every night at half past ten. Wagons-Lits perhaps endorsed the show. Certainly the company name appeared on the posters, which showed women undressing in sleepers they shared with caddish-looking men. The Ancien Élysée was where the can-can had been pioneered, and this 'Voyage en 2 Tableaux' was part of a bawdy continuum, since the theatre would be associated with striptease in the 1940s, and *Oh! Calcutta!* would have a long run there in the 1970s.

The first novel to exploit the racy reputation of the Orient Express was *The Madonna of the Sleeping Cars*, published in 1925. It was by Maurice Dekobra, the pen name of a French playboy called Maurice Tessier. He had once watched a snake charmer in Egypt who had two cobras: 'deux cobras', hence 'Dekobra'. His tale of high life and espionage features a femme fatale called Lady Diana Wynham, who is determined to find 'the imbecile who will cater to my whims and ripen in my garden of Hesperides some golden apples'. *The Girl on the Train* it is not, and the significance of sleeping carriages to the plot is more symbolic than actual: they represent a life of gilded libertinism, and Lady Diana is only seen boarding a train – the Orient Express – at the very end.

Here is Lady Diana's departure from Gare de l'Est:

The early arrivals were wandering through the corridors of *wagon-lits* ... Suddenly I saw a little truck laden with two valises and a toilet case of mauve crocodile which I recognised. I spied Lady Diana following the porter. She was a symphony in pearl grey, from her tiny hat, stabbed through with a diamond ornament, to the tips of her little shoes of alligator skin.

Being a femme fatale, she declares, 'I have a ticket for Constantinople. But I may stop off at Vienna or Budapest. That depends absolutely on chance or the colour of the eyes of my neighbour in the compartment.' It's possible I like this book partly because I'm the only person I know who's read it, yet it sold 15 million copies when it came out in 1925, and it was the first of the night train bestsellers.

It would be impossible to encompass the amount of sex that must have taken place on the Orient Express. The sleepers most closely associated with the the train, the S-class, had (like the later versions of the Lx-class) some single compartments and some doubles. The doubles shared a washroom that could be accessed from the compartment on either side. You were supposed to lock the door against the opposite carriage, but these washrooms are said to have been used for amours. Or they provided a covert means of access, unseen from the corridor, between compartments. But the chap on his fold-down seat at the end of the corridor was a man of the world, and the Wagons-Lits sleeping car conductors were known for the things they did not do, as well as the things they did.

Speaking at the Hay Festival in 2015, Jean Seaton, official historian of the BBC, said that George Howard, who was the BBC chairman from 1980 to 1983, had claimed expenses for using a prostitute on the Orient Express. The expenses form was found in a safe by a newly appointed secretary. The previous incumbent, Jean Seaton said, had suffered a nervous breakdown, and he (this was a male secretary) had deliberately left the expenses form lying about as a warning that his successor 'would have to deal with the chairman and he had to be managed around these young women'.

On the opposite platform at St Pölten stood a double-decker commuter train marked 'Weasel' and decorated with a cartoon of same. You wouldn't call an English train 'Weasel', since it was the nickname of Roy James, one of the Great Train Robbers. I went back to sleep, and woke again shortly after seven at Hegyeshalom on the Hungarian border. There were no passport checks, Hungary being in the Schengen zone, although it had closed its border to migrants. There had been a migrant camp here in the summer of 2015, but now there was only a vast marshalling yard, and no passengers. Yet there were constant announcements, punctuated by what sounded like blasts on a harmonica. We pulled away, passing empty brown fields, with a light rain falling from a grey sky. The conductor knocked on my door with a white plastic tray, on which was a plastic cup of instant coffee and a jam-filled croissant in a sealed wrapper uninspiringly labelled '7 Days'. I took out my map. I was now on the other side of its principal fold, in the place marked 'Eastern Europe'.

BUDAPEST

We arrived at Budapest Keleti station on time at 09.05. My connection – EuroNight 473, named Ister (Hungarian for 'Danube') – would not be departing until 19.10. There is also a day train over the route. It takes only an hour less, and I had missed it anyway, since it had departed at 07.10. There were few historical precedents for how to fill this day. When the Orient Express had speeded up from its 1883 timings it tended to arrive at Budapest late on the second night, in either direction. And there usually wasn't much of a wait, either for those progressing to Bucharest or those heading to Belgrade en route to Constantinople. In February 1896, for instance, the Orient Express arrived at 01.35, departing for Belgrade at 01.45. Coming the other way, it arrived at 02.02.

This is why the famous incident at Biatorbágyi Viadukt, ten miles west of Budapest, occurred at the time it did: 12.20am, on 12 September 1931. The Orient Express was heading west along the viaduct when a bomb exploded. The engine and nine carriages – an unusually long consist – plunged into the ravine below, and twenty-two people died. On board the train were delegates returning to London and Paris from an International Air Transport Association conference in Bucharest. They were among the survivors, but the disaster must have underlined their belief in the superiority of aviation. Josephine Baker was also on board. It is said that she sang her big hit, 'J'ai Deux Amours', to keep up the spirits of the survivors as they awaited the emergency services. Baker knew her way about a train. As a girl, she had played in the railway yards of Union Station, St Louis, and her first husband – whom she married at thirteen – had been a Pullman porter. She does keep coming up in a railway setting. The following is from *Josephine*, by Baker and her fourth husband, Jo Bouillon:

> It was raining that morning in 1925. The Gare St Lazare was teeming with its daily ration of pale, grim-faced commuters. Suddenly the bustling crowd froze. An excited, noisy, gaudy knot of people had just stepped off the Le Havre-Paris train. They were carrying strange-looking instruments and laughing uproariously. Their

rainbow-coloured skirts, fuchsia jeans and checked and polka dot shirts lit up the grey platform ... A tall, willowy girl in black-and-white-checked gardening overalls and an amazing hat detached herself from the group. 'So this is Paris,' she cried. These were Josephine's first words about the city she was to conquer.

The Biatorbágy bomb had been planted by Sylvestre Matuschka, a former officer of the Austro-Hungarian Army, who was arrested near the scene. He was a member of a far-right group called the Arrow Cross League, and a political motive has been ascribed to him. But here are some highlights from his entry on the *Murderpedia* website:

SYLVESTER MATUSCHKA
Classification: mass murderer
Characteristics: Derailment of several trains – Caused the crashes to obtain sexual gratification
Status: Sentenced to death in 1934. Commuted to life in prison. Escaped from jail in Vác in 1944. Never recaptured and his fate is unknown

The viaduct is no longer in use. There are trees growing on it today.

Budapest Keleti station was opened in 1881, so it was only two years old when the first Orient Express arrived, to be met by a military band. In *Stamboul Train*, Graham Greene describes the station as an 'echoing hall', and that is still about right. The arch of the train shed is oddly pinched, like a bishop's mitre, and this mirrors the shape of the carriage roofs within. There was an air of battered grandeur, with classical pillars leading up to high arched windows, some of them broken. A side entrance hall, which might have been a neglected anteroom of the Louvre, contained giant friezes, one showing showing classical figures, including Mercury, all riding upon – or in Mercury's case hovering above – a flat-bed railway wagon. So here were the gods … shunting.

Keleti was freezing and everybody seemed to have a cold. There was a strong, sickly smell of bread and cakes, and the platforms were dotted with little fairy-lit kiosks, tended by muffled-up women. In one alcove, a man was slapping raw, pale pink meat onto a kebab spit. I bought a coffee and a ham roll from one of the kiosks, and consumed these next to a stall retailing dusty old magazines, some of them pornographic. Nearby, a thick brown curtain concealed a recess. Pinned to the curtain was a sign showing the number '18' in a red circle with a red line through it. Presumably this meant that only people over eighteen could enter, rather than only people under eighteen. It was too early in the morning to tangle with whatever lay behind that curtain.

A more inviting doorway was marked 'Wasteels'. Wasteels is a Belgian travel agency, established in 1951, and special-ising in discounted international rail tickets. They used to have an office in Victoria, in the 1970s and 1980s, when that station was still, just about, 'The Gateway to the Continent'. Might they know about the enigmatic sleeper from Bucha-rest to Istanbul?

The office was reminiscent of an infant school, except without the children. Middle-aged, matronly women sat at low desks in a bright room decorated with tattered travel posters. There were tiny green plastic chairs for their clients to sit on. In front of me, a man took his place on one of these. He was clearly not English, but he and the woman communi-cated in English, albeit not for long. 'I want to take a train to Zagreb,' he said. 'You can't,' said the woman, 'the border's closed.' (Zagreb is the capital of Croatia: in 2015 Hungary closed its border with Serbia and Croatia, to stem the flow of migrants.) She told him there was a bus, however.

I was next. 'I'm heading for Bucharest,' I said, at which she began typing furiously on an old computer. 'I already have a ticket,' I said, and she stopped typing and looked cross. 'From Bucharest,' I said, 'I want to go to Istanbul on the sleeper,' and she resumed her manic typing. This seemed promising, but the typing went on too long, and began to be interspersed with sighing pauses. After one final flurry, the woman stopped.

'No,' she said, 'it's not responding.'

'What isn't?'

'The system.'

'But I will be able to book a ticket for Istanbul in Bucharest?'

'Maybe yes. I think so.'

I walked out of Keleti, turning back to look at the arch incorporated into the façade. According to Richards and Mackenzie, this, along with the old Euston Arch (which was un-incorporated), is 'a symbol of the triumph of the railways, the arrival, consolidation and dominance of the new mode of transport'. With the idea of escaping the cold – and killing time in the way that a patrician Orient Express passenger might have gone about it – I rode a modern, bland underground train towards the Gellért Baths. These are on the west bank of the Danube: in Buda, rather than Pest, on the east bank, where Keleti is located; indeed, Keleti is subtitled 'East Station'. The second station of the city, Budapest Nyugati, is subtitled 'West Station', but it too is in Pest, albeit west of Keleti. Budapest Déli Station is in Buda, and is subtitled 'South Station', despite being west of Keleti and Nyugati and south only of the latter. This all becomes slightly less bizarre if it is remembered that the stations' directional subtitles refer to the direction from which their trains arrive, but then again Keleti serves both west *and* east, hence its pivotal role on the Orient Express route.

Gellért Baths has an art nouveau exterior and a classical interior. The place is full of muscular male staff, attendant upon basking Hungarian narcissists. In the steaming turquoise waters of the hot pool, I was half sitting, half floating next to a man of about seventy who had heard me arguing with one of the attendants, who'd stopped me going into the main swimming pool because I didn't have a bathing cap. In order to get a bathing cap, I would have to pay, which would require me to return, by way of labyrinthine cold corridors, to my locker for the money.

'They should supply the bathing cap free with the towels,' said my hot pool companion.

I introduced myself, but he did not do likewise, even though he had initiated the conversation.

I complimented him on his English, and asked if he was Hungarian.

'Half,' he said, smiling enigmatically.

I praised the beauty of Budapest, describing the architecture as 'beaux arts'.

'Buttons and *bows are* ...' the man said, satirising my French accent. 'You are here on holiday?'

I explained that I was travelling along the route of the Orient Express.

'*Why* are you doing that?' he asked, after a while.

'I might write something about it,' I said (because I have found that people become self-conscious if you openly declare that you're a writer).

'You mean you *are* writing something about it,' the man said, seeing through my ruse immediately. 'If you like trains,' he continued, now swimming around in a little circle, 'you will like our Metro.'

'I've been on it already,' I said, not very enthusiastically.

'On Line 1?'

'I don't think so.'

'You will like only Line 1, and you can take it to the Transport Museum, which you will also like.'

That was a thought: I dimly recalled that this museum housed an early Wagons-Lits dining car, a 'teak', that had been sold to Hungary after the 'steels' came in – also that visitors were handed a glass of champagne as they entered this particular exhibit.

For my parting question, I risked asking the man what he made of Viktor Orbán, the right-wing prime minister of Hungary.

'I am persona non grata, as far as he is concerned,' he replied, perhaps rather self-importantly.

Now that, I thought, climbing out of the pool, was the sort of conversation that could have taken place on the Orient Express.

There is some excellent Orient Express dialogue in *The Mask of Dimitrios*, a film of 1944, based on the thriller of the same name by Eric Ambler. It is partly set aboard the train on a westbound run from Istanbul. An insinuating con man called Mr Peters (played by Sydney Greenstreet) shares a compartment with the bemused author Cornelius Leyden (Peter Lorre). Mr Peters, who is perusing a volume called *Pearls of Everyday Wisdom*, introduces himself as 'a man of the world'. He then alarms Leyden by saying, 'Your passport describes you as a writer, and that is a very elastic term.' But then again, as he admits, 'My friend Dimitrios describes me as a spymaster – the term is ambiguous.' Another line of his that seems particularly fitting for the Orient Express is, 'I'm not without friends in Sofia. I assume you know Mr Varza?' When Leyden proposes turning in for the night, Mr Peters says, 'Ah, sleep, the great mercy vouchsafed to us humans', which does nothing for Leyden's attempts to *get* to sleep.

The mysterious man in the baths was right about Line 1. All the charm of the Budapest Metro is concentrated in this, the oldest of the three lines. It is in fact the oldest underground line on the continent of Europe, dating from 1896. The beautifully preserved stations are white-tiled, and not much bigger than a drawing room. Each contains a wooden booth for the sale of tickets. In mid-afternoon, these were all closed, as signified by the pulling across of thick, purple velvet curtains. The trains were like small yellow trams that made electrical fizzing noises as they stopped and started.

I rode Line 1 to Ho˝sök tere (Heroes Square), which is next to City Park, where the Transport Museum is located. I walked for forty minutes through City Park in search of the museum, wondering whether the charming old trolley-buses passing through the park were anything to do with it. (They are not.) On some litter bins, the word 'Migrant' appeared in graffiti, accompanied by an arrow pointing towards the top of the bin. The writers of that graffiti had probably never seen the film *Daniel Takes a Train*, which was made in 1983 and set in 1956, when many Hungarians became refugees and poured onto the trains at Keleti to flee the Russian invasion. I reached the museum to be confronted with a rusty steam locomotive and a sign: 'Closed for Reconstruction'.

***

In Keleti Station at half past five, rush hour was underway, and a female announcer with a sexy voice like Zsa Zsa Gabor was reeling off trains and times. Most trains on the big departure board were locals, and marked 'Személy' which means 'stops at all stations' ('Sebes' means 'stops at nearly all'). But there were also plenty of international services, as befitting a landlocked country in the centre of Europe. The star departure was a sleek red-and-black Railjet (Austrian high-speed) train to Munich via Vienna. Budapest is the most easterly point of the Railjet network. The trains have three classes, so it's like England before 1875, when the Midland Railway abolished second class and began the trend towards two rather than three classes. Although capable of 143mph, the Railjets are strangely antiquated in another sense: the top class carriages have compartments of a sort. The partitions do not extend to ceiling height, but there is a still a sense of cosy seclusion. There were also a couple of not-quite-high-speed Eurocity trains, to Brno and Vienna, because Hungary is part of that international network as well. Eurocity services (which took over from the Trans-European Expresses) only run between 6am and midnight, but they and other fast trains have undermined the need for night trains thereafter. A couple of years earlier, a train for Russia would have been indicated on the board, and it would have gone via Kiev, but in the wake of its Ukrainian intervention, Russia suspended services to EU countries running through Kiev.

I noticed the station restaurant, the entrance bedecked with fairy lights. The interior was wood-panelled, redolent of faded Mitteleuropean glamour. It appeared that the Christmas decorations were still up, with green tinsel entwined around pillars and above the bar. A formally dressed waiter who might easily have been eighty years old approached.

'Can I have a glass of wine, please?'

'Naturally,' he said.

This would have been a good place to have breakfasted,

perhaps on 'soft boiled eggs' (350 forint, or about a pound) or indeed 'bacon and eggs' (850 forint). Other dishes were more exotic, or perhaps made to seem so by faltering English: 'Gentility barbecued pork chops, gypsy style with pommes'; 'Medallions of pork, hunter style with potato croquets'; 'Mozzarella cheese grilled on lava stone'. Particularly intriguing was 'Bakossy camembert cheese with whortleberry sauce'.

After finishing my wine, I returned to the concourse. EN 473 was now displayed on the indicator, but since it was still only 6.30pm, I could think of nothing better to do than to return to the restaurant for another glass of wine.

'I've come back,' I said to elderly waiter.

'Yes,' he said. 'Thank you.'

At seven o'clock, the Ister was ready for boarding.

ISTER

The colour scheme was about right: blue above, white below, with a yellow stripe in the middle. There was one sleeper carriage and one couchette, both probably forty years old. The rest was open seating. My sleeper compartment had wood panelling (or at least wood veneer), in approximation of Wagons-Lits style. On one side was extensive shelving – as if in anticipation of passengers moving in for a week – and a recess for hanging up clothes. On the other side was a dark-blue bench seat with the bunk above, already made up. The carpet was dark grey, thick pile; the blind was black and velvety. The sink in the corner had a plug hole giving straight onto the tracks. On the bunk was a 'dental kit' and a big green serviette, serviceable as a towel. All in all, quite a comfortable and well-ordered bedroom. The Romanian sleeping car conductor popped his head in. 'You like it?' he asked. I told him I did. 'Built by Germans,' he said. 'The Germans is the best!' he added, giving the thumbs up sign.*

'How many stops will there be?' I asked.

'Twenty-five,' he said blithely. 'Some of them are here.' And he pointed to a window label giving the highlights:

Szolnok 20.32
Békéscsaba 21.39
Lőkösháza 22.10
Curtici 23.50
Arad 00.29
Deva 02.45
Braşov 09.20
Bucureşti 12.00

Just after Szolnok, I approached the dining car, taking care to carry all my valuables with me. As I passed two big blokes in leather jackets illegally smoking at the end of the corridor, I congratulated myself on taking this precaution.

The dining car consisted firstly of a serving counter, then a sort of cocktail bar area with fixed high stools; next came the blue dining seats and white Formica-topped tables. There were grey curtains, all closed against the wintry darkness beyond the windows. The vibe was British Rail, circa 1974. I felt a sense of loneliness, since the diner was completely empty, and I couldn't at first even see any maître d'hôtel. Then I noticed a burly, grey-haired chap sitting on a duvet on

---

*When I returned home, I showed a picture of my accommodation to Brendan Martin (no relation), who is one of the leading experts on W-L history, and he diagnosed it as a Swiss-built carriage bought second-hand by Romania. He added that Romanian Railways owned more modern sleepers, bought second-hand from Germany, and that some of the compartments on those have en-suite WCs.

the floor behind the counter with another duvet wrapped over his knees. He was watching a film on a laptop. Behind him, a makeshift curtain concealed what was probably the food preparation area. He stood up and nodded by way of greeting.

'I was hoping to have dinner,' I said, and he nodded again. 'What have you got?' I asked, just as I noticed a menu, fixed to the panel next to the counter.

'That's all sandwiches,' the man said, dismissively.

'Do you have anything hot, then?'

'Pork with frites and Mexican salad,' he said.

'OK, I'll have that.'

'Not frites,' he said, running his hand agitatedly through his hair, 'I mean boiled potatoes.'

'Fine.'

'Do you want a drink?' he said, indicating a variety of wine bottles wrapped in cellophane with the prices – in euros and forints – written on Post-it notes attached to them. I was somehow reminded of the prizes offered in a shooting gallery at a funfair.

'I'd like white,' I said, and the man pointed to a bottle of Riesling for six euros. That was undoubtedly a bargain, however terrible it might be, but I couldn't face a whole bottle, so I opted for a half bottle of Sauvignon for €2.50. I had thought the half bottle I'd pointed to was merely for display purposes, but the man reached for that very one, uncorked it, and poured it into a plastic glass.

'Do you have any ice?' I said.

The man nodded, and ducked behind the curtain, returning with another plastic glass, this one frosted over. I said, 'You don't have any actual ice, do you?' The man nodded again, and disappeared once more behind the curtain. I heard what might have been a sound effect of Chris Bonington going up K2. The man then returned, slightly out of

breath, with a plastic glass full of shards of ice, and only now
– the man having left the curtain slightly open – did I notice
a silent woman in the food preparation area. She was taking
meat out of a fridge.

'Your food will take twenty minutes,' said the man, and
he sat back down on his duvet, and opened his laptop again.
I ought not to be too shocked at the duvet. In the heyday
of Wagons-Lits, anyone wandering into a dining car in the
small hours might see the staff sleeping in hammocks suspended from the roof. The question of where the W-L staff
spent the night obviously perplexed Vladimir Nabokov. In
Speak, Memory, he recalls a childhood journey on the Nord
Express. The underlining is mine:

> I would put myself to sleep by the simple act of identifying
> myself with the engine driver. A sense of drowsy well-
> being invaded my veins as soon as I had everything nicely
> arranged – the carefree passengers in their rooms
> enjoying the ride I was giving them, smoking, exchanging
> knowing smiles, nodding, dozing; the waiters and cooks
> and train guards (whom I had to place somewhere)
> carousing in the diner; and myself, goggled and
> begrimed, peering out of the engine cab at the tapering
> track ...

After five minutes, a smell of frying meat began to per-
meate the carriage. This would be the first time I'd have a
properly cooked – as opposed to microwaved – meal on a
train since the dining cars were removed from the York to
London services in 2011.

The dinner was delicious, the pork cooked in herbs, and
accompanied by a well-dressed salad. But when, after ten
minutes, I'd consumed it, there was nothing left to do but

return to my compartment. Dinner on a night train ought to be an *event*, not a quick pit stop. It certainly was for George Behrend. Here he is on the Nord Express in the 1960s, making the best of that period of supposed decline in W-L standards, when buffet cars were replacing diners:

> Two menus are available in the buffet car, the small one omitting either cheese or sweet. Both begin with *Julienne d'Arblay* soup, served in those familiar big blue cups. The entrée is *Timbale Milanaise* ... After this the *chef de brigade* comes round with slices of mouth-watering veal on a silver platter. The *Côte de Veau fines herbes* is accompanied by *Pommes Cocottes* (cooked in butter) and creamed spinach. For this is not one of the most expensive menus; it is ordinary, adequately bourgeois, which means that it is elegantly served, carefully prepared and subtly tasteful.

In *Stamboul Train* by Graham Greene, the character called Myatt eats a remarkably similar meal on the Orient Express in the 1930s, but a Behrend-like enthusiasm has no place in Greene-land. Myatt 'dipped his spoon into the tasteless Julienne; he preferred his food rich, highly seasoned, but full of a harsh nourishment'. He then chooses a medium Burgundy, a Chamberltin 1923, to drink with the main course of veal, 'though he knew it a waste of money to buy a good wine, for no bouquet could survive the continuous tremor'. Whereas Behrend says, 'The rattle of glasses and the swaying motion of the car, mixed with the mellowing effect of the Company's Listrac, give the meal a pleasant ambience.' (Listrac claret was practically the 'house red' of the post-war Wagons-Lits.)

Behrend lamented the lack of appreciation of Wagons-Lits 'gastrology' among his fellow countrymen, whom he found more concerned about cost than taste, and failed to show any imagination when it came to those liqueurs: 'for our Englishman it is invariably Cointreau, and he has extremely odd ideas about how the flavour is improved by a smut from the engine'. (The English, apparently, liked to open the windows in the dining or buffet cars.) The liqueurs on the Wagons-Lits were always served from large bottles, not the miniatures of today, which are well on the way to being as negligible as chocolate liqueurs.

At 22.10, dead on time, we pulled into Lőkösháza. Here we took our leave from Hungary and the Schengen zone, so there was a passport check. At 22.40 we set off again, and I went to bed. I was awoken at ten to midnight by a loud rapping on the door. I blearily climbed down and unlocked the door, to be confronted by a uniformed Romanian woman, who said 'Passport check,' then turned aside, saying, 'My colleague will look', because I was wearing only boxer shorts and a T-shirt. We were at Curtici, just inside the Romanian border. Here was a neat encapsulation of the virtues of the Schengen agreement: outside it, you are not only checked when leaving one country, but also when entering the next one. My passport was scrutinised for a long time by a uniformed male, who said 'Welcome to Romania' when he returned it. During the stop at Curtici – which lasted about an hour – I climbed into my bunk and went back to sleep. Something caused me to awake in the small hours. The train was moving, and there was a man in a grey hoodie standing by my bed. He held a packet of cigarettes.

'What the hell are you doing?' I said, sitting up.

'Oh,' he said, completely unfazed, 'I was looking for the sleeping car conductor.'

There was about a 5 per cent chance of this being true. In spite of the Thello incident I had neglected to lock the door after the second passport check, but I had put my passport and wallet under my pillow. As the man exited, with an aggrieved look, the thought occurred to me: 'What if I'd been a woman?'

In his very droll work, *The Great Railway Bazaar* (1975), Paul Theroux describes an episode of Orient Express voyeurism that is no less sinister for being juvenile. He is on the Direct Orient Express. The train is going through Switzerland at breakfast time, and Theroux has just failed to find the dining car (because there was no dining car):

> On my way back to Car 99 I was followed by three Swiss boys who, at each compartment door, tried the handle; if it responded they slid the door open and looked in, presumably at people dressing or lounging in bed. Then the boys called out 'Pardon, Madame!' or 'Pardon, Monsieur!' as the occupants hastily covered themselves. As these ingenious voyeurs reached my sleeping car they were in high spirits, hooting and shrieking, but it was always with the greatest politeness that they said, 'Pardon, Madame!' once they got the door open.

I woke again at about eight, aware of that old-fashioned railway rhythm: di-dum-di-dum, the sound of jointed, as opposed to continuously welded, rail. The sound went well with the scene beyond the window: thin trees on a hillside, a fast-flowing rocky river (the Olt), smoke rising from the chimney of a ramshackle house, and bright, cold sunshine.

In the dining car, the steward's duvet and laptop had been packed away. He seemed in a brighter mood than the night before, and his female companion was actually laughing, albeit into a mobile phone. Breakfast, like dinner, was inexplicably delicious: thick, sweet coffee and a ham omelette. There were now other people in the dining car, although nobody else was eating. Some of them watched *me* eat, with faint scepticism. They seemed a very ascetic lot, determined to forswear Wagons-Lits-type fun. Was it possible they couldn't afford breakfast? But they all had smartphones ...

We came to Braşov, evidently a pretty, medieval town, but the train traveller sees nothing but a low, modern station and a scrapyard. This is the stop for 'Dracula's Castle', or rather Bran Castle, a medieval fortress marketed as such. In the novel, Jonathan Harker goes to visit the Count by train, following the Orient Express route from Munich to Vienna to Budapest. But if he is *on* the Orient Express, he doesn't say so. Once in Romania, Harker takes a train to the small town of Bistritz (known as Bistriţa today), which the Count had commended as the nearest to his 'Castle Dracula'. Bistritz is in the North Carpathian Mountains, whereas Braşov is in the South Carpathians. There are several candidates for the true inspiration of Castle Dracula, which is presumably as Bram Stoker intended, because he makes sure that Harker 'was not able to light on any map or work giving the exact location of Castle Dracula'.

Harker does namecheck the Orient Express later on, when he returns to Romania to confront the horrible Count: '15 *October. Varna.* We left Charing Cross on the morning of the 12th, got to Paris the same night and took the places secured for us on the Orient Express. We travelled night and day, arriving here at about five o'clock.' It's about as perfunctory a description of a 2,000-mile journey as you could imagine. But Stoker knew his trains. In *The Railways: Nation, Network & People*, Simon Bradley points out that in 1882 Stoker organised a very successful sixteen-week railway tour for Henry Irving's theatrical company, adding 'Perhaps the railway logistics recurred to mind when he came to write *Dracula*, the pages of which include the text of a very plausible legal document covering the nocturnal despatch by Great Northern Railway goods train of fifty boxes of vampiric soil.'

My rail atlas marks the sixty-mile stretch from Braşov to Ploieşti as one of its 'selected scenic rail routes'. But the Transylvanian landscape was at variance with the Dracula films: pretty instead of Gothic; mountainous, but not severely so. We did keep going through long tunnels though, and because a loose connection had caused the lights in my compartment to stop working, I was plunged into complete darkness every time; but the day seemed sunnier at each re-emergence.

We were also higher at every emergence, because we were climbing steadily. There were half-hearted enterprises by the tracks: quarries, logging mills or factories that had either long since closed down or never got going. The consistent feature was a complete absence of people. As the landscape flattened the factories became more purposeful-looking, with human beings appearing in their vicinity. We were approaching Bucharest, and the moment of truth about the onward sleeper to Istanbul.

THE CONTRACTING LINE

It was 11.40. In twenty minutes we would be arriving on time at Bucharest. In theory, the Bosfor sleeper for Istanbul – operated by CFR, or Romanian Railways – would be leaving at 12.50. I had taken the precaution of making a cancellable booking at a Bucharest hotel, but it seemed we would make this tight connection, if the Bosfor existed.

The compartment door was open, and the sleeping car conductor was passing by. Asked whether he'd ever heard of the 12.50, he gave his trademark thumbs up, but he added: 'You check with my friend, though.' He pointed along the corridor, to another railway official, an altogether steelier-looking character, and possibly a ticket inspector. Even as I began describing the 12.50, this man was shaking his head.

'Not possible,' he said.

'But I was told I could buy a ticket for it in Bucharest.'

'There might be tickets,' he said derisively, 'but there are no trains.'

'So I can't get a train from Bucharest to Istanbul?'

He shook his head. 'Not from Bucharest. From Sofia, maybe.'

He was proposing to shunt me off the route of the very first 1883 Orient Express onto the 1889 version, which had, like the Simplon Orient Express, gone to Istanbul via Sofia. As an Orient Express calling point, Sofia had a perfectly good historical pedigree. But to go there from Bucharest would be to go backwards.

Approaching Bucharest we passed sidings full of red or blue 'vagons de dormit'. In this wide, almost landlocked country, in a region lacking high-speed trains, sleeper business is profitable. You can take sleepers from Bucharest to Arad, Cluj-Napoca, Oradea, Timişoara, Tulcea, Suceava. Surely they could spare a couple of carriages for a run to Istanbul?

We pulled into Bucharest Nord station, the main one in the city, and our terminus. It was brightly coloured, scruffy, crowded, with a McDonald's a prominent feature, and a market going on in a hallway beyond the main concourse. About 50 per cent of the people in the station were smoking, since indoor smoking is not banned in Romania. I walked fast towards a booth on the concourse marked 'Informaţii'. I didn't glance backwards to check the departure board, so I didn't know what, if anything, was leaving at 12.50. The thing was to buy a ticket. Seeing that a party of backpackers was closing in on Informații, I broke into a run, which excited a big black dog – one of many strays on the station – who gave chase, barking. I stopped, and he stopped. He wagged his tail, as though in apology. I still had time to be first in the queue for Informații.

In answer to 'Do you speak English?' a bored-looking woman shrugged, then indicated a booking hall on the other side of the market. Here, at the international ticket window, was a less bored woman.

'I'd like a ticket for a night train to Istanbul,' I said, and she smiled mysteriously. She typed something into a computer, printed out a page, tore off a strip and started making corrections by hand. Eventually, she handed over a piece of paper about three inches long and one inch wide. It read as follows:

București N. 12.55 [amended in pen to 12.50] – Gorna
   Oreahovița 18.17 TREN
Gorna Oreahovița 19.00 – Dimitrovgrad 23.10 AUTO/
   TREN
Dimitrovgrad 23.27 – Kapıkule 02.30 AUTO [but the word
   'AUTO' had been crossed out]
Kapıkule 02.56 – Çerkezköy 05.44 TREN [the words
   'Çerkezköy 05.44 TREN' had been crossed out]
Çerkezköy 06.00 [again, Çerkezköy was crossed out] –
   Istanbul 07.50 AUTO

This wasn't the sleeper train called Bosfor, but it was a method – however convoluted – of getting overnight from Bucharest to Istanbul, and so completing an Orient Express-type journey. It was a shame Çerkezköy was so determinedly crossed out. The Orient Express had got stuck in a snowdrift there in 1929, which had inspired Agatha Christie to write

Murder on the Orient Express. Nevertheless, the start and end timings were very close to those of the apparently mythical Bosfor train, and there was no mention of Sofia – a moral victory over the doom-monger of the Ister.

Asked whether any of these trains were sleepers, the woman shook her head:

'No beds,' she said.

'What does "Auto" mean?'

'Bus.'

'Why are some things crossed out?'

'The arrangements are changing all the time.'

'Why?'

'Because the line is … contracting.'

She laughed, possibly aware that her English was slightly off. She presumably meant that contractors were working on the line – in connection with the Marmaray Tunnel project – rather than that the line was shrinking. I decided to take up my hotel room and make a night of it in Bucharest, so I asked the woman to date the ticket for tomorrow. It cost the equivalent of thirty-five pounds: not bad for 300 miles of railway travel, even with an admixture of buses, and indeed Romania is known among backpackers for the cheapness of its trains.

In two TV adaptions of Simenon's Inspector Maigret novels, Budapest has stood in for Paris, but Bucharest might have been a better bet. It would be cheaper to film in, and is bursting with Parisian-style neoclassical architecture, especially in the Old Town, where most of the restaurants and bars are conveniently clustered. In a short TV film about the Orient Express, made in 1971, Ian Nairn said of Bucharest, 'You feel that, like Paris, you want to use the city. You can put it on and wear it.' Budapest, by contrast, he had found 'rather standing on its architectural dignity'.

This film is mainly remembered for the scene filmed at Munich. After some uncharacteristically dainty reflections on the rebuilt post-war city – 'Everything feels a bit safer for the pedestrian than it used to be ... They've built in arcades all over the place' – Nairn went to the Oktoberfest, a fatal move for a man for whom ten pints of beer was an aperitif. He blunders through the crowd, elbowing people aside in a manner hardly Reithian ('Excuse me, mate'), while giving one of the great, inebriated pieces to camera: 'This is not a beer festival, it's more of a convulsion.' His essential critique was that too many tourists were involved in this legitimate 'expression of German identity'. As Jonathan Meades says, in his introduction to the repackaged films in 1990, 'Ian Nairn on the Orient Express? Sounds wrong somehow. But this was made before the train was sprayed with essence of corporate hospitality [he must be speaking of the tourist train, the Venice Simplon Orient Express]. It was a real train then, with a destinational purpose, besides leisure.'

In Bucharest, I went to look at Ceauşescu's celebrated folly of a parliament building. It took twenty minutes to traverse the front of it. Ceauşescu and his diplomats and aides – always travelling in first class – helped sustain the Orient Express in its later years. They were among the few Romanians who could afford to use it.

THE LONG NIGHT

I had read that while Romania had many sleepers, it had no diners, and so, walking back to the station the next morning, I bought a bottle of mineral water, a packet of dried apricots, a Mars bar, a small loaf of bread (which would turn out to be cake), two cheese-and-ham rolls and a packet of processed cheese.

The departure board showed the first of my trains, the 12.55, as terminating at Sofia, but I would be leaving that train – and the line to Sofia – before it started heading west in earnest. I would be doing this at Gorna Oreahoviţa, where a connection would take me south. I had not been able to find this place – the lynchpin of my entire journey – on my railway map. Nor could I find 'Gorna Oryahovitsa', as it is also known, but Google offered the assurance that it was 'an important railway junction in northern Bulgaria', and I had located the likely intersection of lines, and determinedly written the name on the map.

With half an hour to kill, I sat on a platform bench, and watched the trains; a far more interesting exercise than it would be in Britain. Most were loco-hauled (both electric and diesel), sometimes with carriages that appeared to date from the communist era, but there were also brand-new double-decker diesel multiple units. The black dog came up, and I gave him half the cake-bread. On the opposite platform a man with a long-handled hammer was tapping the carriage wheels of a newly arrived train. He was testing their soundness. If they rang with a true note, they were un-cracked. (Today in Britain, wheels are tested more discreetly, in depots, by means of ultrasound scanning.) A man with a hose started watering a flower display in a hanging basket; the dog went off to lick up some of the water leaking from it. Having finished with the newly arrived train, the hammer man was now absent-mindedly tapping his hammer against a buffer stop. The danger of equipping a man with such a hammer might be that he starts neurotically testing the soundness of everything, including eventually his wife's head.

The 12.55 now shambled into the furthermost platform: three ancient-looking red-and-cream coaches and a diesel loco. It was a 'Regio' service, the humblest and slowest category. But it was compartment stock, and I knew I would like this train. The compartment held six brown-and-grey vinyl seats and a wide openable window, which is all you really need on a train. As I settled in, I heard from the corridor a small American voice: 'Do you like kryptonite?'

The speaker was a boy of about five. He was followed by his mother, who was hauling two big suitcases and saying, 'Why would I like kryptonite? Kryptonite can kill Superman!'

Stepping out of my compartment, I said, 'You're not going to Istanbul, are you?'

'That's the idea,' said the woman. 'We have to change at Sofia, I think.'

I scotched that old wives' tale, and told her about Gorna Oreahoviţa.

'*Where?*' she said.

We agreed to consult later, and she went off and found a compartment.

The train departed on time, and began dawdling through the sunlit countryside. We would be crossing the Romania-Bulgaria border at Giurgiu, travelling over a line built by the British firm of John Trevor Barkley between 1865 and 1869, on a commission from the King of Romania. Some fields had been set on fire, to prepare them for the new crop. Whenever we passed a river bank, a certain part of it seemed to have spontaneously become a rubbish dump. We passed small oilfields, and spooky, giant grain silos. A ticket collector appeared: he didn't flinch at the sight of the word 'Istanbul' on my ticket, but merely made a note on the back. I mentioned Gorna Oreahoviţa, and he said, 'Ask again in Bulgaria.'

We came slowly into Videle: a red-brick bungalow of a station building; three yellow dogs sleeping on the platform; a water tower. Here we left the main line, and we were on un-electrified single track (hence the diesel loco) almost hidden by the grass growing between the sleepers. I know a man who once walked across Europe to Istanbul, and in Romania he was nearly run down by a train, the line having been hidden beneath grass.

At 4pm we came to Giurgiu, the border station: specifically, Giurgiu Nord. A uniformed official approached from the handsome, Italianate station building. He boarded the train and asked to see my passport, then nodded politely and turned and walked away with it. This was obviously going to be a long stop, so I walked along the corridor of the almost-empty train, to confer with the American woman. I will call her Sarah. Her son was watching an animated *Superman* film on a laptop while eating Pringles. Without looking up from the screen, he held up the Pringles tube, inviting me – with the single word 'Sir' – to take one. Sarah was apprehensive that the passport man would need proof of the boy's paternity. 'Where's papa?' Romanian officials had tended to ask her, during her month in the country. She was divorced and 'goofing about in Europe' for a few months while between jobs. One of the big suitcases held schoolbooks for her son, so she could keep up his education en route. She was taking the train from Bucharest to Istanbul because it would have cost her 600 dollars to fly with the boy.

Standing on the platform was an American man, nothing to do with the woman. He wore wraparound shades and a baseball cap. 'Just looking at the loco,' he said. 'It comes from Detroit, of all places.' (It had been made there, by General Motors.) I asked whether he was going to Istanbul. 'No I am not,' he said emphatically. 'I checked on the Internet, and it said "Don't go to Istanbul."' He was going to Sofia instead.

As we looked on, the GM diesel loco was detached, and an electric loco was put on. (Both Romania and Bulgaria have a higher percentage of electrified lines than Britain, as do Hungary, Austria, Germany, France and Switzerland. Top of the tree is Switzerland, with no un-electrified lines). The driver was guided backwards by a series of whistle blasts from a platform guard, like a sheepdog.

We pulled away, and began trundling over the Danube. We were on what is apparently the longest steel bridge in Europe. It used to be called, in that mawkish, communist way, 'The Friendship Bridge', but now it's 'Danube Bridge Number 1'. It was quite rusty. The Bulgarian town of Ruse, looming ahead, seemed full of smoking chimneys, cranes and cooling towers. Ruse has also changed its name. It used to be called, less poetically, Rustchuk, and it has beautiful neo-baroque architecture in the centre. It was Rustchuk when the passengers on that very first Orient Express had called there. At that point they were on a boat, which they had boarded at Giurgiu. There was no bridge in those days. At Rustchuk they were put on a different train, borrowed by Nagelmackers from Austria, and taken to Varna, where they would sail for Constantinople. (Rustchuk, incidentally, is a pivotal location in John Buchan's novel *Greenmantle*. Buchan may well have become aware of it while on the Orient Express, on which he travelled in spring, 1910.)

At Ruse, there was another passport check. Afterwards, flat plains give way to hills, and we began heading south. The original party, aiming for Varna, would have gone east. A mood of depression apparently prevailed. They had been greeted sullenly by a few Russian soldiers at Rustchuk, Bulgaria being under Russian control at that time, and they had not been warned about the maritime element of the route. Nor had they been warned, until now, that the stretch to Varna was bandit country. Opper de Blowitz sat on the train with his pistol in his hand.

Bulgaria would always be a bête noire for the Orient Express. It was the last piece in the jigsaw for Nagelmackers when he'd been assembling the original route. In the 1930s, the Wagons-Lits company had to contend with King Boris III. He was a rail enthusiast and a member of the Bulgarian railwaymen's union, who treated the Orient Express like his own personal garden railway. He liked to travel on the footplate, preferably taking the controls. It is said that, in 1934, he was on the footplate when a blowback of flames from the firehole set the overalls of the driver alight. King Boris then doused the flames, and took over the controls, saving the driver and possibly the train by driving it on to Varna. There is a darker version of this story, according to which Boris caused the blowback by over-firing, and the driver died.

In communist days, officials tried to belittle a train considered ideologically unsound. In 1949, an American journalist, Roy Rowan, reported in *Life* magazine that 'The Bulgarians flag the train at every mudhole.' Dining cars might not be attached as promised, and meals had to be taken 'ashore' – not on the train.

In *On the Old Lines* (1957), Peter Allen, historian, sometime deputy chairman of ICI and a member of the Stephenson Locomotive Society, described a post-war run on the Simplon Orient Express: 'From Paris through to Trieste, it was a pretty respectable fast train by any standards. Next morning, however, as we got near Ljubljana, the first Yugoslav town of any size, we were clattering along through farming country in pretty disreputable company, some very elderly coaches attached to the back of us and some cattle trucks next to the engine.' Things got worse, and 'We ran through the Bulgarian border as a local, stopping at all stations.' Incessant shunting of the train always made it hard to keep track of the fourgon or baggage wagon, so that, as the explorer Barbara

Mons reported in her book, *High Road to Hunza* (1958), 'it proved impossible to apply the maxim – "never lose sight of your luggage"'.

All that said, the Bulgarian ticket inspector was amiable, and spoke decent English. He confirmed that Gorna Oreahoviţa was where I'd put it on my map – which was just as well, since all the station nameplates were now in Cyrillic, if they appeared at all. (What always did appear on the platforms was a smart stationmaster in a red cap.)

I asked the ticket inspector what had happened to the sleeper to Istanbul. 'Stopped,' he said.

'For how long?'

'Two years.'

Gorna Oreahoviţa was a dark, deserted station, with an underpass leading towards several platforms, none of which were numbered. Sarah and I chose one set of stairs at random, and came up next to a train. We wanted the connection to Dimitrovgrad, in eastern Bulgaria. Was this it? The indicator board was blank. A guard was leaning out of a carriage window. 'Is this for Dimitrovgrad?' I asked, and he slowly shook his head. So we just stood on the platform for the next quarter of an hour, with the train (electric loco, ancient compartment stock) simmering away alongside us, and the guard intermittently looking down at us from various windows and doors. A female guard now emerged from a station building and boarded the train. Sarah asked her, 'Is this the train for Dimitrovgrad?' and she shook her head. It was only five-to-seven, but the station had essentially closed except for this one train. It *had* to be the service for Dimitrovgrad, which, according to the itinerary, would be departing in five minutes. It was then I remembered having read that in a certain Balkan country, the people shook their heads to mean 'Yes' and nodded to mean 'No'. We boarded the train.

The journey now became vague. It was pitch black outside, apart from illuminated signs that often seemed to be high above us, or elevated factories, made luminous and ghostly by pale grey concrete. There was no water in the WC, either for the taps or the flushing of the loo. That ought not to have mattered because the toilet was just a hole onto the tracks. Yet still the toilet reeked, and the reek permeated the compartment of lumpy green vinyl seats. On that original Orient Express, Edmond About had – according to E. H. Cookridge – been 'impressed by the fresh towels, tablets of soap, and vials of toilet water beside the washbowl – a service, he mentioned, that was not provided even in the most expensive hotels that he frequently patronized in all parts of Europe'. As for the toilet itself, he noted that a servant stepped into the water closet, to clean it after every use.

We arrived at Dimitrovgrad on time at ten past eleven. We were now on the line that had formed the home straight for both the Orient Express and the Simplon Orient Express, although this particular Dimitrovgrad did not exist as a town until the late 1940s. There is another Dimitrovgrad (formerly called Caribrod) in Serbia. Both towns are named after Georgi Dimitrov, a Bulgarian communist leader who favoured the creation of a Balkan Federation. (He was in Germany in the 1930s, and was charged with complicity in the Reichstag fire. Dimitrov defended himself eloquently in court, and was acquitted.)

We stepped down with the one remaining passenger on the train: an old woman with gold teeth, who I assumed to be Turkish. The train to Kapıkule was due at 23.27; it was now 23.22. Besides us travellers, three people remained in the bleak, dark station of Dimitrovgrad: two policemen smoking in the station building, and a man coming along the platform jauntily swinging one of the wheel-testing hammers. He banged it against a few wheels of the train from Gorna. The possible Turkish woman asked him a question and he made no response at all. Did this imply some geopolitical tension? It bothered me that she had felt the need to *ask* a question, because I'd put her down as somebody who knew the ropes. The train from Gorna pulled away empty, leaving behind a deeper silence than before. It was now 23.27 exactly. (In *Dracula*, Jonathan Harker says, 'It seems to me that the further east you go the more unpunctual are the trains. What ought they to be in China?' This had not been my experience, until now.)

At 23.32, a train approached – but it was a freight, and it ran through the station. After another five minutes, another headlight approached, which gradually became an electric loco pulling a single carriage. It was the train to Turkey: the ghost train of the Orient Express, that 'Magic Carpet of the East', 'The King of Trains and the Train of Kings'.

The carriage was fitted with dingy blue open seating, with ugly headrests. There was one passenger – a youth who was asleep – and another male-and-female team of guards, who asked us to write our passport numbers and other details on a form. Sarah's son – 'a real trooper', according to his mother – said, 'I can cross another two countries off my map!' Soon we were ambling through the darkness at forty miles an hour. We called at a couple of stops, and at the second one, both the youth and the woman with the gold teeth had disembarked. (So she *wasn't* Turkish.)

We exited Bulgaria at Svilengrad, where our passports were checked and forms collected. In 1952, the border between Turkey and Bulgaria was closed, and the Simplon Orient was advertised as terminating at either Svilengrad or, if the situation in Bulgaria was too dangerous, at Sofia. At 3am we pulled into Kapıkule, in Turkey. It was here that the dining cars were belatedly attached to the westbound Orient Expresses, no doubt to the relief of the passengers, who had probably expected them to be present from the 'off'. The station name was spelt out in red neon on top of a bland 1970s building. We stepped off the train to be greeted by half a dozen Turkish customs men, some in uniform, some in plain clothes. Turkey-to-Bulgaria had been an aspiration of many migrants, and the crisis had made hotspots of all the crossing points. We were not desperate refugees heading west, but whimsical tourists heading east. Even so, the head man of the border guards – a good-looking chap in a leather jacket – seemed anxious to make us feel at ease.

'Welcome to Turkey,' he said. 'Show visas please. Paper visa or electronic both OK.' We were shown into a bare room. After half an hour, a hatch connecting our waiting room with the adjacent office was opened and a Turkish policeman was revealed. He slowly lit a cigarette, then muttered 'Passports.'

The customs men now ushered us towards an outhouse containing a metal detector and a silent, very tall man. I put my own bag through the machine, then helped Sarah with hers. As we were walking towards the coach that would take us to Istanbul, the X-ray man called to one of the customs men, who asked us to return to the outhouse. Something suspicious had been discovered in Sarah's suitcase. At this, I protested: 'This bag is nothing to do with me. I was only helping the lady!' The leather-jacketed customs man looked at me with narrowed eyes. The suspicious object, it turned out, was a metal statue of Superman of unusual density. Everyone laughed, except the leather-jacketed man, who had not been impressed by my moment of un-chivalry. 'You!' he commanded, 'Help the lady again with her luggage.'

We boarded the coach for Istanbul. 'Nothing spells fun,' said Sarah, 'like a four-hour bus ride.' But the coach was made cosy by many rugs on the floor. It was manned by a driver and three colleagues, or maybe they were just friends, since they didn't seem to do anything apart from exchange jovial remarks with the driver, and make a fuss of Sarah's son. Watching the Turkish motorway unfold, I reflected that here was something we had in common with the passengers on the original Orient Express: while travelling on what was supposed to be a railway journey, we had made our final approach to the Turkish capital on something other than a train. For that party of 1883, the fourteen-hour voyage by which they were, like W. B. Yeats in his poem, 'Sailing to Byzantium', was not pleasant. The engine of the steamer smoked badly, and the sea was rough. Nobody was interested in the elaborate dinner prepared by a Viennese chef.

After a couple of hours, we stopped at a service station, and were invited to use the toilets in a restaurant apparently kept open especially for that purpose. An hour later, we were driving through the city walls of Istanbul. If we'd come in on the train, we'd have been skirting the Sea of Marmara beneath the walls of Topkapı Palace.

At 06.00, we pulled up. 'Sirkeci Station!' the driver announced proudly, and we had reached the terminating point of the Orient Express, or the car park adjacent to it.

It was still dark, but I could read a plaque outside the station, which began, 'The Orient Express which takes off from Paris, brought its passengers to the terminal for many years.' The station was open – in the sense of it being accessible to the public – and illuminated by pretty orange lights, but no trains would be leaving that day, and whether Sirkeci will ever return to normal service is uncertain. A couple of vagrants slept on the concourse, and there were about twenty cats, padding loftily about and cutting each other dead. The station has circular and arched windows of stained glass, and delicate iron pillars holding up a glass roof. A placard propped against one of these pointed towards the Orient Express Restaurant, which *would* be opening later in the day, a possible pointer to the future of Sirkeci: as a leisure amenity or heritage centre.

Since 2013, the station has been closed to trains because of the Marmaray Tunnel project. The tunnel – running under the strait to the Asian side – opened in 2013, and can be traversed on trains accessible from the Metro station below Sirkeci. It is the work to extend the commuter line using the tunnel that has closed the station, and that work had stalled.

The restaurant has a terrace abutting one of the two platforms, and I sat down there and ate the last of my processed cheese, and drank the last of my mineral water. (I had said goodbye to Sarah and her son, who'd gone off in search of a taxi.)

When I emerged from the station it was raining, and there was nothing golden about the Golden Horn. The choppy grey waters reminded me of Hannay's arrival in Istanbul, as described in *Greenmantle*:

> I don't quite know what I expected – a sort of fairyland Eastern city, all white marble and blue water, and stately Turks in surplices, and veiled houris, and roses and nightingales and some sort of string band discoursing sweet music. I had forgotten that winter is pretty much the same everywhere. It was a drizzling day, with a southeast wind blowing, and the streets long troughs of mud.

This contrasts with Buchan's own memoir of visiting the town. 'Constantinople,' he wrote, 'is pure Arabian Nights. My experience varied from lunching in state with the Sultan's brother and dining at Embassies to chaffering with

Kurds for carpets in a sort of underground Bazaar. I don't know any place where one feels history more vividly.' These two seem inverted. It ought to be the latter, rather than the former, that it is the fiction.

THE PERA PALACE

I put up my umbrella and set off across the bridge for Pera, which had been a new suburb in 1892, when Nagelmackers opened the Pera Palace Hotel to accommodate his travellers arriving on the Orient Express at Sirkeci, which had opened in 1890. The Wagons-Lits office and its agents were also lodged at the Pera Palace. Some effete types would have been carried to the hotel in sedan chairs, thus reverting at Sirkeci from the nineteenth to the eighteenth century. The original party of 1893 were taken to the Pera in horse-drawn carriages, having disembarked from their steamer. They had been met at the dockside by Turkish dignitaries and the Belgian Ambassador, but a greater honour was in store for Opper de Blowitz. He would be granted an audience with the Sultan himself, and since Abdul Hamid II was officially the 'Emperor of Powerful Emperors, the Sole Arbiter of the World's Destiny, Refuge of Sovereigns, Distributor of Crowns to the Kings of the World, Ruler of Europe, Asia and Africa, High King of the Two Seas, and Shadow of Allah Upon the Earth', this must be counted a signal honour.

In those days, Constantinople was to be approached with caution. Its hectic streets were frightening, in the grip of an unknowable morality, or possibly none at all. Among the travellers' accoutrements recommended by George Bradshaw in his *Hand-Book to the Turkish Empire* (1870) was a Deane & Adams revolver. But by the time Nagelmackers launched the Orient Express, Turkey was presenting a smiling face. Or, a smiling face was being painted on it.

In 1878, at the Congress of Berlin, Disraeli had attempted to prop up Turkey (the 'sick man of Europe'), in the face of antipathy from Russia and the Balkans. The Sultan had promised reform. On the strength of these developments, the firm of Thomas Cook placed an advert in *The Excursionist and Tourist Advertiser* on 19 April 1884, proclaiming that 'political and military troubles, and brigandage' in Eastern Europe were at an end: 'We have decided that the time has now arrived when we may without doubt do everything we possibly can to induce travellers to visit these interesting districts.' (Henri Opper de Blowitz, by the way, was a beneficiary of the Congress of Berlin twice over. Not only was his joyride on the Orient Express enabled by its diplomacy, he had also made his name as a journalist by leaking its conclusions before they were published.)

I arrived at the hotel, to be greeted with embarrassing deference. In 1896, that Wagons-Lits propaganda sheet, *The Continental Traveller*, had said of the hotel, 'It enjoys the most perfect air on account of its situation.' It had then pointedly added, 'The sanitation, the furniture, and the comfort are English.'

In his short story 'Turkish Night', Paul Morand was his usual charitable self about the Pera Palace: 'The hotel was unbearable: sneaky faces, loose mouths, fat noses, receding chins, charred crepe eyelids, sharp Pera eyes. A shrill pistol-shooting orchestra played to smoking-room seats covered with false Bokharas lit by mosque lamps made from soda bottles.' That was in the early 1920s. A couple of years ago the hotel was (to use a word that would have made Morand's lip curl) refurbished, and I found it flawlessly stylish: a soft-focus film set of silver chandelier-light, white marble, burnished brass and rich red Turkey carpets.

On gaining my room, I closed the velvet curtains against the grey sky, and went to sleep. Even travellers who'd arrived in Istanbul on the proper Orient Express were exhausted by the journey: a combination of excitement and overindulgence giving way to stress and perhaps a few hours of actual deprivation (if the last dining car had failed to appear). At the end of his documentary on the Orient Express, Ian Nairn, looking even more dishevelled than usual, perches on the buffer stop at Sirkeci. 'My impressions of the whole journey?' he says, in a shaky voice. 'I'm so physically shattered, it's hard to sort 'em out – a kind of shock therapy right through Europe, this one ...'

★★★

I hadn't booked into the 'Agatha Christie Room', number 411. That was twice the price of my own sufficiently splendid quarters, and anyway its provenance is questionable.

In *An Autobiography*, Christie described her first run on the Orient Express, undertaken in 1928 soon after her husband, Archie, had said he wanted a divorce. 'It was settled at last. I wrote to my lawyers and went to see them. Things were put in train.' That phrase might have been meant literally, because she did then board the train to Istanbul. On it, she met a Buchan-esque 'Dutch mining engineer', who, on the approach to what they both called 'Stamboul', advised her to stay at the Tokatlıyan Hotel: 'You are quite safe *there.*' Except possibly from him, because he added: 'I will call for you at nine o'clock.' The flirtation fizzled out, and the Tokatlıyan Hotel closed down in the 1950s. Christie progressed further east by train, to Iraq, where she met her second husband, Max Mallowan, an archaeologist.

The two began a phase of almost commuting on the

Orient Express, shuttling between England and Mallowan's excavations. According to the travel writer Andrew Eames, 'on further occasions she sometimes chose the Pera Palace'. I will take Eames's word for it, having read his authoritative and enjoyable work *The 8.55 to Baghdad*, in which he pursues every possible connection between Agatha Christie and the Orient Express.

Eames did stay in Christie's room, and found it 'far more modest' than others in the hotel bearing plaques indicating that they had been favoured by the likes of Marshal Tito, Mata Hari and Greta Garbo. He explains how 'The designation of room 411 as hers was largely the work of a glossy American psychic and self-publicist called Tamara Rand.' In 1979, Rand was recruited by Warner Brothers to promote a projected film about Agatha Christie's famous 'lost weekend'. Rand obligingly had a vision of Christie (three years dead by then) getting off a train, then entering a room – number 411 – of a Pera Palace-like hotel. Thus was an awkward situation rectified, because the fact is that in *Murder on the Orient Express*, which is the foundation stone for all this mythologizing, Poirot stays at the Tokatlıyan Hotel, where he meets M. Bouc, the Belgian director of W-L, a man whose natural habitat surely ought to have been the Pera Palace.

***

I woke up at lunchtime, and opened the curtains to see that Istanbul had got its act together: sunshine, the reverberating call to prayer, wheeling seagulls. Early travellers on the Orient Express might have thought the world came to an end in Constantinople, only to find that it started up again on the other side of the Bosphorus. I myself took a ferry across to the Asian side – one of those wide, bouncing boats, with the sunlight flashing in through the windows – and walked to Haydarpaşa Station, dating from 1909, and described by Eames as rising 'like a proud neo-German schloss complete with turreted corners, directly from the quayside, where it is surrounded on three sides by water'. This was the Asian counterpart to Sirkeci, and remains its counterpart, in that it too has been closed by the Marmaray Tunnel project.

The tunnel does not run from Sirkeci to Haydarpaşa, as traditionalists, fond of that east-west railway double act, would have liked. It goes from Sirkeci to Üsküdar, which is north of Haydarpaşa, leaving the latter dangerously out on a limb. The high-speed line being projected from Ankara to Istanbul might come into Haydarpaşa, or it might not. At the time of writing, it terminates at Pendik, east of Istanbul, and Haydarpaşa is apparently being eyed by the speculators. Meanwhile, it is given over to dusty sunbeams, and another colony of cats.

Nagelmackers had perpetuated his vision on this side of the water. The Wagons-Lits company had an atelier, or workshop, at Haydarpaşa, and it despatched trains from there, allowing Orient passengers to continue east. (They were taken across the Bosphorus in special Wagons-Lits launches.) Most famously, there was, from 1930, the Taurus Express to Aleppo, with carriages and connections to Tehran, Mosul, Baghdad, Beirut and Cairo. But travel that way lay well beyond the territory depicted on the badge of the British Railwaymen's Touring Club, I'm glad to say.

I spent the rest of the day shuttling between the Pera Palace and the main tourist street, Istiklal Avenue, using an alley-way about which a friendly hotel doorman had tipped me off. Istiklal has an antiquarian bookshop of the kind you might find in Oxford, but it's not easy to get a drink on that street. You have to go down the alleyways to the north. I wondered whether the bars and pubs were thinning out under the more Islamic society promoted by President Erdoğan. I discussed this with a barman. 'Perhaps,' I suggested, 'most Turks don't drink much anyway?' 'Like hell they don't,' he said, and he pointed out that modern Turkey had been founded by a brilliant alcoholic: Kemal Atatürk.

In the early days of the Orient Express, British diplomats made their own fraught calculations. Turkey, at the helm of the crumbling Ottoman Empire, may have been 'the sick man of Europe', but it was still gingerly embraced as a counterweight against Russia. At the time of my visit, the European Union was engaging in a similarly wary clinch, in order to secure Turkey's help in the migrant crisis. Turkey can exact a high price for its support, but it didn't exactly choose its pivotal position, and it was also *paying* a high price, in the form of Islamist attacks.

When I flew back on a British Airways flight from Istanbul, the plane was only a third full. We were told to congregate in the middle before take-off, for balance, but that we could spread out once in the air. That was on Saturday 12 March 2016. The following Saturday, an Islamic State suicide bomber blew himself up on Istiklal Avenue, at the junction with the alleyway that had formed my cut through to the Pera Palace. Five people died, including the perpetrator. Thirty-six people were wounded, including twenty-four Turks. Looking in detail at the news reports, I was satisfied that neither Sarah nor her son were among the casualties.

5

THE SUD EXPRESS

I was back in Paris for a journey on the Sud Express, which was no hardship of course. Paris is the railway city par excellence. The Parisian stations were polished and set like so many jewels by Baron Haussmann, architect-protégé of that great rail enthusiast, Napoleon III. The approaches to the Gare de l'Ouest (Montparnasse) were opened up by Rue de Rennes, and Haussmann framed the Gare St Lazare by the creation of the Place de Rome. In 1855, the northerly prong of Haussmann's 'Grande Croisée' was formed of the Boulevard de Sébastopol and its extension, the Boulevard de Strasbourg, which is like a red carpet flamboyantly bowled by this 'Attila of the Straight Line' towards the classical façade of the Gare de l'Est. The Boulevard de Magenta was extended to reach the new Gare du Nord, although compared to Est, Nord is tucked away, like a masterpiece kept in a cupboard.

For Wolfgang Schivelbusch, author of *The Railway Journey: Trains and Travel in the 19th Century*, even the 'Grands Magasins' of Paris are railway-related: 'As Haussmann's traffic arteries are connected to the rail network by means of the railway stations, and thus to all the traffic in its entirety, the new department stores, in turn, are connected to these new intraurban arteries and their traffic.'

Here is more from Schivelbusch about how the department store is essentially a railway phenomenon (and this fairly typical passage should help the reader decide whether they ever want to read another word by him or not):

The department store encourages the kind of perception that we have called panoramic. To recapitulate its essential characteristics as seen in the context of the train journey: as speed causes the foreground to disappear, it detaches the subject from the space that immediately surrounds him, that is, it intrudes itself as an 'almost unreal barrier' between object and subject. The landscape that is seen in this way is no longer experienced intensively, auratically (as by Ruskin, the critic of rail travel), but evanescently, impressionistically – panoramically in fact.

Certainly the glass-and-iron roof of the cavernous Galeries Lafayette department store, on Boulevard Haussmann, suggests a railway station to the extent that you can't believe a full-sized gleaming locomotive isn't somewhere about the premises, with commensurately large price tag attached.

The Gare de l'Ouest of Haussmann's day has given way to the Gare Montparnasse of today, the third one to be built on the site, and from here, I would be starting my Sud Express journey. But it could easily have been elsewhere, because the starting point of the Sud Express has flitted about.

***

The service was started by Nagelmackers in 1887, running from Calais to Lisbon via Irun in northern Spain. As mentioned, Nagelmackers also inaugurated the Nord Express from St Petersburg to Paris in 1896 with the idea of connecting it to the Sud, the fulcrum being his home town of Liège, but the through-link was never forged into one train, and the Russian Revolution, and the descent of the Iron Curtain, would kill the project

When it began, the Sud Express was one service but two trains, because the Iberian track gauge encountered at the border was – and is – different from the French: five foot six, as against the standard gauge of four foot eight and a half, disseminated by George Stephenson to more than half the railways in the world. While passengers heading south changed at Irun, those coming back the other way – from Lisbon to Calais – changed at Hendaye, just inside the French border. Hendaye and Irun are separated by the river Bidasoa, and a signalman's nightmare is created by the existence of both track gauges on the bridge over the river, which is officially called the Santiago Bridge, but also known as the International Bridge.

From as early as 1890, the Sud Express spurned Calais, starting instead at Gare du Nord. Yes, Gare du Nord for the Sud Express, because the departing trains immediately ran around the Ceinture to point south. Originally, the two trains forming the Sud were both sleepers, but in 1900 the first of the two became a day train, and began leaving from Gare d'Orsay at around noon, arriving at Irun at nine-thirty in the evening. (By now, the Sud Express was running three times a week, whereas at first it had been weekly.)

In 1900 the brand new Gare d'Orsay must have presented a Jules Verne scene with its combination of electric trains and antique, beaux arts splendour. In the Paris flood of 1910, the tunnel connecting that station to its parent terminus, Gare d'Austerlitz, was inundated, so the Sud Express terminated for a while at one of the humbler stations of the Paris-Orleans Railways: the one at the southern Parisian suburb of Juvisy. A booklet called 'Orsay', available from what is now the museum, states:

> The Gare d'Orsay, under more than five metres of water, was nicknamed Gare d'Ys, Ys being the name of the legendary Breton city believed to have been submerged in the 4th or 5th Century. People came to catch a few large fish and look at their reflected image floating in the water.

The accompanying photograph shows an electric luggage ramp – whose base was presumably on one of the submerged platforms – rising from the murky water towards the rococo, gilded clock, like the appendage of some robotic monster from the future. Incidentally, the Sud Express at this point was only hauled by an electric locomotive for the trip through the tunnel to the sister station of Gare d'Austerlitz. There, the nineteenth century resumed, and a steam locomotive was attached before the train began its journey south.

The *Thomas Cook Continental Timetable* for 1931 shows the train still departing from Orsay, at 10.50. In the following year, one of the best Maigret novels, *The Madman of Bergerac*, appeared. In this, the Inspector departs on a sleeper from Orsay to Villefranche, but the exoticism of the station was lost, either on him or his creator, Simenon, hence the aridity of the following:

> Later that afternoon, having purchased a first-class ticket for Villefranche, Maigret boarded the train at Gare

d'Orsay. The guard reminded him to change trains at Libourne.

'Unless you're in the sleeper compartment, which gets hitched to the next train.'

The detail of that 1931 departure from Orsay, by the way, contains the reassuring words 'Pullman car', and in the interwar years, the French leg of the Sud Express was the service that made most use of the blue-and-cream Wagon-Lits day cars.

Orsay stopped being a main-line station in 1939, when only a few suburban services were left dribbling away from the lower levels, and the Sud Express shifted to Gare d'Austerlitz. In 1973, it fused again into one train, running directly to Lisbon, thanks to having bogies that could be detached and replaced with ones of the different gauge. But it began to lose its W-L identity, because these through carriages were couchettes, not sleepers. In the late 1970s, the restaurant car of this through train became a 'Grill Express', then a bar car. The through service was killed by the advent, in 1989, of the TGV Atlantique from Gare Montparnasse to Irun, which made it quicker to do the journey as in W-L days: in two stages.

The name Sud Express is still occasionally used in Spain. But the man on the end of the London booking line for Spanish railways (RENFE) stopped me in full flow, saying, 'Sorry, but you keep talking about the "Sud Express" and that confuses me.' He would rather I spoke of the 18.50 RENFE Trenhotel departure from Irun to Lisbon, even though that is referred to in the European Timetable as the 'Sud Expresso'.

This train perpetuates the second half of the old Sud Express. I asked the RENFE man if I could have a press ticket. He said he'd get back to me. After ten days, I pursued the matter, and he said my application had been forwarded to Portuguese Railways (CP) and they had not replied. Out of revenge, I therefore bought my ticket through the London office of Deutsche Bahn, where I spoke to a neurotically efficient German, who had a habit of muttering, while typing on his computer, 'Yes, yes, this is all going through smoothly ... no unexpected problems here at all ...'

He set out the options with great trenchancy. A Gran Clase sleeper would provide sole occupancy with en-suite shower and toilet (and a complimentary small bottle of port). A Turista Clase two-bed sleeper involved the risk of sharing with one other person. The Turista four-bed might involve sharing with three others. I opted for this last one – at a cost of £70, half the price of Gran Clase – and the efficient German said, 'Of the six berths remaining on this train, four are in one compartment, so I'll book you into that one, and there's a chance you'll have it to yourself.' (Actually, I'd have preferred to share, feeling I'd been making too many journeys as a sole occupant, but it would have been rather clammy to say so.)

The outstanding question was how to duplicate the *first* half of the old Sud Express. It was possible to take a French sleeper from Gare d'Austerlitz to Irun (a service that will have ceased by the time this book appears). But I'd had enough nocturnal anxieties at Gare d'Austerlitz, and if W-L had been able to dispense with a night train to Irun as early as 1900, it should be possible to get by without one in 2016. This dictated one of the TGV Atlantiques to Irun – which is why I had ended up at Gare Montparnasse.

THE TGV ATLANTIQUE

The 'new' Montparnasse was opened in 1969, but I prefer the previous incarnation, which I have seen only in photographs. The façade featured high-level lunette windows, through one of which an engine crashed in 1895, having leapt the tracks and careened across the concourse. It killed a female newspaper vendor – she was taking over her husband's pitch for a few minutes – and was left dangling for several days, causing a PR headache for the Compagnie de l'Ouest. Of all the things you do not expect to fall onto your head, a steam locomotive must be near the top of the list.

The 'new' station – 'a characterless curtain-walled slab', according to Steven Parissien in *Station to Station* – is grey, modernist and multilevelled, but like Euston in London it feels subterranean because of the banishment of natural light. Whereas there is no excuse for the oppressive roof of Euston there is at least something on top of Gare Montparnasse: the Jardin Atlantique, which is always very peaceful, like a zoo from which all the animals have escaped. The station is flattered by contrast with the adjacent Tour Montparnasse, fifty-nine floors of sinister black brutalism, and such an aesthetic triumph that the city banned buildings over seven storeys in the aftermath of its erection. (The tower used to house the French hotel chain Accor, into which the Wagons-Lits company was subsumed in 1991.)

The train was packed, and not a duplex. It comes to something when a passenger complains of a train being only one storey high, but I had been spoilt by the previous TGV, which *had* been a duplex. In second class, the high backs of the seats – albeit stylishly angled like the wings of big birds – contributed to a slight sense of claustrophobia. But the colour scheme was warm: orange and purple, whereas first class was cool, with grey and lime. Christian Lacroix, designer of the interiors of the Atlantiques, irritated SNCF by mischievously inverting the usual hierarchy, whereby first is cosy and second less so.

The first stage of the journey takes place under a land-scaped canopy, the Coulée verte, which hides the line. At Courtalain there is a junction, one line going west to Brittany and the other south-west to Tours. Ours went to Tours, which we reached after about an hour, and where our train slowed, since that is where the high-speed facility stopped. But it will be continued all the way to Bordeaux from 2017.

At 2.30pm – just after Poitiers – the buffet car was impen-etrably crowded, owing to the French habit of all doing everything at the same time. I heard a northern-accented British woman asking the maître d', with exasperation, 'But haven't you got any *tea* tea?' 'We don't 'ave tea for milk,' he said, proffering a variety of exotic infusions like a fanned pack of cards. The man accompanying the woman was called Len, and he was from Liverpool. He too would be taking the Sud Express for Lisbon – 'because I don't fly'. He would be in Gran Clase accommodation.

'I'm in Turista,' I said, 'but perhaps we'll meet in the res-taurant car?'

'Not sure we'll be mixing with the riff-raff,' he joshed.

After Len had quit the buffet car, it was gratifying to see a French woman explaining to the maître d' how to make a cup of tea using Earl Grey *and milk*.

At Bordeaux, 80 per cent of the passengers got off the train. While we were stopped at the station, I turned to the woman in the seat next to me, who spoke good English, and said, 'No offence, but I'm going to move, so we can both spread out.' '*Wait*,' she said, and over the next three minutes, the train filled up again. (The woman explained that she knew this line well, since her parents lived in Biarritz.)

We were late into Biarritz: six o'clock instead of ten-to, and I began to get anxious about the connection at Irun. But I took comfort from what the reassuring German booking clerk had said: 'No way are they not going to wait for the passengers from Paris. That would mess things up for so many people!'

SUREXPRES

Summer was latent in Hendaye: a clear evening sky, but a breeze ruffling the palm trees and the Atlantic waters, the streets all but empty. As we approached the International Bridge over the river Bidasoa, the Iberian gauge tracks came into view alongside us. It is strange to see something so familiar as a railway track in a bigger size than you're used to. You can't quite believe the track is different. It's as though you yourself have shrunk.

In *Blood, Iron & Gold*, Christian Wolmar writes, 'Of Europe's major nations, Spain was the most reluctant to join the railway age.' When it did so, in the 1830s, it chose a five-foot-six-inch gauge (which is a polite way of saying five-foot-five-and-twenty-one-thirty-seconds of an inch), lumbering its neighbour, Portugal, with the same white elephant. Wolmar again: 'The isolationist Spanish government made a political decision on the basis of military considerations, since it was felt that a change of gauge at the frontier would hamper any invading army.' It was France – which, like most of Europe, had run with Stephenson's standard gauge of four foot eight and a half – that Spain had in mind. Stephenson had tried to interest Spain in four foot eight and a half, but the government had shunned him just as they generally shunned Europe. In fact, as Wolmar points out, 'France never showed more than a cursory interest in invading its Iberian neighbour.' In fact, the obstructionist five-foot-six gauge might have been more useful in France for fending off Germany than it was in Spain for fending off France. Meanwhile, it held back the Spanish economy by making railways more expensive to build. More land was required to accommodate the wider gauge, which pointed up the virtues of *narrow*-gauge railways, and many of those were built, compounding the operational confusion. That the Spanish high-speed trains use the standard gauge is tantamount to an admission that the five foot six was a mistake. (The RENFE high-speed trains use German and French technology developed for the standard gauge.)

The other country that adopted a defensive railway gauge was Russia (five foot), and the ambition of Nagelmackers is shown by the fact that his Russia-to-Portugal Nord-Sud scheme would have involved *two* gauge changes. But Nagelmackers could take these things in his stride. A gauge change was an opportunity to show off, and the broad gauge could be taken advantage of. In 1884, he had begun running a Madrid-to-Portugal service, using coches-camas (sleeping cars) that took advantage of the extra width by having armchairs in the corridors.

We were only slightly late into Irun: half past six instead of twenty past. The Sud Express was scheduled to leave at 18.50. It waited on the opposite side of a station building that would once have been the customs hall. Here, the 'Surexpres' was given star billing on the departure board, outranking trains to Brinkola, Pontevedra and Miranda de Ebro. It constituted half a dozen white carriages with an electric loco on the front. The carriages, cordoned off behind a rope, like an exclusive nightclub, were unusually wide but low – and so were boxy, like a line of caravans. The train uses the Spanish TALGO technology first introduced in the late 1940s. TALGO stands for Tren Articulado Ligero Goicoechea Oriol, which means light articulated train. The bogies consist of only two wheels, not four, and they are shared between the back of one carriage and the front of another, which is supposed to give smoother riding over the long and curvaceous Spanish lines.

My compartment was untenanted. There were six seats of a quite pleasant light-and-dark-green check, the beds not yet being made up; there was a stainless steel sink in the corner, betokening that this was a sleeper, not a couchette. The compartment was set at an angle, like the German ones at Munich. The chef du train came to check my ticket. I'd been told that, as part of the general collapse of the Schengen agreement, border controls had been reintroduced between France and Spain. But the chef du train dismissed the idea with some contempt: I would not be needing my passport after all. 'I come back at eight to make up the bed,' he said. 'Bed', singular, so perhaps I would not be sharing?

We pulled away from Irun. Twenty minutes later, we stopped at San Sebastián, and I watched fatalistically as a thin, reserved-looking chap of about my age with a backpack on his shoulder boarded the train and made unerringly for 'my' compartment. I indicated that, until the beds were made up, he could have the three seats on one side, and I'd take the other three. He smiled briefly in acknowledgement. 'Do you speak English?' I asked. 'No,' he said, and he began making a phone call. To minimise the excruciation of trying to look elsewhere as he spoke quietly but intently in Spanish, I quit the compartment again. I went to the WC (perfectly logically ordered and clean), and then there was nowhere else to go but to the restaurant car. This was like an American diner, with high, cushioned stools at a bar, and a place for dinner set at each one.

It was a descendant of 'Coches-Camas Cafeterías', which began to replace W-L coches-comedor on the train as the world became more informal in the late 1950s. These were created by remodelling the end compartments of some of the S-type sleepers that ran on the Sud Express. A small kitchen was inserted for preparation of the dreaded (if you were George Behrend) 'snacks', which were sold over a bar with high stools. There was also a settee that, when the passengers had gone to bed, folded into a double bunk for the crew of two. The cafeteria offered Spanish 'champagne'. At least, noted Behrend in 1962, 'it is no longer disguised among the French champagnes on the wine list as "Sleeping Car Sparkling, special cuvée A. & G.", as it was in 1902'.

All the stools at the present-day bar were occupied by a cheerful crowd, whose average age was about sixty-five. Most were Spanish. The diners were being served by two breezy Portuguese men, who combined so harmoniously in the adjacent kitchenette – the one putting a plate into a microwave, the other switching it on – that I thought they might be an item. They were equipped with half a dozen microwaves, but anyone ordering steak had it freshly cooked on a griddle. Cooking in the Wagons-Lits restaurant cars was done by coal-fired ranges until the very end (the late 1970s). According to one Wagons-Lits researcher, 'The future looked bleak for the trains, so it wouldn't have been worth doing a re-fit.' In any given diner, the range was nicknamed by W-L staff 'the Piano'.

Another chef du train – one of about three who seemed to be aboard – came into the car, and I asked him where we would be stopping. He kindly handed me his iPhone, open at a page where the stops were listed, and then disappeared. I began noting down the stops, but gave up after half a dozen. There were seventeen in all.

Len turned up – not for a drink: 'I've just had half a bottle of wine in the compartment.' He had also eaten. 'The secret to enjoying European sleeper train travel,' he said, 'is a good Marks & Spencer's salad.' I showed him the list of the stops, and he said, 'Perhaps it's like a Parliamentary train – required by law to stop at all those places.' He believed the Sud Express to be an important service: 'You know it's the quickest way of getting by train from north Spain to Portugal?' (Nonetheless, the Portuguese government's Strategic Plan for Transport, published in 2011, envisages the closure of the Sud Express.)

Len is a big traveller, but never by plane. He'd been a fan of the Trenhotels between Paris-Barcelona and Paris-Madrid, operated by the French-Spanish partnership called Elipsos. (They were killed off in 2013 when the TGVs began running from Gare de Lyon to Barcelona via Perpignan, at the other – more futuristic – end of the border from Irun. Passengers can then change at Barcelona for the Spanish high-speed route to Madrid.) Further back in time, he'd ridden the car-carrying sleeper train from Calais to Berlin, operated by Deutsche Bahn. He'd liked that train, and I took a sadistic pleasure in telling him that there are no longer any car-carrying trains from Calais.

The mode is deemed uneconomical, even if it is good for the environment. (All those cars going at seventy miles an hour with their engines switched off.) Car-carrying trains are associated with the 1960s and 1970s, when the car was king, but they ought equally to be associated with the 1830s and 1840s, when private carriages were often carried by train, their wealthy owners sitting inside, as though reluctant to capitulate entirely to this new transport mode. According to Mark Smith, the Man in Seat 61, the Dutch Autoslaap trains to Italy were 'a wonderful overnight experience', with 'an elegant restaurant car serving a 3-course dinner with great wine too'. They stopped in 2014. A Dutch company called Treinreiswinkel runs a car-carrying sleeper from Düsseldorf to Verona, and one from Düsseldorf to Vienna is operated by Austrian Railways (ÖBB). The French run several Auto-Trains, heading broadly south from Paris Gare de Bercy. But only the cars have the excitement of overnight train travel: their owners must go by ordinary day trains. Motorail trains in the UK stopped in 1995, bringing the curtain down on a world of nocturnal services between places apparently randomly paired: Cambridge-Edinburgh, Newcastle-Newton Abbot, Brockenhurst-Sterling. As a rule, the attached sleepers were second class only.

Len explained that, as well as his Marks & Spencer salad and bottle of wine, he always brought with him on a sleeper a door-locking contraption for supplementing the existing locks. He retreated to his compartment and came back with the clamp-like device. I told him I'd been robbed on the Thello train, and he shook his head at my naivety.

Len didn't like to fly, but he wasn't scared of terrorists – or rather, he thought it was absurd to take precautions against them. He'd met an American couple on the TGV Atlantique who'd boarded at Bordeaux, having flown there from Amsterdam, being determined to avoid Paris, which they considered too dangerous after the Islamic State attacks of November 2015. They were now aboard the Sud Express, presumably unaware that Islamic State claims much of the Iberian Peninsula, as having once been Muslim territory.

Len went back to his compartment, and I ordered dinner: Parma ham and olives for a starter, cod in garlic sauce for main, with 'seasonal fruits' (in practice a dry bit of pineapple) to follow. It wasn't bad overall, and the cost – sixteen euros – included another can of beer.

I finished eating as we called at Vitoria, where nobody got on, and nobody got off. By now, I was alone in the dining car. I was oppressed by the thought of the taciturn Spaniard in the compartment. Should I delay my return so that he could fall asleep undisturbed? Or perhaps he was *waiting* for me to return, so as to get the disruption I would cause out of the way, and we could both settle down? I decided the best policy was to order half a bottle of vinho verde for six euros. After a further half an hour, there was no putting off bedtime.

The silent Spaniard had left the door hospitably propped open. He was lying on one of the two top bunks fully dressed and reading a paperback. In the small litter bin next to the sink was a single neatly crushed can of Diet Coke, suggesting an abstemiousness on his part that made me feel guilty. (Might be one of the 25 per cent of the Spanish population who is unemployed?)

I removed my outer clothing, and self-consciously washed my hands and brushed my teeth. I was about to take occupation of the lower bunk on the opposite side – the number of which corresponded to that on my ticket – when I realised that the Spaniard would be able to observe me diagonally from his elevated vantage point. I didn't *want* to be observed, and no doubt he did not want to observe me, so I took the bunk directly beneath his. Having climbed beneath the comfortable and clean duvet, it struck me that I might now be occupying a berth someone else had booked, and would be expecting to occupy at a later point. But it was too late to do anything about that.

The Spaniard now began another muttered phone call, as I worried about the following:

1. Should I have closed the door?
2. Should I have closed the curtains?
3. Who would switch off the light?

I watched apparently nondescript Spanish countryside, shrouded in greenish gloom, as it rolled past the window. I quite liked the curtains being open. It would be like going to sleep with the television on and the sound turned down.

At eleven o'clock, the Spaniard finished his phone call, climbed stealthily down from his bunk, and went to the lavatory. He returned, shutting – but not locking – the door, climbing back into bed and turning off the light. He was emerging as the alpha male in this situation, leaving me to second guess all his actions. He had not closed the curtains. *Why* not? And why had he not locked the door? An obvious answer presented itself: he knew we were about to be joined by another passenger.

At twenty past eleven, we slid into the hazy orange light of a deserted railway station, verbosely designated Valladolid Campo Grande. It was deserted except for one traveller, a muscular young man carrying a rucksack and a skateboard. He entered the train, then stomped along the corridor to our compartment. I pretended to be asleep as he undressed to his boxer shorts in the dark. There was a fifty-fifty chance that I was lying in his bunk. If so he didn't raise any objection, but just climbed into the lower bunk on the opposite side. So it was that I spent the next seven hours trying to pretend I was not aware of this character as he alternately slept, lay awake in various postures, sometimes under, and sometimes on top of his duvet. I did not sleep at all, and felt repeatedly jostled, in spite of the TALGO bogies, and the broad gauge, both of which are supposed to give a smoother ride.

The low point came at the big junction of Medina del Campo, north-west of Madrid, at midnight. We approached the station through an industrial landscape, sliding past a frighteningly high concrete silo that I couldn't see the top of, however much I craned forward in my bunk. We pulled into the empty station directly next to an energy-saving lamp that, over a cycle of about a minute, flared from a low glow to a bright dazzle. This continued for twenty minutes until we rolled slowly out of the station. Some gentle buffering took place, denoting a change of engine. (The electric loco is replaced with a diesel here.) We then rolled slowly *back* into the station, the compartment window becoming once again perfectly aligned to the light. The torture resumed for another half an hour, the timetable requiring us to spend an hour in total at Medina del Campo. I would have got up to close the curtains, but the skateboarder – lying complacently with hands behind his head – gave every indication of being awake and enjoying the show. There was always a lot of messing about at Medina del Campo. The opening, in 1895, of the line running west from there to Fuentes de Oñoro on the Portuguese border gave the option of cutting out Madrid, which the Sud Express had previously passed through. The option wasn't always taken, and the train would divide at Campo for either Lisbon or Madrid.

We pulled away, and Spain continued to unfold beyond the window. Perhaps it is considered rude to close the curtains on Spanish trains; but then why *have* curtains? This did feel like a very foreign train. It seemed significant that it had not – well, not since 1890 – originated at Calais. In Holy Week of 1900, W-L offered an excursion to Seville, using the Sud Express as far as Madrid. A poster, in the shape of a minaret, depicted old Seville, and a Semana Santa procession led by figures in pointed hoods and masks. The Sud Express differed in other ways from the standard trains de luxe. While the service was suspended during the Spanish Civil War (both sides helped themselves to the W-L rolling stock), the Spanish portion of the service continued to run during both world wars, Spain being neutral. In 1943, indeed, W-L had introduced a new Spanish service: 'Lusitania', operating from Madrid to Lisbon, and parent to the current Spanish Trenhotel sleeper service of that name. The Lusitania carriages, and some of the other W-L sleepers and diners in Spain, were painted silver, in the hope that it would deflect the heat of the sun better than dark blue, but it showed the dirt, and so the silver was ditched in 1959. (Lusitania, incidentally, was a Roman province of Iberia.)

At 2.30, at the border town of Fuentes de Oñoro, electrification resumed, and so we changed locos once again. We reached Mangualde 03.46. At 18.37 on 11 September 1985, a few miles west of here, the Sud Express, heading towards Spain, crashed headlong into a local train. The line was – and is – single, and trains were supposed to pass each other using the loop at Nelas, west of Mangualde. The local was proceeding towards the loop, believing the Sud Express to be running late, but the express had made up time. Approximately 150 people died, making it the worst rail disaster in Portuguese history.

At 06.30, after Entroncamento, there came a loud rapping on the door. I opened it, and one of the chefs du train looked in, saying, 'Forty-five minutes to Lisbon Oriente!' thus waking up the other two. While they stayed in their bunks, I furtively put on my trousers and shirt, but in the gloom of dawn I couldn't find my boots. Rain lashed against the window and – as I discovered while walking along to the buffet in my stockinged feet – it had leaked in at the carriage ends, forming puddles at the interconnections. Another black mark for the TALGO system. So it was with wet feet that I ate the breakfast being cheerfully doled out by the two Portuguese: strong, sweet coffee, orange juice and a plate with three pastries on it.

At 07.20, I disembarked at Oriente. Lisbon was in the grip

of an Atlantic storm, to which the spectacular architecture of this modern station – a soaring roof held up by neo-Gothic pillars – left me fully exposed. (There were no walls, so the rain blew in from the sides.) All my fellow passengers scurried to the exits on the lower levels of Oriente. If they were excited at their arrival, they had a funny way of showing it, but perhaps they had other business immediately in hand. The Sud Express had always been a staging post to further adventures, and many of those on board would have been connecting at Lisbon for the steamers heading for Cape Town, Buenos Aires, Madeira, Rio de Janeiro, Montevideo. In any case, I remained on the beautiful, limestone-tiled platform, savouring the wildness of the weather, illuminated by the gentle orange lights of the station, which occasionally flickered, as though slightly daunted by the storm.

LISBON

After a wash in a (probably haunted) gentleman's lavatory located in one of the deserted subterranean galleries of Lisbon Oriente, I took a Metro downtown, disembarking at Restauradores. Here, at Rua 1 de Dezembro, a vision from the past emerged with the aid of clearing rain and strengthening sun: the Avenida Palace, a neoclassical hotel, commissioned by Nagelmackers and opened in 1892. The architect was José Luís Monteiro, who had also been responsible for the building next door, completed in the previous year. While the Avenida Palace looks like a hotel, the building next door looks like a strange kind of church, except for the Starbucks set into the façade. The apparent absence of any railway lines notwithstanding, this is in fact a railway station: called Central Station when it opened in 1901, it later became known as Lisbon Rossio. In *Station to Station*, Steven Parissien writes that Rossio

'drew inspiration from the Maneuline architecture of the Portuguese Renaissance. The two horseshoe-shaped entrances
recalled a time of Portuguese greatness, of the wealth and
opulence of the Portuguese Empire before the ignominious
Spanish annexation of 1580.' I walked inside and, yes, there
were trains (they come in via a tunnel, as with Gare d'Orsay),
many of them going to the suburb of Sintra. Parissien adds
that 'the interior is a great disappointment'. The side walls
of the train shed feature pretty tiled medallions advertising
Portuguese regional produce, which do look like the kind of
decorations you see on the wall of an upmarket delicatessen.

The design was controversial. Monteiro took some flak
over it, so he was perhaps relieved at the commission for the
more conventional hotel. A suspended walkway connects
the third floor of the hotel with the station. This was for
the use of VIP arrivals on the Sud Express. I myself merely
walked from the street into the hotel, but only after a couple
of enjoyable days spent in Lisbon with my wife, who arrived
courtesy of easyJet, having 'no interest whatsoever' in going
there by sleeper train.

I wandered through a plush, pinkish lobby towards the
bar, which was neatly spoiled by the presence of a widescreen
TV showing football with the sound turned down. A woman
was playing piano with all the restraint and delicacy of the
late Liberace. On the other hand, a glass of decent white
wine was a relatively modest five euros. No railway memorabilia was on view. I approached the reception, meaning
to ask, indignantly, why not, but as soon as I mentioned the
name of Nagelmackers, the desk clerk reached for a box containing numerous A4 envelopes of good-quality paper. 'In
English?' he said, and he handed over what turned out to be a
very comprehensive, if quite fruity and erratically translated,
history of the hotel:

A private orchestra flooded the rooms with music during their famous Saturday balls, and while the dancing pairs challenged love, spies from everywhere looked for conspiracies. A special Night Service, characterised by an exquisite French 'a la carte' cuisine, sustained the hours, and 'seasoned' the most fierce emotions. The aromas of Parisian fragrances filled the air with the faint and sweetish scent of a decadent monarchy.

Sometimes the Sud Express terminated at Santa Apolónia Station, situated on the banks of the Tagus, and the oldest of the four in Lisbon. But most of the international traffic was concentrated on Rossio from the 1890s until the 1950s, so those 'Parisian fragrances' must have included the 'aroma' of the steam-hauled Sud Express, fuming away directly next door.

6

THE BERLIN NIGHT EXPRESS

THE NENE VALLEY RAILWAY

This journey on the night train from Malmö to Berlin could be said to have begun in Cambridgeshire.

The Nene Valley Railway (NVR) is a preserved railway near Peterborough. It has track clearances that can accommodate the bigger continental loading gauges, and is home to many foreign vehicles, which are being restored under the auspices of its subsidiary, the International Railway Preservation Society (IRPS), as quickly as funds allow, which is not very quickly. The IRPS is restoring, amongst other things, a German shunter, a Danish loco, a Swedish loco and British vehicles including some Travelling Post Offices (TPO), one of which, TPO M30272M, was on the train robbed in the Great Train Robbery. These will be exhibited in a Night Mail Museum, which combines the two interests of Phil Marshall, founder of the IRPS: night trains and mail trains.

One railway journalist raised an eyebrow at mention of the NVR. He said its collection was ill assorted, like a 'railway zoo'. But for some of us, a visit to the line is the next best thing to taking a foreign railway holiday. Two minutes off the AI, you're on the pretty country lane leading to its headquarters, Wansford Station, once an important junction of the Great Northern Railway, whose early-Victorian station building looks even older, being Jacobean in style.

At Wansford you enter the NVR dreamworld, as presided over by Phil Marshall, who lives in a flat on the station and works round the clock on the restoration of the rolling stock. Phil is one of the leading British authorities on W-L matters, and a nice chap, but he is also very busy. Whenever I see him, I am guiltily aware that I am keeping him from some essential task – not that he consciously guilt trips me, it's just that he's always holding a paint pot or a spanner.

After picking Phil's brain, I visit the rambling second-hand bookshop. Amid the thousands of dusty volumes (all about railways, of course), are back numbers of the *International Railway Preservation Society Journal*, which often covers Wagons-Lits matters. For instance, one article, entitled 'In Lament of Oostende Atelier', opens:

> There can be no greater place to stir the emotions than the spiritual home of WL, Oostende Atelier ... The hall that once echoed to the music of the riveter's gun and the banter of its workers, lies ghostly silent. Only the rattle of the wind blowing the tin sheet roof breaks the silence, while the echoes of our footsteps call back from its walls ... Outside is a heap of ashes that was once the Teak Restaurant car 2101.

A short walk from the bookshop brings visitors to W-L sleeping car number 3916, fading to sky blue under its tarpaulin, as mentioned in the chapter on the Nordland

Railway. It was built in 1949, and is a veteran of the Nord Express. The gantry alongside gives a view of the dark corridor, and closed compartment doors. The view through the windows of another Wagons-Lits veteran undergoing restoration – dining car number 2975 – is more rewarding: you can see luggage racks, an old suitcase, dusty pink lampshades, marquetry (whereas number 3916 was built to an austere post-war specification, and had no marquetry even when brand new). According to the NVR website, 'Number 2975 was built in 1927, and was used mainly in Switzerland, which is probably why it survived the War. It was brought to England for the filming of Stephen Poliakoff's television play of 1980, *Caught on a Train*, which is set on an Ostend-to-Vienna night train.'

Standing opposite this mouldering pair is a rake of pristine midnight-blue carriages, much more evocative of the golden days of the trains de luxe, to the extent that a visitor might wonder why the Nene Valley bothers with 3916 and 2975. On the carriage sides are enamel plaques reading

Le Train Bleu
(London) Calais-Paris
Nice-St Remo

There are cosy-looking compartments, and a 'Voiture-Salon-Bar' with beautiful marquetry and banquette seats. 'Actually, they're nothing to do with Wagons-Lits at all,' a volunteer at the NVR brutally pointed out, on my first visit. 'They're from the Belgian state railway in the 1930s. There's a clue *here*,' he said, indicating a sign below the communication cord that read 'Noodsein', meaning 'Alarm'. 'This was never a bar car, either,' he added. 'We converted it from ordinary seating.' The NVR runs Blue Train-themed dining evenings in these cars. In a nifty piece of legalese, they are referred to as 'licensed Wagons-Lits-style carriages'. The mocked-up bar car will strike many visitors as being mysteriously familiar, because it stands in for a W-L dining car in the version of *Murder on the Orient Express* made in 2010 by ITV, and starring David Suchet as Poirot. In fact, there was never any bar car on the Orient Express, but for filming purposes, it is easier to muster the dozen suspects in a bar car than a restaurant car, which is where Poirot convenes them in the novel.

At some point during my NVR visits, I ride up and down the seven-mile line in the orange-and-yellow Swedish diesel rail car called Helga. In Sweden during the 1960s Helga covered 1,996,000 km, which, as the NVR website points out, is the equivalent of going to the moon and back two and a half times. On coming to England she did a melancholic stint as a static exhibit at the Bygone Village, Fleggburgh, Great Yarmouth, then served as a shelter for rainy-day picnics at Tweddle Animal Farm near Hartlepool. Helga is superbly ergonomic, with comfortable seats and a handhold wherever you want one. She is also incredibly wide, like a boat – a pleasure steamer, with the semicircle of windows at either end, through which the pleasantly bland fields on either side of the line quietly unfold. Whatever else is not happening on the NVR, Helga will be running.

It's fun to see novices climb on board, and slowly work out the foreignness. The door of the WC is marked 'Toalett'. The loo itself is a sort of porcelain tube, at the bottom of which is ... nothing: a hole giving onto the tracks. About two out of every three people who go into the Toalett come straight out again, exclaiming to their friends: 'It goes straight onto the tracks!'

But for any student of European sleeper trains, the main

goal of a visit to the NVR is a few minutes of Phil Marshall's time, and in early summer of 2016, I managed to collar him. He was driving a dumper truck, but very slowly, and so I was able to walk alongside him for a while. After mentioning the journeys I'd so far made, I sought a recommendation for one final trip.

'Take the Berlin Night Express,' he shouted over the noise of the truck's engine, 'From Malmö to Berlin! It's run by a private firm called Snälltåget! They put the train on a boat across the Baltic! It's the most authentic Wagons-Lits type experience!'

'Why?'

'Because it's like the Night Ferry!'

THE NIGHT FERRY

First things first: the Night Ferry was not a ferry; it was a train. It did run at night, though. It ran from Victoria to Dover, where it – or most of it – was shunted onto one of several special train-carrying ferries. These then sailed for three-and-a-quarter hours to Dunkirk, where the train was taken off and ran on to Paris Gare du Nord. The journey also happened in reverse, and one or two carriages ran through to Brussels, after being taken off at Lille.

The Night Ferry first ran on the night of 5 October 1936, featuring specially made sleeping coaches from the Compagnie Internationale des Wagons-Lits. They were slightly smaller than the usual W-L rolling stock, being designed to fit the smaller British loading gauge. Even so, the Night Ferry – with perhaps ten of those sleepers, a restaurant and kitchen car, a buffet car and varying quantity of ordinary Southern Railway carriages – was a very heavy train, and in steam days it needed to be hauled by two locomotives. The foremost of these had a circular name board on the smoke-box door, like the end of a giant cotton reel. It bore the words 'Night Ferry, London-Paris', and the image of a yellow crescent moon on a pale-blue background.

The carriages were called F-class (for Ferry). There were nine compartments, each with an upper and lower bunk. If a single traveller required sole occupancy that was counted as first class, and the fare was accordingly higher. They were not wood-panelled – that would have been a fire-hazard in the boat hold – but were made of melamine, which was painted brownish to suggest wood. The exteriors did follow the W-L template however, in that they were dark blue, which was unusual in Britain, and people who observed them on the move, running through Kent at about ten o'clock at night, remarked that they seemed to disappear, being essentially the colour of the night – all except the shuttling yellow light from their windows.

On arrival at Dover, those in the ordinary carriages would walk onto the boat. Those in the sleepers would sleep – or they might have done, if they were exceptionally tired or drunk, because if they weren't woken up by the jerking of the shunting; or the susurration of the sea water as the level was adjusted in the train ferry dock (so as to get the link-span, by which the train boarded the boat, to the right level); or the rattling of the chains by which the carriages were secured in the echoing hold; or the shouting of the blokes who performed this action, then the motion of the sea on a rough night might have done the job – because the Night Ferry offered the novelty of being seasick on a train. There was a porcelain seasickness bowl in every compartment, and luggage was secured in a net. This blurring of travel categories was part of its fascination. There was a lifebelt in every compartment, and those boarding the sleepers had to walk through customs while still in London. The station called Dover Ferry was the only timetabled passenger calling point in Britain with no platform.

It's not that a train ferry was unprecedented, even within Britain. They had been used to cross the Firths of the Forth and Tay before the waters were bridged in 1890. In 1924, a train ferry from Harwich to Zeebrugge in Belgium was inaugurated, but this was only ever used for freight, which was carried in special white wagons with foreign lettering on them. Sleeper carriages were sometimes put aboard, but there was nobody inside them: they were for export.

The Harwich train ferry – or a good miniature model of it – was in effect the star of Alfred Hitchcock's film, *Number 17*. 'The rambling narrative of jewel thieves, mysterious detectives and hanging bodies borders on the incomprehensible,' says Peter Ackroyd in his biography of Hitchcock, but when train time comes, things do pick up. The half-ridiculous, half-compelling climax involves freight wagons crashing onto the ferry, in scenes suggestive of Hitchcock playing with toy boats in his bathtub. The train ferry dock at Harwich survives but is rotting away; the installation at Dover is now a gravel depot.

On the Night Ferry, there was also the disorientation of travelling on what was really a French train in Britain. As Michael Williams writes, in his enjoyable book, *The Trains Now Departed*:

> For all its life the Night Ferry was an enclosed world of its own, characterised by the charming Gallic argot used by the staff. Thus the bellows connection between the carriages was known as a *soufflet*, the trolley for light refreshments as a *vente ambulante* and the conductor's hat as a *képi*.

Also the potty, stored under the sink, was called a 'vase de nuit', and passengers were spared the inscription common on such receptacles in purely British sleeping compartments: 'This utensil is not to be used for solid matter.' In the early days, the conductors were all French, and according to George Behrend, writing in 1962, one of them 'happens to live in London, the only staff member of WL to do so'. I imagine this character as living in a small terrace near Victoria, a dapper, impeccably dressed man (even when not wearing his Night Ferry uniform of chocolate brown with gold piping and brass buttons), who, on his mornings off, walks briskly to the one café in London that serves croissants – in those days when croissants were not ubiquitous and terrace houses near Victoria did not cost 2 million pounds. Being French, the Night Ferry was erotic. Commuters at Victoria, arriving from Croydon or Haywards Heath, would peer jealously through the carriage windows to see the tousled red blankets, strewn pages of *The Times* and lately abandoned breakfast trays.

Today, the train would be called elitist. Immediately after the war, complimentary packets of Palmolive soap, bearing the crescent moon and stars, were supplied, even though soap was being rationed. The Duke of Windsor was a regular on board, and there was special provision for the famous: they could be served breakfast on a tray in their compartments, sparing them the need to appear in the restaurant car. One such VIP was Winston Churchill, and on 16 December 1951, the train stopped at Sevenoaks to collect him (his country seat was at nearby Westerham), the only time the Night Ferry picked up a passenger before Paris.

In the 1960s, a single sleeper fare to Paris was about ten pounds. The man who fired the locomotive that hauled it to Dover was probably on about twenty-five a week. Later, the train suffered the decline usual among W-L services, and it became less French. W-L ceased to operate the train in December 1976, when its management was transferred to SNCF, with BR employees as attendants. It was plagued by strikes in its later years, and eclipsed by aeroplane travel. The Night Ferry came to be viewed as a sort of stately home on wheels, its old-fashioned grandeur appreciated more by its users than its operators.

The International Railway Preservation Society has produced a bilingual book called *Ferry Boat de Nuit 1936–1980/ Night Ferry 1936–1980*, containing memoirs of travelling on the service. One is written by a chap called Tom Scharf, who was on the very last running of the Night Ferry, on 31 October 1980, with his friend Graham: 'I must confess to a certain amount of dismay at the very utilitarian mushroom-beige paint finish along the corridor and the compartment doors ... I shared a compartment with Graham who provided champagne to mark the occasion. We had both dressed in suit and tie out of respect to the old train.' Tom Scharf was slightly alarmed to find himself crunching through chunks of coke spilled from the stoves, located at the corridor ends, that heated the carriages.

The book is decorated with reproductions of moody paintings, showing nocturnal scenes of carriage loading, usually in the rain, with a few lonely figures in trilbies and macs standing about. Sometimes the *contrôleurs* at Dunkirk would board the ferry for a nightcap of gin and orange; then they'd have to board the tug that pulled the ferry clear of the docks, in order to return to the port. One of the memoirists recalls some important – or self-important – men turning up at the Dover dockside in a fast car, and demanding to be admitted to the train, evening fog having stopped flights from Heathrow. They were given permission to board, but became agitated at the time it was taking to get the water level in the dock right. I imagine there must have also been some anxious moments at Dover for the most famous fugitive to use the train: Ernest Marples.

If you live in York, as I once did, and you regret the fact that there's no longer a direct train from there to the pretty seaside town of Whitby; or if you're a regular at the Glastonbury Festival, but you're annoyed that you can't get there directly by train; or if you wonder why Britain is bothering to spend 40 billion pounds to create High Speed Two from nothing when the old Great Central Railway might have provided a ready-made route much like the one proposed, then you can blame Dr Richard Beeching, because he closed all those lines as chairman of British Railways. But who – in 1961 – had made Beeching chairman of British Railways? It was the Minister of Transport, Ernest ('Ernie', as he liked to be known) Marples. If your property is blighted by the noise of a motorway, you might also be able to blame Marples, because he owned a construction firm that specialised in road building.

He was among that dangerous generation of public servants who found themselves middle aged at the time of the 'youthquake'. They wanted to join in. If they'd simply bought fast cars or had sex with much younger women (Marples did both), the bad effects might have been confined to their families, but they inflicted their mid-life crises on the nation. If they inherited an old house they would purge it of such grotesqueries as high ceilings or fireplaces. If they were town planners they instigated 'comprehensive redevelopments', involving the building of car parks. If they were railwaymen, they thought Euston was beautiful, and they closed railway lines. From the rail enthusiasts' point of view, the only thing that can be said for Marples is that, while he helped ruin Britain with his Darwinian notion of 'the motorway of life', he also did some small things to check the motorist: he introduced single and double yellow lines, parking meters, traffic wardens and the MOT test, hence the graffiti appearing along the length of the M1, which he had both opened at transport minister, and helped build as a businessman: 'Marples must go'. He did go, in late 1975, and it still seems unjust that, when faced with an unpayable tax bill, arising from years of tax evasion, he should have been whisked away from justice by a train: the Night Ferry. From Paris, he entrained to Monte Carlo, where he died in 1978.

On the last night of the Night Ferry, the indicator on Platform 2 at Victoria read 'Au Revoir Mon Ami', and the driver waved a copy of the *London Evening News*, which died on the same day. There was a crescendo of whistles from the other locomotives as it sighingly left Victoria for the last time. One of the sleeper cars, number 3792, is preserved at the Shildon annexe of the National Railway Museum, so in the case of this vehicle at least, 'au revoir' was correct.

THE TRAIN FERRY PERFECTED

A month after speaking to Phil Marshall, I was on a plane approaching Copenhagen. I had discovered that while it costs about 300 pounds to fly from London to Malmö, it costs only thirty pounds to fly to Copenhagen, which might as well be a suburb of Malmö, since the opening of the Øresund Bridge, which connects the two cities, in 2000. As we began our descent, everybody looked left, and there *was* the Øresund Bridge. On the Danish side, the crossing of the Øresund strait begins with a tunnel before the bridge takes over, and cars appeared to rise out of the sea to traverse the bridge, like amphibian cars of the future, blithely taking everything in their stride.

The Øresund Bridge supplies the premise for the TV thriller *The Bridge*: a body is found exactly halfway along it, triggering bureaucratic complications that are apparently very compelling. I've never seen *The Bridge*, or the British spin-off, *The Tunnel*, which pedantically transfers the corpse to the middle of the Channel Tunnel. Before the building of the bridge, the Øresund strait was traversed by a train ferry, and it was in the Danish archipelago that the art of the train ferry was perfected.

According to *Railway Wonders of the World*, a British traveller to Copenhagen in the early 1930s would have proceeded as follows. He would begin by taking the ferry from Harwich to Esbjerg. There, in the evening, he would board a through sleeper carriage on a train for Copenhagen, which would have journeyed the fifty-five miles across Jutland to Fredericia. From there, the carriage would have been put on a train ferry for the two-mile crossing of the Little Belt. 'By smart working,' wrote the anonymous author, 'the train is run on to the ferry steamer in fifteen or twenty minutes; the crossing itself takes fifteen to twenty minutes, and another fifteen minutes is needed at Strib to run the trains off on to land again and re-marshall.' The train then ran across the island of Funen for fifty-two miles, bringing it to Nyborg, on the west side of the Great Belt, where the train was put onto another train ferry, which sailed for eighteen miles to Korsør on the eastern side of the Great Belt: a process that took nearly two hours. From Korsør, the train ran to Copenhagen.

From 1935, a bridge across the Little Belt replaced the Fredericia-Strib train ferry, which had been operating since 1872. In 1997, the Great Belt Fixed Link, combining bridges and a tunnel, made redundant the train ferry from Nyborg to Korsør, which had begun in 1883.

The operation of a train ferry is a now a *dying* art. Whereas the British Night Ferry would have been thought of when it started as something akin to a boat, by the time it had ceased to run it would have looked like something akin to – but not as good as – an aeroplane. (There was a half-hour check-in for the service, although it wasn't called that.)

Today, there are half a dozen freight-only train ferries operating in the Baltic. The Berlin Night Express is the only service marked on my European Railway Map with the line of blue dashes reserved for *passenger* train ferries, but this says more about the map than the facts of the case. A passenger train ferry runs from Rødby in Denmark to Puttgarden in Germany. It carries diesel trains from Copenhagen to Hamburg, but no longer at night. My map connects Rødby and Zealand with *red* dashes, to which the map key offers no clue. But written above the dashes is '2021', which must denote the year in which an 'immersed tunnel' between these two places, the Fehmarn Belt Fixed Link, is scheduled to be completed. What use this information is to the purchaser of the map in 2016 I don't know. There is also a train ferry running from Villa San Giovanni in southern Italy to Messina in Sicily, for the trains running between Palermo and Naples. The Strait of Messina is only a couple of miles wide, and barely a millimetre on my map, so there probably wasn't room to fit the line of blue dashes.

***

Half an hour after landing at Copenhagen, I was crossing the bridge on the train, which runs on the lower deck of the bridge – so there isn't the same sensation of rising porpoise-like out of the water as you would have in a car. On the platform at Copenhagen Airport, my passport had been checked. As a result of the migrant crisis, the Schengen agreement had been partly suspended in Sweden. And my ticket had just been checked by a train guard in civvies: camouflage shorts and a hooded top. I only knew he worked for the railway by the laminated ID card dangling around his neck, and by his interest in my ticket, which would be otherwise unaccountable.

As we approached Malmö, I was looking at my notes.

The Berlin Night Express goes from Malmö to Berlin, but the interesting core of the journey is across the Baltic, between Trelleborg in Sweden and Sassnitz in Germany. This route was served by a train ferry from 1909, and the vessel in question is very famous (among people who like ferries). It was called *Drottning Victoria*, and it was built by Swan Hunter in Newcastle, and remained in service until 1964, at which point most of the trains carried – whether by day or night – were foreign. There were direct services from Malmö to Moscow, Budapest, Belgrade, Prague, Gdansk, Hamburg and elsewhere.

In April 1917, Vladimir Lenin crossed from Germany to Sweden on *Drottning Victoria*, en route to Finland Station in what was then called Petrograd. This was facilitated by the German government, anxious to bring the war in the east to an end. Lenin had sworn to sue for peace if he obtained power and – equally promising for the Germans – to trigger a class war within Russia. In *The Life and Death of Lenin*, Robert Payne wrote that it served German interests to 'hurl the revolutionaries like a bomb upon Petrograd'.

The Germans had obtained the consent of the neutral Swedish government to send Lenin across Sweden rather than through the German lines to the east. Lenin and about thirty of his colleagues began their journey in Zurich, their place of exile. The journey was famously made in a 'sealed train' but this was more like a sealed carriage in an ordinary scheduled train, the seal taking the form of a chalk line in adjacent carriages, guarded by German police. Why the seal? To prevent Lenin infecting ordinary Germans with the revolutionary virus, and to prevent the Provisional Government in Russia finding out what was going on. According to Payne, most of the Bolsheviks, but not Lenin, smoked incessantly on the train. Lenin drank a lot of beer but objected to the smoking, and decreed that it should take place only in the lavatory. When it became obvious that there would be a massed rush to the facility, Lenin designed a system of regulation. Karl Radek, evidently one of the more amusing Bolsheviks, recalled that Lenin 'cut a piece of paper in two and distributed permits. For every three tickets of category "A" for the legitimate use of the premises there was one smoker's ticket. This naturally evoked further discussions about the value of human needs, and we acutely regretted that comrade Bukharin was not with us, as a specialist in Böhm Bawerk's theory about marginal utility.'

The Germans arranged for excellent meals to be served on the train, so as to give the impression that everything was going swimmingly in their country, but from the window Lenin saw starving people in the passing villages – and very few young ones among them. At Karlsruhe and Berlin there were long delays, which apparently disappointed Lenin, who had the same high regard for the efficiency of German railways as everyone else. One imagines him checking his watch, and shaking his head, like some petulant commuter.

The train reached Sassnitz on the night of 12 April, and the Bolsheviks were transferred from the sealed carriage to a sealed room, where they spent the night. They crossed the Baltic on the next morning and, rather disappointingly, neither the train nor even the sealed carriage was put onto the boat. One Swedish expert on the route sent me an email saying, 'There were probably other cars [carriages] on the Drottning Victoria but for some unknown reason, Lenin's car remained in Sassnitz, and he took another train from Trelleborg.'

In both wars, the train ferry was operated by our old friend MITROPA. After the Second World War, MITROPA survived as one of the few joint stock companies in East Germany, where it provided the railway catering. It then served reunified Germany until 2002. (Lars von Trier's black-and-white expressionist film of 1991, *Europa*, concerns a young American lured into a pro-Nazi conspiracy hatched by a sinister railway company called Zentropa, a deliberate echo of MITROPA. The idea of a sinister railway *catering company* would be absurd, so Zentropa is a railway in the fullest sense.)

'After the Second World War,' according to my Swedish correspondent, 'the Ferry route faced a lot of problems.' This was because Sassnitz found itself in the GDR. 'The trains to Berlin,' he wrote, 'ended in various stations, but from 1955, traffic was re-established with Berlin Zoologischer, in West Berlin, as the end station.'

The passenger services were operated by Swedish and German state railways until 2000, then deregulation kicked in. In 2001, the German private operator, GVG, took over from Deutsche Bahn on that side of the partnership. In 2012, one of the private Swedish operators, Snälltåget, took over on the other side. Snälltåget – owned by the French transport multinational Transdev – also operates day trains to Stockholm, and sleeper trains to the ski resorts Åre and Vemdalen. These sleepers operate between Christmas and Easter, whereas the Berlin Night Express is a summer service only.

ALL WINDOWS DOWN

The train from Copenhagen took me to a platform beneath Malmö Central Station. Since the coming of the Øresund line in 2010 the subterranean level at Malmö has been busier than the upper one, and the station proper had the peaceful air of a railway museum on a quiet day. It dates from 1856, and is barn-like, with a white timber roof and red wooden beams. I walked to the enquiry desk to make sure the Berlin Night Express would be leaving on time at 17.00. 'I can confirm that is correct,' came the unflappable Scandinavian response. I was curious about the name of the operator. Snälltåget apparently has a punning double meaning. The Swedish connotation is 'nice train', but there is also an echo of the German 'schnell'. 'So it means fast train as well,' said the consultant, 'but in fact it is not really a fast train at all.'

'But it is nice, I hope?'

'That is for you to decide.'

I had four hours to kill before train time – and I had a headache, which increased my susceptibility to the disorientating effects of the north European summer. Platform 1 was decorated with small oak trees planted in tubs and festooned with fairy lights, suggesting Christmas, but it was a day of blazing sunshine and seagulls wheeled loudly over the station (which is next to docks), suggesting another topographical dimension altogether. On the wall of Platform 1 were big black-and-white pictures of the station in the early twentieth century. It was beautifully austere, with people sitting on wooden benches, as in a church. I wondered whether any of those people were waiting for the one Wagons-Lits service that had touched Malmö: the Nord Express.

Platform 1 was accessible through a variety of very clean and well-managed shops, including a pharmacy, where the emphasis was on podiatry: corn plasters, insoles, sensible sandals. This means of access must have helped both the shops and the station. It was one of a number of good railway ideas I'd noted. On the train from Copenhagen there'd been transparent polythene bags on hooks to act as litter bins. In the subterranean station of Malmö there had been moving images on the platform walls, projections of countryside scenes, to alleviate the depression of being in a tunnel. Just outside Malmö Station proper, an iron sculpture of a bike was mounted atop a pole, to signal the presence of a bike store. In 1935, *Railway Wonders of the World* had observed, 'Sweden was one of the first European countries to recognise the benefit of an attractive city station in drawing business to the railway, and the salesmanship side of her railway undertaking has been very well developed.'

The streets near the station were wide, quiet and reminiscent of Britain in the 1950s, with many sweet shops, clothes shops with slightly battered mannequins in the window and a population of sinewy cyclists, some riding wooden bikes. It was hard to believe there had been serious race riots in Malmö in June 2015, and that it has a reputation for ethnic tension and gun crime.

A strong wind seemed to buffet me with redoubled vigour every time I turned a corner, making my headache worse. I had got up too early, having been worried about the running of the Gatwick Express from Victoria. It was subject to disruption, the RMT union being engaged in shadow-boxing with the Govia Thameslink Railway, which was 'evolving the role of the conductor'. Conductors would no longer be required to close train doors, 'so they can spend more time helping passengers'. It was hard to believe the trouble was not related to the terrible nomenclature of the privatised railway. GTR is a subsidiary of Govia, which is a joint venture between Go-Ahead Group and Keolis. GTR runs the

Thameslink, Southern and Great Northern rail franchise. (That might sound like more than one, but it's 'franchise', singular.) Within the *franchise* GTR runs the Thameslink, Great Northern, Southern and Gatwick Express *services*. I trust all that is perfectly clear?

In the event, I had arrived at the airport on time, but having slept for only a couple of hours.

Returning to Malmö Station, I wondered whether this troublesome breeze might be whipping up the waves on the Baltic. Even by the admission of Snälltåget, the Berlin Night Express was 'liable to cancellation at any time' (whereas the Night Ferry never missed a single running because of rough seas). There was a new man at the station help desk, but he was as unflappable as the other: 'We have a three-class warning system, and the wind today is not even class one.'

By now the train was in the station: five venerable sleeper carriages of ribbed steel, like the 1950s 'P'-class of W-L. Like the P, these carriages were unpainted except for the word Snälltåget, written large in multi-coloured lettering. Snälltåget might be owned by a multinational, but the impression was of a hippyish train, the railway equivalent of a VW camper van with a 'Nuclear Power? No thanks!' sticker on the bumper. At four fifteen, the passengers were already arriving: mainly young couples and their young children, who were being lifted up to peer through the windows. Varying numbers of beds were made up in the compartments, which were all couchettes. The maximum number was six.

Somebody who looked like a student came along and propped a sign on the platform asking that passports be shown to officials of the train before boarding. Two officials were ushering people aboard the train in a friendly way: both had high-visibility vests and long blonde ponytails, although only one of them was a woman. The woman ticked my name off a list as I climbed up. She had very long, pale-blue artificial fingernails, so she would probably not be chaining down the carriages in the ship's hold.

It turned out that the extremely efficient press officer of Snälltåget had reserved an entire compartment for me, which made me feel guilty, since every other compartment was packed. One of the bunks was folded down, with enough clean bedding for six heaped on it. The upholstery was blue, and the armrests on the seats – about the size of breeze blocks – were detachable, so I could have chucked them all on the floor and stretched out along the length of the seats. There was a curtain, and an openable window, so the carriage was not air-conditioned, but I immediately liked my sunlit, old-fashioned quarters, and as we pulled away dead on time, I was reminded of Philip Larkin's poem, 'The Whitsun Weddings':

> All windows down, all cushions hot, all sense
> Of being in a hurry gone.

After fifteen minutes along what is known as the Continental Line, we had reached Trelleborg. Poised for loading onto the boat, we waited in the middle of a wide marshalling yard, with freight wagons on either side, and seagulls swooping overhead. What was missing, in comparison with the Night Ferry, was *night* (the sun still shone brightly), arc lights and a steady English rain.

FS *SASSNITZ*

I walked into the corridor, opened the window and stuck my head out, joining half a dozen others doing the same. Our locomotive was wandering away, revealing the yawning hold

of the ferry, into which we would soon be pushed. A very perfunctory diesel shunter – like a big go-cart – now buffered
up to the rear. The driver was doing that thing that always
lessens my confidence in any professional: checking his
messages on his mobile phone. But for all I knew, he would
receive the instruction to start the manoeuvre in the form
of a text message. My understanding of shunting is weak (I
offer the excuse that it, like the operation of train ferries, is a
dying railway art, what with all the fixed-formation trains). It
bothered me that the man on the shunter could have no sight
of the front of the train he was about to push into the boat
hold. Surely this was an accident waiting to happen? When
I got home, I mentioned this to my eldest son, who is quite
technical, and he thought about it for two seconds before
saying: 'Well, presumably the train's the same length every
time, so he'll have a mark to stop at.'

An announcement came: 'We will now be joining the
ferry!' and the shunter started up. We were indeed sent in as
one train, whereas the longer Night Ferry train was split into
four when loaded.

My compartment came to rest right alongside a big black
four-by-four. Another announcement said we could either
remain on the train, or walk to the upper decks, where we
could take advantage of two restaurants or the duty free
shop. There had been a similar option on the Night Ferry,
but unannounced, and more low key. It was about midnight
when that train was put on the boat, and passengers were
supposed to be asleep. There was a saloon bar on the boat,
however – latterly denoted 'the lorry driver's mess'. There
was also a service hatch that rattled open at about midnight
so the train manager could sell duty-free cognac, whisky and
bourbon to insomniac passengers.

Before quitting the Snälltåget train, I collected my

valuables. (Unlike all the motor cars, the train would not be locked for the crossing.) I then walked along to sample the 'Toalett'. There was a notice about not smoking in the WC. The rather droopy threat was in accordance with the hippyish ethos of the service: 'Smoking could mean you have to leave the train.' Unlike the toalett on the Nene Valley's Helga, this one did not flush straight onto the tracks. These carriages might be old, but they were house-trained. In the case of the Night Ferry carriages, the toilets did discharge straight onto the tracks, so they were parked over receiving pits on the boat. The smell could become nauseating as the night wore on. Then again, the smell of this current boat hold – petrol fumes – was not doing much for my headache, as I stepped down from the train onto a one-foot-wide steel platform. A man, securing the train with chains threaded through its mooring rings, nodded at me. He said that on an evening like this, when – in spite of the wind – the sea was nearly flat, they only secured the front and end carriages. Had he heard of the Night Ferry? He frowned: 'No.' So I explained about it. When I'd finished, he said, 'Adolf Hitler ... you heard of Adolf Hitler, right?' I confirmed this. 'When he visited Sweden in the war, he came by this train ferry.' Surely this could not be true, because Hitler never visited Sweden. But perhaps my mention of the Night Ferry had subliminally triggered the thought. The Night Ferry was surprisingly one of those British institutions admired by Hitler – another was the Grand Hotel, Scarborough – and Hitler said he wanted to 'roll into Britain'. Evidence in support is the fact that in 1940 the Nazis destroyed everything at Dunkirk except the train ferry dock.

To access the upper decks, it was necessary to press a button that released an airlock, allowing a sliding door to open. The ferry was called FS *Sassnitz*, and it was like a

modern-day cross-Channel ferry but smaller and more inno-
cent. There was no Costa Coffee, for a start. The self-service
restaurant, which had a 1970s school dinners atmosphere
about it, was called 'Everyone Deserves a Break'. (There
was also another, posher restaurant, of the 'Wait-Here-To-
Be-Seated' kind.) I took a wood-laminate tray and began
pushing it along the self-service counter, but at the sight
of the pork scallops in bread crumbs, and salmon steaks,
I returned the tray to its place. The food looked like decent
canteen fare, but I wasn't up to eating.

On the deck, happy Europeans were sitting around in clus-
ters of white plastic chairs. Some were sipping beer or wine,
in a restrained way that nevertheless increased my nausea. I
was leaning over a railing looking out at the Baltic, when I
noticed a woman smiling at me from a nearby chair. I asked
if I could interview her. 'Go ahead!' she said, her English
shamingly good in that familiar way. 'Why take this night
train instead of flying to Germany?' I asked. 'Well, first of
all,' she said, 'I'm not on a train. I think *you* must be on the
train, but I'm a foot passenger. In Sassnitz, I'll pick up a hire
car, and then drive to Poznań.'

A young girl, nearby on the deck, was happily wafting her
arms to mimic the roll of the ship. I felt a sweat breaking out
on my forehead. 'Poznań's in Poland,' my interviewee was
kindly explaining. 'I work in Malmö, but I live in Poznań.
I could fly there for about the same price, but you see, I am
travelling with my companion.' She gestured to a crate half
hidden behind her chair. A small dog lurked inside. It slowly
dawned on me (the Polish woman watched the process with
amusement) that there were many dogs, and other pet carrying cases on the deck around us. Perhaps this was the future
for night train ferries. I blurted something of the kind. 'Yes,
there's even a dog toilet,' the Polish woman said.

'Oh,' I said, 'I haven't seen that.'

'Well, it's not so beautiful.'

My thoughts ranged over my European odyssey: my encounter beneath the 'Accueil' sign at Gare d'Austerlitz, the stolen euros, my cravenness as the Turkish customs post. Perhaps this comedy of embarrassments could only have had one culmination: the emetic of Brexit, which had occurred a couple of weeks previously.

I was definitely feeling seasick. I thought I should lie down. I did have a sleeper train at my disposal, and a packet of Nurofen in my soap bag. So I descended the five steel floors to the car/train deck, and pressed the airlock.

The train was largely empty. It was extraordinary to walk along the corridor. There was a feeling of light bounding as the train rose and fell. Entering my compartment, I couldn't see how to access the top bunk (the only one folded down). Something could be pulled out of the side of it that initially looked like a ladder, but this turned out to be only two feet long, and proved instead to be a railing to stop you rolling out. They had almost exactly those railings on the Night Ferry. The only way to the top must be to fold down the middle and lower bunks, and step up using them. I made up the lower one, swallowed two Nurofen, and squirted water into my mouth from the tiny hole in one of the six cartons of mineral water that had been left for me on a complimentary basis (but minus the straws that surely ought to have been attached to them). I closed the curtain and got into bed. For a few minutes, it was touch-and-go as to whether the unaccustomed buoyancy of the train would send me scurrying along the corridor to the sink, but then the Nurofen kicked in, and I fell asleep.

***

I awoke refreshed after an unknown period of time. I was not aware of the movement of the ship. Perhaps we had been shunted off the FS *Sassnitz*, and were stopped at some German signal. I opened the curtain, and there was the black four-by-four. I found my mobile phone and checked the time. Eight o'clock. I had slept for two hours, and so I still had two hours of the four-hour crossing left.

I enjoyed those two hours. I had a quarter bottle of wine, then a meal, then another quarter bottle of wine, which I drank on the deck. By now the sun had coalesced into a red ball, low on the right side of the ship. Gradually – on that same side – the chalk cliffs of the German island of Rügen loomed out of the gloaming. Those cliffs are famous. They were painted by Caspar David Friedrich – for example in *Chalk Cliffs on Rügen*, which shows three figures gazing pensively through a jagged 'V' in the chalk. As usual with this painter, the symbolism is of death, but it's a daytime scene, and one of Friedrich's less glowering works.

At ten-thirty, a hooter blared, and the ferry began reversing into Sassnitz harbour. An announcement was made: 'Would drivers please return to their cars and train passengers please return to … the train.' I descended into the hold again.

The bow doors were open. A very big bloke in a high-vis jacket was regulating the level of the linkspan projecting from the dock, to match its tracks with those in the ferry's hold. The rails were set in grooves, so it was a matter of matching these up rather than the rails, and the grooves would help keep the train on the rails as it rode over the crack. It seemed fitting that the operator was big, even though he was doing nothing more strenuous than pressing buttons on a control panel.

A shunter pulled our train out of the hold, and propelled

us to a lonely platform of Sassnitz Fährhafen Station (or Sassnitz Ferry Terminal Station). There, an electric locomotive was attached. But nothing else happened. We simply stood there, surrounded by freight. Then some German police turned up. Perhaps an emergency passport check was taking place? Another crack in the Schengen ideal? But the focus seemed to be one particular compartment in the next carriage along. After about twenty minutes, the police took a young, smartly dressed man off the train, and began questioning him under one of the platform lamps. I walked through to the carriage from which he'd been taken, and saw the German chef du train in his own compartment, which bore all the hallmarks of permanent residence, with books, magazines, biscuit tins; one bed was made up for sleeping, another as a sofa. He was very friendly, and seemed completely unconcerned by whatever the police were up to. I asked him about the delay. 'Oh,' he said, 'we stay here until three.'

'Is that normal?'

'Yes, normal. Ever since they made the ferry leave so early from Sweden.'

So here was that familiar sleeper train tactic: holding the train so it reaches its destination at a civilised time.

'So this delay is nothing to do with the police?'

'Oh no,' he said, waving away the idea.

Just then a policeman came up and, politely excusing himself, interrupted us. He addressed the chef du train in German of course, but he was clearly indicating the young man on the platform, who was still being questioned by one of his colleagues. The only word I could make out was 'Afghanisch'. Evidently the young man was Afghan. But this seemed to be fine, because the news of his nationality was being imparted with a sort of wondering smile by the policeman – an amused 'Whatever-next?' tone. If the Afghan had ever been a suspect, he was no longer, and he was now climbing back aboard the train with thanks and goodbyes all around.

Asked what he made of the Brexit, the chef du train shrugged. 'To me, it's nothing. The politicians can sort that out. But when you were beaten by Iceland in the European Championships ...' That, he seemed to think, was the real disaster for Britain.

I returned to my compartment. A crescent moon hung above a distant car park, which reminded me of the Night Ferry logo, and so in turn the book I had brought with me: *Night Train to Paris*, a thriller of 1952 by Manning Coles ('Triumph number fourteen for Tommy Hambledon, the amiable Secret Service man.' *Daily Telegraph*). Coles was two people, both with impeccable thriller-writing CVs. Adelaide Frances Oke Manning had worked for the War Office in World War One. Cyril Henry Coles had worked in British Intelligence during the war, often behind enemy lines. They later became neighbours in East Meon, Hampshire. In *Night Train to Paris*, a strait-laced English solicitor called Logan has accidentally got mixed up in some international espionage. Finding his life in danger, he decides to flee to Paris, in order to consult with his more worldly twin brother. He opts to travel on the Night Ferry: 'Once aboard the train he would be quite safe.' He is certainly still in one piece on arrival at Dunkirk, which provides the best scene in the book:

> He was awakened again by the train being shunted once more; he sat up, pulled aside the blind and looked out. There was no moon, but the scene was illuminated by arc lamps high and lonely on tall standards; there were many railway lines and beyond them the sterile unevenness

which marks the site of bombed houses. There was a road with men cycling along it to work – and somewhere in the background, a ship.

Logan goes back to sleep, only to be awakened soon after by a persistent tapping on his door. It is the chef du train, wishing to return Logan's passport, or so Logan assumes.

In *The Ipcress File*, the entertaining film of Len Deighton's entertaining novel, Michael Caine (as Harry Palmer) is also fleeing a criminal gang by means of the Night Ferry. He too makes the mistake of opening his compartment door in response to an enquiry about his passport. There is a special DVD edition of *The Ipcress File* featuring a commentary by the American director Sidney Furie and the English film editor Peter Hunt. Even though the Night Ferry sequence is short, I was hoping for some revelations, but Hunt remains entirely silent during this part, while Furie says, 'I love English trains, with their compartments and … things.' (The Night Ferry was a *French* train.)

The real Night Ferry appeared in the 1974 Christmas Special – the very last episode – of the BBC sitcom *Steptoe and Son*. Michael Williams again:

> … it shows rag-and-bone man Harold dispatching his father abroad so that he can have Christmas alone with his girlfriend – in Bognor Regis. But sharp-eyed viewers may have noticed that the coaches were showing signs of their years.
>
> By the end of the 1970s British Railways were no longer putting much effort into publicising the train, and some ticket offices even denied its existence. The Paris-Dunkerque breakfast car was withdrawn and replaced by a snack-vending machine, although hot meals were

restored after furious protests by passengers. Another blow came when computer-aided automatic landing was introduced for planes at Heathrow airport, diminishing another source of revenue for the train, since it was always well patronised on foggy winter nights when there were likely to be severe air delays.

The sleeper carriage expert, Brendan Martin, had told me his abiding memory of the Night Ferry was the feeling of sheer relief as, after all the shunting in the small hours at Dunkirk, a French electric loco was attached to the train, and it began speeding smoothly towards Paris. At 3am I experienced something similar, as the Berlin Night Express finally started becoming ... if not an express, then at least a moving train. Like Logan, I managed to switch out the light after making 'careful study of an embarrassing array of knobs and switches' located above the compartment door.

TERMINUS

At half past six, the chef du train announced over the intercom, 'We are approaching Berlin, which is our terminus. Change here for Warsaw, Utrecht, Budapest' and too many other places for me to write down in my notebook. Before Berlin there would be a tunnel. 'And I want to inform you not to pull the emergency brake in the tunnel,' the chef du train added. I was reminded of a not-very-funny 'funny' railway book of 1959, written by C. Hamilton Ellis and called *Rapidly Round the Bend*: 'Everyone is well-behaved on a German train. The Travel-guests are forbidden in a Notsmoker to smoke, in the wagon out to spit, their boots on the bolsters to place, unprotected hatpins to carry, out to lean, before the train halts to open ...' The anti-foreign Edwardian journal called

Travel used to go in for this kind of heavy-handed satire of German railway officialdom – which was put to shame by the chef du train's sign off: 'Thank you very much for travelling on Snälltåget, and I hope you will have a very nice day.'

After the tunnel came the Stadtbahn, the viaduct that carries trains from west to east of the city, or the West to the East, as used to be the case, and politics has frequently checked those trains. We passed Ostbahnhof, then Fried-richstrasse, but we didn't get as far as the former endpoint of the Berlin Night Express, Zoo Station, since we termi-nated at Hauptbahnhof. This is now the principal station in Berlin, and it is a 'new' one, in that it's a rebuild – opened in 2006 – of the Lehrter Bahnhof, which dated from 1871. Hauptbahnhof is multi-levelled, like several stations on top of one another, and the train movements are advertised to the city in that they are visible through the glass walls. Top billing, as it were, goes to the pretty mustard-and-red trains of the S-Bahn, which come in at the highest level, even above the white ICE trains of the high-speed network.

I disembarked from the Berlin Night Express and ascended to one of the most hygienic station lavatories it has ever been my privilege to use. It was called 'Rail and Fresh', and well worth the one euro entrance fee. At the exit, a notice read 'Please disinfect your hands', and C. Hamilton Ellis did come to mind again. Now it was breakfast time. On the Night Ferry, breakfast was always the main meal. Some people took dinner on the train, but since it left Victoria at around ten o'clock (the departure times varied), quite a few went straight to bed on boarding. Everyone took break-fast, however, compounding the pleasure of Paris looming. In the 1960s, it was eight shillings for the 'Le Meat Break-fast', which involved that French rationalisation of eggs and bacon: oeufs au plat, with ham instead of fatty bacon, and more than one egg. It was served, along with chipolata sausages, tomatoes and mushrooms, on a scorching metal plate taken straight from the coke-fired range and wrapped in a white napkin. As on all the Wagons-Lits, the tea, coffee or hot chocolate was served in soup bowls, to guard against spillage.

I myself breakfasted off a couple of muffins, at the Hauptbahnhof branch of McDonald's. Then it was out into Berlin on a very hot sunny morning, past the Reichstag, through the Brandenburg Gate, and along Unter den Linden, which was like a diplomatic theme park, with its modern embassies, hotels and a Starbucks. A new S-Bahn station is being constructed below Unter den Linden, and where the building works are screened off from pedestrians, there are displays showing the history of the area, which was flattened by bombs in the war. The architecture was more beautiful before, and even though the historical displays urged me to think of the good and bad in German history, I was focused on the bad.

I walked for ten minutes to a sad display of crumbling brick Romanesque arches, with a modest public garden attached. This might have been the ruin of a church or monastery. In fact, it used to be Anhalter Station, which, unlike the stations on the Stadtbahn, points south. It first opened in 1841 as little more than a halt, and was rebuilt on a bigger scale in the 1870s. Here is what Roger Moorhouse has to say about it, in *Berlin at War*:

> The rebuilt Anhalter Station served rail traffic to the
> south, initially in the direction of Leipzig, Frankfurt and
> Munich, but by the early decades of the twentieth century,
> it was also serving destinations as far afield as Athens,
> Rome and Naples. By the 1930s it was handling over

40,000 passengers a day, with trains leaving, on average, every four minutes. It soon became known as Berlin's 'Gateway to the World'.

It was also Hitler's gateway, in his expansionist phase. His private train was stored there; it was to Anhalter – bedecked with swastikas and laurel wreaths – that he returned after the victorious French campaign in 1940. It would become associated with the movement of troops to the front, and of 9,000 Berlin Jews to the camp at Theresienstadt. If this station symbolises the particularly railway-oriented aspect of Nazi hubris, it is fitting that a certain blue carriage should have ended up there. The voiture-restaurant in question, number 2419, could not have got there as a result of any normal running. Wagons-Lits was evicted from Germany in the Second World War, as it had been in the first, so this had to be a special situation.

Number 2419 was a brand-new dining car when, in 1918, the Supreme Allied Commander, Marshal Foch, recruited it into his private train. He had the kitchen taken out, and customised it as a mobile office. The Armistice of 11 November 1918 was signed in this car, when it was berthed in a siding in the forêt de Compiègne, with the rose-coloured, silk-shaded lamps lit at 5am, when the signing occurred.

After the war, number 2419 was returned to regular service with W-L, albeit briefly, on a couple of excursion trains running from Gare de l'Est. There might have been an opportunity for one or two playboys, making small talk over the hors d'oeuvres, to say, 'Did you know, darling, that the Armistice that ended the war was signed in this very carriage? Waiter! Another gin and tonic, please!' But the French woke up to the significance of the carriage, and it was exhibited in Les Invalides in Paris, where it looked rather embarrassed, being an essentially frivolous object, to be displayed behind a guard of honour of a dozen cannons. In 1927, it was returned to the hallowed spot in the forest, the location now given the fate-temptingly tranquil name: the Glade of the Armistice.

On 22 June 1940, Hitler had the carriage moved back to exactly the original signing place, and the Armistice with defeated France was signed in it at 3pm on that day. Number 2419 was then taken to Berlin, and exhibited in the Lustgarten. In his *Berlin Diary*, the American journalist William Shirer wrote, on 8 July 1940, 'The historic Pullman car [not quite right] of Marshal Foch arrived in Berlin today. Pending final arrangements it will be placed in the Anhalter freight depot.' The roof of Anhalter Station collapsed after a bombing raid of late November 1943. In her 1968 memoir *The Past is Myself*, Christabel Bielenberg described how 'propaganda posters hung unnoticed in red and black tatters from the shrapnel-pitted walls ... the windowless trains ... carried a rudderless crowd of soldiers, civilians, refugees and evacuees along diverse routes to uncertain destinations'. A raid of February 1945 reduced the station to something not much more substantial than its present condition.

At about this time – the chronology is unclear – the carriage was moved to the small town of Crawinkel. When an American armoured column entered Crawinkel, an SS detachment set 2419 ablaze to stop it being used for another armistice, which would have put the French two–one up. Parts of the carriage survived the fire and were returned to the Glade of the Armistice, where they are exhibited together with an exact replica of 2419, built in 1950.

Car number 2419 was tussled over because it had been the venue for the signing of a document. But it also happens to have been, like any Wagons-Lits car, a symbol of peace, or at least of international cooperation. Since we are speaking of documents being signed, let us remember that, before the first Orient Express could run, contracts had to be struck between Wagons-Lits and the Eastern Railway Company of France, the Imperial Railways in Alsace-Lorraine, the Grand Duchy of Baden State Railways, the Royal Württemberg State Railways, the Kingdom of Bavaria Lines of Communication, the Royal Imperial Office for the Operation of State Railways at Vienna, the Imperial and Royal Austrian State Railways and the Royal Rumanian Railways. That the company's long-distance trains were necessarily sleepers increased their romance, but did not necessarily add to their virtue. Today, sleeper trains do seem virtuous. They are better for the environment than their rivals, the high-speed trains and the aeroplanes.

They do not make money, however, so their future looks uncertain in Western Europe. But my Swedish correspondent, who wished to remain nameless ('I have no need for crediting,' as he put it), concluded his potted history of the Berlin Night Express with a surprisingly severe injunction: 'It may be off topic, but a book about European night trains must not end pessimistic.'

Well, here goes. As already mentioned, Austrian Railways, ÖBB, will take over some of the sleepers given up on by Deutsche Bahn, which ought not to be too surprising. After all, why would Austria, located in the centre of Europe, give up on sleeper trains? As I came to the end of writing this book, I had a conversation with a man who works as an analyst at a London bank. Admittedly, he is a rail-enthusiast, but he is always governed by the balance sheets: 'Night trains?' he said. 'Oh, they'll survive somehow. I mean, it's a no-brainer. Travel increases all the time; planes will never be allowed to fly between midnight and 6am because of noise

– and you save a hotel bill.' If Paris is no longer the 'ompaha-los', the baton has been passed to Moscow. In 2009 Russian state railways, RZD, commissioned 200 sleeping cars from the German firm Siemens. These are mainly for domestic use, but sleepers run from Moscow to Vienna, Cheb, Prague, Warsaw, Krakow and Helsinki, among other European cities, and the list would be longer were it not for the Ukraine crisis. I have mentioned the Moscow-Nice and Moscow-Paris sleep-ers, and there are suggestions at the time of writing that the Russians might yet go beyond loaning a couple of carriages to the Paris-Nice Intercité de Nuit. The rumour is that they might bid to run all of the surviving, apparently doomed, French sleepers. When asked about the Russian rationale, one railway journalist replied, 'It's a putting-up-two-fingers thing,' which made sense: Russia propping up a European institution, and gaining the kudos that comes from operat-ing night trains.

This book has been written as a lament. But if it turns out that my tone is misconceived, and the European night trains will not disappear into a permanent darkness, I will be only too glad.

ACKNOWLEDGEMENTS

For supplying historical information and insight, I would like to thank, in no particular order: the International Railway Preservation Society, especially Brendan Martin, Christopher Elliott and Phil Marshall; the SNCF Society; Colin Rolle of the Railway Employees & Public Transport Association; Chris Jackson, editor of *Railway Gazette International*; John Scott-Morgan; Julian Pepinster; Dame Frances Cairncross; Tim Johnson of the Aviation Environment Federation; John Stewart of HACAN; Brian Riddle of the National Aerospace Library; Nigel Harris, editor of *Rail* magazine; Bob Gwynne at the National Railway Museum, York; the staff of the National Railway Museum, Shildon; Lars Igeland of Friends of the Earth, Sweden; Dr Werner Reh, of Friends of the Earth, Germany; Susie Cox, of the P&O Heritage Collection. All factual errors are entirely my responsibility. For supplying press tickets, I would like to thank Eurostar; Voyages SNCF; the Nordland Railway; Snälltåget.

LIST OF ILLUSTRATIONS